ROAD TO FREEDOM
A JOURNEY FROM OCCUPIED TIBET

ROAD *to* FREEDOM

A Journey from Occupied Tibet

THE TRUE STORY OF THE SEARCH, DISCOVERY, AND ESCAPE OF A REINCARNATE LAMA

Marya Waifoon Schwabe

Foreword by His Holiness the Dalai Lama

LUMINARE PRESS

WWW.LUMINAREPRESS.COM

Printed in the United States of America

Cover Design by Claire Flint Last
Cover Photo by Diego Hangartner

Photography by Shogen Rai, Chiu Leong, Paul Murray, Ritsuko Tokura-Ellsworth, Greg Herbst and Michael Schwabe

Luminare Press
442 Charnelton St.
Eugene, OR 97401
www.luminarepress.com

Nechung Dorje Drayang Ling
Wood Valley Temple & Retreat
P.O. Box 250, Pahala, HI 96777-0250
www.nechung.org

LCCN: 2020913711
ISBN: 978-1-64388-398-4

DEDICATED TO

HIS HOLINESS THE FOURTEENTH DALAI LAMA

NECHUNG RINPOCHE

OUR ROOT AND LINEAGE TEACHERS

THE TIBETAN PEOPLE

AND

ALL PEOPLE WHO LIVE UNDER TYRANNY

TABLE OF CONTENTS

Venerable Nechung Rinpoche, Lhasa, Tibet in the mid-1940s

In 1983, our teacher Nechung Rinpoche, a Tibetan lama, passed away in exile in India. In 1987 and 1993, following clues provided by His Holiness the Dalai Lama and the Nechung Choekyong, Chief State Oracle of Tibet, my husband Miguel and I, along with a Nechung monk from India named Thupten, set out to find Nechung Rinpoche's reincarnation in Chinese-occupied Tibet. This is the true story of our search, his discovery, and harrowing escape.

THE DALAI LAMA

FOREWORD

This book tells the story of the discovery of the present reincarnation of the Nechung Rinpoche. His predecessor, Thupten Konchok passed away in Dharamsala in 1983. The lineage of the Nechung Rinpoches began with Ogyen Thinley Choephel, a high lama of Mindrolling Monastery who moved to Nechung Monastery in the 1880s.

The previous Nechung Rinpoche lived at the Nechung Dorje Drayang Ling Buddhist Center in Hawai'i where he gave Buddhist teachings to Western students, among whom were Marya Schwabe, the author of this book, and her husband, Miguel. Following his passing away, Marya, Miguel and a monk from Nechung Monastery here in Dharamsala travelled to Tibet looking for a likely candidate for their late teacher's reincarnation. To their credit, they eventually located the young boy and brought him to India, where he has been educated and received spiritual training.

In this book Marya recounts the exciting tale of their journey, while at the same time revealing many aspects of Tibet's religion and culture. The story is also an example of how setting a goal and taking a realistic and determined approach to fulfilling it eventually lead to success.

May 3, 2014

Introduction

Reincarnation

The concept of reincarnation and afterlife is, and has always been, a mystery to human beings. Where does the consciousness go after departing the physical body? A common belief is that one ascends to heaven, joining loved ones and God in whatever form the holy being takes and in accord with each culture and religion.

Another conviction is the notion of past and future lives. Human beings have the potential to direct their deeds toward ultimate goodness, creating positive disposition and results; or, to the contrary, may spiral downward to negative tendencies. In most cases, life is a combination of both. Dependent on physical, verbal, and mental actions, the consciousness is imprinted with habitual patterns that create causal conditions for future births, whether they are fortunate or unfortunate.

Tibetans accept reincarnation as a reality. This is reflected in their philosophy of life which emphasizes the cultivation of loving-kindness, compassion, and tolerance. These principles are practiced in conjunction with the elimination of afflictive emotions and actions. Thus, individuals can imbue their mental continuum with virtuous qualities in order to achieve good rebirths and gain freedom from the cycles of existence.

Over the centuries, Tibetans have refined a system of mystical proportions for identifying the reincarnations of influential lamas.[1] Recognition came from the guidance of spiritual masters who offered their wisdom, insight, and divinations. Other methods

---

1. *"La" means high in terms of learning and wisdom; "Ma" means mother (e.g., someone with exceptional compassion, like a mother caring for all living beings as her only child). Therefore, a lama is someone with incomparable qualities and boundless compassion. A lama may be a celibate monk/nun or a layperson.*

included predictions by oracles, visions in sacred lakes, and other accepted signs. In the cases of preeminent lamas, delegates from monasteries would seek explicit direction from His Holiness the Dalai Lama and a prediction from the Nechung Oracle. In some unique cases, lamas leave personal letters with the place of their rebirth, parents' names, and other instructions. Vivid accounts of previous lives can be found in some autobiographies—including clear recognition of assistants, friends, family, and personal possessions.

The reincarnation of a person merits recognition if his or her predecessor's activities have brought great benefit and significant spiritual influence to a community of practitioners. Searches are conducted when the child is relatively young by members of the deceased lama's household, monks, or officials who have a stake in the process. Thereafter, the discovered child is given the title Rinpoche[2] or Tulku,[3] and is regarded with utmost esteem.

Nechung Rinpoche's Lineage

Nechung Rinpoche's reincarnations can be traced back to the great master Padmasambhava. Along with King Trisong Deutsen and Abbot Shantarakshita, Guru Padmasambhava was primarily responsible for the establishment and dissemination of the Buddhist doctrine in eighth century Tibet. His achievements touched countless lives, the principal ones being his twenty-five chief disciples, each of whom achieved extraordinary accomplishments. Nechung Rinpoche is an emanation of one of those disciples, Langdro Konchok Jungne, who was later recognized as the Treasure Revealer, Terton Ratna Lingpa (1403–1479), a highly revered lama of Buddhism in Tibet.

Later, Rinpoche took rebirth as Ogyen Thinley Choephel of Mindrolling Monastery in Central Tibet. In the 1880s he left Mindrolling to reside in a hermitage below Nechung Monastery located five miles west of the capital city Lhasa. He became the mentor and spiritual guide of the eighth Nechung Kuten[4] Shakya Yarpel and was a

2. *Rinpoche or "Precious One" is a title of distinction achieved by various means: a) an ordinary person rises to such a position by his/her own merit through study, meditation and realization, b) identified to be the reincarnation of a high lama.*

3. *Tulku or "Buddha's Emanation Body" is a realized being who takes birth in a physical form.*

4. *Kuten is the human Medium or "physical base" for a Protector of Dharma (Choekyong). Such a protector is known as an oracle when he/she appears during a trance through a human Medium.*

teacher to many Nechung Monastery monks. In 1891, following a prophesy by the Nechung Choekyong, Thinley Choephel was sent to Eastern Tibet by the Tibetan Government to retrieve some *termas*, or "hidden treasures" that had been discovered by the great Treasure Master, Terton Sogyal Orgyen Lerab Lingpa. As directed, Thinley Choephel went, and returned with these priceless items—a statue of Guru Padmasambhava and a sacred Guru Yoga text—and presented them to His Holiness the Thirteenth Dalai Lama who enshrined them in the Jokhang Cathedral in Lhasa.

After Ogyen Thinley Choephel's demise, there was a debate between the administrations of Mindrolling and Nechung as to which monastery his reincarnation would belong, since both monasteries considered the lama to be affiliated with them. To resolve the dispute, they sought the counsel of the Tibetan government who determined that he should be the Nechung Tulku. Subsequently, the Thirteenth Dalai Lama recognized and ordained Thupten Konchok Palzangpo (1917–1983) to be the second reincarnate lama of Nechung Monastery.

The Search for Nechung Rinpoche's Reincarnation

Nechung Rinpoche (Thupten Konchok) was a tantric Buddhist master with remarkable abilities. He had clear visions of his future, and while in Tibet, he commissioned an artist to create a map of his life's journey on a lacquer table. It had scenes that depicted people, places, and a path that led to a temple surrounded by tall trees in a tropical setting.

He was a member of a Tibetan government delegation sent to Beijing in 1955. At the request of the Chinese government, he remained for several years to teach the Tibetan language at China's Minority School. Despite this role as a teacher, he was imprisoned in Lhasa on two occasions after China's occupation of Tibet in 1959. In 1962, he miraculously escaped to India during a period of radical crackdown.

Rinpoche came to Hawai'i in the autumn of 1975 and established a temple on the Big Island identical to the one that he had envisioned decades earlier in Tibet. He initially named the sanctuary Shing Lung Gonpa (Wood Valley Temple), then in 1976 it was incorporated as Nechung Dorje Drayang Ling (Small Immutable Place of Melodious Sound), the same name as his prestigious monasteries in Lhasa, Tibet and

Dharamsala, India. The decades of political turmoil in Tibet and his journey to Hawai'i helped activate the latent conditions for my husband Miguel and me, and our karmic reunion with Nechung Rinpoche. We had the extraordinarily good fortune to live and work with him for almost eight years at the temple in Hawai'i. Rinpoche tutored us day and night and became our beloved spiritual master. He taught us the Tibetan language, Buddhist philosophy and unveiled the mysteries of Tibetan culture which we grew to love and embrace. Here in Hawai'i, Rinpoche lived until May 1983, when he returned to his monastery in northern India and passed away after a brief illness.

Miguel and I had a theoretical concept of the process of how reincarnate lamas were discovered and recognized from accounts in the biographies of eminent lamas. The notion of putting these principles into action firsthand was compelling, as was the wish to locate the incarnation of our teacher. Together with the Nechung monks in India, we sought the guidance of His Holiness the Dalai Lama and made repeated requests for his advice.

In 1987, His Holiness apprised us that Nechung Rinpoche had been reborn in Central Tibet. This news was exciting but we were apprehensive. To search for a lama in a free society is one matter, but to take on that challenge in a communist occupied country—where freedom of religion and speech do not exist and where fear, oppression, and surveillance abounded—seemed nearly impossible.

We spent the summer of 1987 in Lhasa, the capital city of Tibet doing research with Thupten, a close friend who was a monk from Nechung Monastery in India. Those months, though productive in establishing contacts and gaining knowledge of the territory, yielded no tangible results.

As our sojourn came to a close, trusted confidants advised us to leave the country at the first opportunity as rumblings of unrest were stirring and danger was in the air. We heeded the warning, and rapidly departed. Shortly after we reached India, the world woke up to news and images of eruptions of violence in Tibet and arrests and killings of innocent Tibetans. The Chinese army had once again imposed martial law, and Tibetans were attacked for holding civil demonstrations.

At that time, the leaders of the People's Republic of China (PRC) had no particular interest in the rebirths of lamas. It wasn't until 1995 that the communist regime determined that it was politically advantageous to get involved with the tradition of reincarnation. The Tenth Panchen Lama[5] had passed away in 1989 and since he was one of Tibet's

---

5.   *Of the four main lineages of Tibetan Buddhism (Nyingma, Sakya, Gelug, and Kagyu), the Panchen Lama is of the Gelug lineage and the head of Tashi Lhunpo Monastery in Shigatse, Tibet.*

most illustrious lamas, invariably his reincarnation was chosen by His Holiness the Dalai Lama. In 1995, a six-year-old boy named Gedhun Choekyi Nyima was recognized by His Holiness to be the Eleventh Panchen Lama. The boy quickly disappeared into Chinese custody, and to this day his welfare and whereabouts are unknown. He became regarded as the world's youngest political prisoner. In that same year, another candidate for the Panchen Lama was appointed and enthroned by the Chinese government. Henceforth, the "Chinese Panchen" lacks legitimacy and credibility in the Tibetan community. This interference with the selection of reincarnate lamas was unprecedented.

Historically, the search and confirmation of reincarnate lamas have strictly and singly been the purview of the Tibetans. This is a unique aspect of their religion and culture that the PRC has ignored since communism gives no credence to the cause and effect of karma, nor to past and future lives. Moreover, the Chinese government has no knowledge of the methods and processes used to identify reincarnate lamas. Nevertheless, the PRC now makes claim to be the only entity with the authority to find and choose the successors of "living Buddhas."

In 1993 we were delighted to receive further clues from His Holiness the Dalai Lama, including the year of Nechung Rinpoche's birth, the names of his parents, and his residence in Lhasa. With this knowledge, we journeyed twice into Tibet that summer, determined to find the young lama and escort him safely to India. Our task was inimitable and the mission unfolded with unexpected developments and risks that tested our ingenuity and reinforced our beliefs. The accounts of the precarious escapes from Tibet of both the previous and the current Nechung Rinpoche are recounted herein. Names of the people who played key roles in this story, both in Tibet and India, have been modified to protect their identities. Likewise, we have omitted photographs of Rinpoche's family and members of our team for the same reasons.

It is my sincere wish that sharing our experiences will shed light on the situation in Tibet, as well as illuminate the beauty of her people and richness of her culture.

—Marya Waifoon Schwabe
Nechung Dorje Drayang Ling
Wood Valley, Island of Hawai'i
January 22, 2014

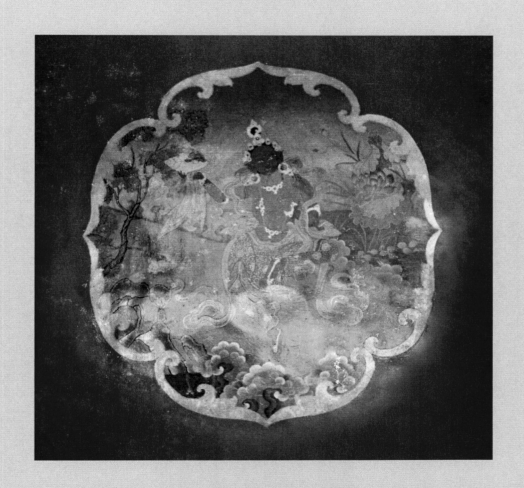

Offering goddess mural in Lhasa temple

THE EARLY YEARS:
1949 to 1983

Tibet 1949 to 1959 and Beyond

Tibet was a sovereign nation with her own distinct culture, language, and government. In 1949, the People's Liberation Army (PLA) of Communist China, under the guise of "liberation," began to invade Eastern Tibet (Kham) and northeastern Tibet (Amdo). Over the next ten years, the Chinese government stationed large garrisons of troops throughout the region, and the PLA occupied more and more territory, expanding its control and domination of the people, resources, and way of life.

Determined to find a compromise to regain Tibetans' freedom, in 1954 His Holiness the Dalai Lama traveled to China at the invitation of the communist government. He was accompanied by the Panchen Lama, an entourage of Cabinet ministers, clergy, and officials of the Tibetan government. The Dalai Lama met with Mao Zedong and other senior leaders of the People's Republic of China (PRC) in an attempt to find a formula for peace between Tibet and the PRC. The expedition lasted nearly a year.

During this time, His Holiness was still a teenager guided by his teachers and trusted aides. The Nechung Oracle gave repeated warnings and ominous predictions for the future of Tibet. He recommended many antidotes for averting the hostilities and minimizing the damage of the invasion. In the following years, acting on his cognition and in corroboration with the Oracle, the Dalai Lama attempted to negotiate a resolution to the conflict. Alas, this was to no avail. Chinese officials violated all verbal and written agreements, instead, using force to overpower the Tibetan people.

After His Holiness' 1954 visit, another hundred Tibetan representatives including Nechung Rinpoche were selected by the Tibetan government to go to China. The Chinese leadership intended to show that improvements to infrastructure in mainland China had indeed resulted from the revolution, and that similar progress could also be achieved in Tibet. At the close of the tour, Chinese officials stipulated that someone from the group remain to teach Tibetan to the Chinese administrators and the Tibetans assigned Rinpoche to this post.

While working in China, Rinpoche witnessed the atrocities and deception perpetrated by the Red Army in the name of the revolution. Religious and cultural persecutions were rampant, and there was a total collapse of social and economic development in the territories of the new emerging China. Rinpoche foresaw with clarity the incalculable harm that the PLA would inflict upon his beloved homeland and her people.

When Rinpoche returned to Tibet, conditions had deteriorated in Lhasa. Tension had escalated and the demands of the Chinese leaders became more unreasonable and suspicious, causing fear and alarm among the Tibetan people. The country's plight seemed bleak and insurmountable. The Nechung Oracle was consulted repeatedly in closed sessions and His Holiness the Dalai Lama was advised to leave Tibet. Reluctantly, in March 1959, he escaped to India with his mother, family members, and tutors.

On March 10, 1959, as the Tibetan people marched peacefully together in solidarity to voice their desire for freedom, the Chinese army crushed them with unprecedented violence. After this 1959 massacre, the Red Guard detained many monastics who were unable to flee and the majority were forced to give up their ordination vows. Countless Tibetans were arrested, imprisoned, tortured, and killed. During the subsequent Tibetan diaspora, nearly 100,000 Tibetan refugees fled into exile to the neighboring countries of India, Nepal, Sikkim, and Bhutan where they were granted political asylum. Of the 115 monks at Nechung Monastery, only six[6] managed to escape safely to India. Nechung Rinpoche was not among them. Since Rinpoche was Nechung Monastery's reincarnate lama, he was imprisoned; it was part of the Chinese effort to selectively isolate high lamas, aristocrats, and those who held important positions. They were cruelly humiliated and beaten in mock public trials to demonstrate the PRC's dominance over these influential individuals.

---

6. *Later on, Rinpoche and another monk escaped. This made a total of eight Nechung monks who fled to India.*

Nechung Dorje Drayang Ling Monastery in Lhasa, Tibet, pre-1959

Central to Buddhist practice is the cultivation of loving-kindness and compassion, even toward those who harm you, and the practice of tolerance and forgiveness in the face of aggression. As such, the mind is trained to overcome harmful afflictive emotions. Lamas and deeply committed practitioners like Rinpoche conducted themselves with dignity and maintained the integrity of their spiritual beliefs even when there was severe physical agony and suffering. They realized that the pure nature of the mind could not be touched and the resilience of the human spirit could not be shattered. Numerous stories of such triumphs have been recounted and recorded into history.

Nechung Rinpoche knew that outward resistance was futile and that it was more astute to give the appearance of cooperation. He worked hard in prison to appease his captors and in time convinced the wardens that their communist indoctrination had been effective. Believing that Rinpoche showed signs of rehabilitation and loyalty to the Chinese "motherland," they released him on his own recognizance. Chinese officials were pleased to have such a high-profile lama join their cause. Rinpoche was given a government administrative position. He earnestly attended to his duties; indeed, he was so proficient that he earned additional responsibilities. With his coworkers, he shared his dreams of moving up in the Communist Party, finding a Chinese wife, and having a family. His display of patriotism and reform was so skillful that he won the complete trust of his handlers. All the while, amidst his daily routine, Rinpoche made plans to escape. His flight had to be perfectly engineered as evading scrutiny under martial law was no easy matter. If discovered, the punishment would likely be more persecution, or worse, a bullet in the back of the head. Rinpoche patiently bided his time, intent on keeping his focus on the day he would be free.

The Sacred Mask

Rinpoche's escape depended on a foolproof plan with the means to execute it. Centuries earlier, trade routes had been established between Kalimpong—the point of entry from India to Tibet—and Phari—a border town at the highest elevation. It became one of the most established routes in and out of Tibet. Although Tibet was under lockdown, the Chinese army still allowed some people to keep their travel permits for commerce. Rinpoche was acquainted with a family of merchants who had long traded goods between Lhasa and Phari.

One such merchant was named Trinley, the father of one of Rinpoche's former students. Each time Trinley came to town, he made contact with Rinpoche whom he trusted. In their conversations, they would share mutual feelings regarding the Chinese invasion of Tibet. Trinley wanted to do something to help the cause but felt powerless. After many encounters, Rinpoche broached the subject of leaving Tibet and asked if the trader would assist him. As expected, the first reaction was fear and hesitation, but in time, he agreed to do it, and they developed a detailed strategy.

The escape was to take place in late spring when the weather was slightly warmer. Identification papers similar to Trinley's were drawn up for Rinpoche. The two were comparable in physique and height, so Rinpoche could don the clothing of his counterpart—a heavy wool *chuba* and a fedora. A chunk of turquoise would be attached to his ear to designate social class. To someone who didn't know better, Rinpoche's appearance would match the merchant's profile well enough.

A few days before his escape from Lhasa, Rinpoche made one final trip to Nechung Monastery. Most of the monastery buildings had been sealed, yet Rinpoche knew that a priceless artifact for the Nechung Choekyong remained hidden in one of the chapels. It was a material base for the supernatural protector entity, referred to as a "mask," so divine that only the Dalai Lama sees it. It was critical for him to retrieve it and take it to His Holiness.

The day of Rinpoche's visit to Nechung Monastery was quiet. Though its buildings were still intact, access was restricted and curfews enforced. Since civil liberties were constrained, the faithful no longer frequented monasteries and temples, and Chinese soldiers and paramilitary guards were now in charge of these holy centuries-old buildings. They used them for army barracks and storage facilities, stationing themselves to monitor dissident activity and purposely keep people away. In contrast to times past when the compound vibrated with life and the rhythmic, youthful voices of novice monks reciting and memorizing scriptures could be heard, the now empty courtyards echoed an uncanny silence. No one stood where innumerable pilgrims had once prostrated and prayed. Chapels where assemblies of ordained monks used to chant in chorus were now hollow shells.

Rinpoche could not allow memories of bygone days to distract him. He walked swiftly through the courtyard toward the temple where the sacred object was concealed. Besides some feral dogs, no living being was in sight. As he entered the building, he stopped with a jolt. A Tibetan man dressed in Chinese clothes stepped out of the shadows and stared suspiciously at him. "Hey! What are you doing here?" he yelled.

Rinpoche, dressed in layman's clothes, was unidentifiable as a lama or anyone of importance; but he recognized the watchman to be a monk from Drepung.

"I came to see the monastery and pray for all the people who have died," Rinpoche said softly. "May I have a few minutes alone?"

The "monk," visibly moved, nodded. Eyes downcast, he replied, "All right, I'll be outside."

As he stood at the Protector shrine, Rinpoche closed his eyes and prayed. Few knew of the existence of the mask, let alone its location. Carefully, stealthily, he extended his hand under layers of colored scarves to find the sacred object. He touched it; it filled his opened hand. Elemental, it was encased in its original wrapping, and just as Rinpoche intuited, it was still untouched and undefiled. He had recovered an article so precious to the Nechung Choekyong that traditionally *no* mere mortal could view it—it was *only* to be opened and perceived by the wisdom eyes of His Holiness the Dalai Lama. Rinpoche slipped it quickly into his satchel and held it under his jacket close to his heart. Despite the bleak circumstances, he was filled with confidence and ready for his journey.

As the designated escape day approached, Rinpoche feigned illness and requested to be excused from work. Since he had been reliable and rarely took time off, he was given a leave of absence without questions. Coworkers dropped by periodically to check on him, and, as intended, Rinpoche told them that he was convalescing. He aroused no suspicions.

"I'm almost better, thank you," he would say. "I'll be back in the office soon."

Instead, in the early hours before dawn on a cold, brisk morning, Rinpoche, disguised as the merchant, walked out of his apartment toward an awaiting truck. He arrived at the covered vehicle before anyone else and took a seat on a side bench in the back. As the other travelers gradually filed in, Rinpoche looked for two people—an old friend named Zungjuk Rinpoche, whom he had invited to come with him, and Trinley's employee, Jampa, who had been assigned to assist the lamas.

Nechung Rinpoche was glad to see them, but the last wave of passengers sent a surge of adrenalin through his body. Several soldiers had stomped in with firearms exposed, their sharp eyes scanned everyone on board, then took seats alongside them. Rinpoche tipped his chin down, allowing the fedora to shade his face, and pretended to drowse to eliminate the possibility of drawing attention. Some of his fellow travelers did the same. Moments later, the engine roared to life and the truck and its human cargo along with the sacred mask, bounced into the darkness headed toward Phari.

As he rode in the army truck, Rinpoche silently recited the prayers he had learned long ago. This gave him great comfort since his faith in the powers of the Protectors was unwavering.

A Daring Escape—1962

Spring had not yet arrived on the arid Tibetan Plateau. The morning air was chilly and a light coat of frost covered the scanty vegetation. The road was bumpy, and every now and then the truck jolted and bounced its passengers off their seats.

Rinpoche felt the tires roll over every inch of that gravelly highway, knowing that with each passing minute, he was closer to the border.

He huddled under his warm, woolen overcoat, listening to the heavy breathing and occasional snoring of the other passengers. The hypnotic hum of the engine had lulled them to sleep. With half-opened eyes, he watched the countryside fly by through the flapping canvas covering the back of the truck. As he continued toward his destination, Rinpoche knew that this was farewell. The transient nature of the temporal world was blatantly clear—everything that he had cherished was gone and his beloved country had changed beyond recognition. The harsh reality affected him immensely, leaving a feeling of profound renunciation.

Soon, he saw signs of approaching civilization, clusters of houses with people moving about, attending to animals and tasks in the early hours of another day. Here in the rural areas, life seemed to exist in a gentler way. Outwardly at least, there appeared to be fewer signs of havoc and devastation. The truck passed through one community after another. When it reached a tiny village before Rinpoche's destination of Phari, Jampa stood up and tapped on the truck's roof.

"Stop! We're getting off here!" he shouted. The truck screeched to a halt, kicking up huge clouds of dust.

This was it—time to make their break for the border. Internally, Rinpoche's heart beat wildly and fear gripped him; yet, as usual, he maintained his calm demeanor. He casually picked up his small bundle of belongings and leapt over the tailgate. Someone watching might have thought that the three men had relatives in the area and had simply come for a visit.

Meanwhile, back in Lhasa, Rinpoche's disappearance had finally been discovered. Anticipating this discovery, Rinpoche had stuffed bulky items under his bedcovers to resemble a reclining body. At first, when a colleague came to check on him, he indeed thought that Rinpoche was sleeping. But during a return visit, he found it unusual that the figure had not moved. The ruse bought a little extra time. Now the alarm of Rinpoche's escape spread rapidly through the ranks of the Chinese officials, and an alert was sent out to pursue and capture the politically valuable lama.

Everyone suspected that Rinpoche had headed for Phari since it was one of the most established routes out of Tibet. Generally, the Chinese would locate escapees by notifying local authorities who would track down and capture them. The most efficient way to communicate at that time was by telegraph. Unbeknownst to the lamas—and as fortune would have it—all telegraph lines between Lhasa and Phari were down.

The fugitives, Nechung Rinpoche and Zungjuk Rinpoche, along with their guide, Jampa, had to make their way to the border crossing without being detected. It was getting late in the afternoon and crucial that they make it before dark. Thankfully, Jampa knew the terrain. They began climbing quickly, winding their way up the mountain, to the pass that was visible in the distance. They needed a good vantage point to plan their next step. Upon reaching the summit, they could see the entire area, including the road leading to Phari and the glaciers that encircled the region.

"Over there is the border of Bhutan," Jampa said pointing. "It's the nearest boundary. You need to get down there on your own. This is as far as I can take you. I must leave now and make it to Phari before dusk. The very best of luck to you!" With that, he retraced his steps back down the mountain.

A vast glacier separated the two lamas from Bhutan. There was no vegetation, no indications of any trails, not a trace of any course taken by living beings. There was nothing but brilliant whiteness.

"How will we get down there?" Zungjuk Rinpoche asked anxiously. "Perhaps we should go to Phari and take the conventional route out of Tibet."

Nechung Rinpoche surmised that by now, his absence had been detected and a manhunt was underway. He knew the authorities would undoubtedly search for him in Phari, so going there was out of the question. What he didn't know was since the telegraph lines were down, a brigade of soldiers had been sent by road to pursue him. He somehow sensed the pursuers were close and that there wasn't a minute to spare.

"I'm heading straight down the hill. Now!" Nechung Rinpoche declared. "Follow me!"

He laid down a piece of woolen cloth, sat squarely on it, and pushed off. With his walking stick as a rudder to guide him, he glided swiftly down the smooth slopes of the glacier. Zungjuk Rinpoche slid down right behind him, following the path indented in the snow. It was as if they had wings soaring through the vast openness of pure unadulterated space.

Although a painstaking search was carried out throughout the town of Phari, no one resembling Rinpoche's description was ever found.

In Exile

T he escape of the two lamas was nothing short of a miracle. The twosome made their way to Bhutan, where they found shelter and provisions at a camp established for refugees fleeing from Tibet. It was a short reprieve for much needed rest and recuperation. Nechung Rinpoche offered prayers and expressed gratitude for the grace of His Holiness the Dalai Lama and the protection of the Nechung Choekyong; and for Trinley and Jampa, who had stayed behind, possibly discovered to be accomplices and punished. With India as their destination, and seeing His Holiness as their goal, they soon moved on to the town of Mussoorie in the hills of northern India.

News quickly spread throughout the Tibetan encampments that Nechung Rinpoche had made a safe passage from the iron grip of the communist Chinese. The Nechung monks in exile celebrated Rinpoche's safe arrival in India. The escape exemplified the accomplishments of a great master and validated the power of blessings and protection.

Approximately 100,000 Tibetans followed His Holiness the Dalai Lama out of Tibet into exile. They had been torn from their homes and loved ones and witnessed injustice and indescribable atrocities. The painful wounds of loss and tragedy were raw. Yet, they were fortunate to be alive—even if they had nothing more than the clothing on their backs.

Nepal, Sikkim, and Bhutan would adopt the refugees to varying degrees. India, in particular, contributed to the enormous efforts of resettlement by assigning large parcels of land to serve as camps and settlements for the deluge of Tibetans crossing the borders. Much of the cooperation with these host countries was dependent on the skill of the Dalai Lama in negotiating with government leaders on behalf of his people. These charitable acts of hospitality gave the refugees a place to begin rebuilding their lives and reestablish their culture in another land. In South India, many of the tracts of land were in desolate, dust-blown areas, parched by intense heat. Unable to adapt to the extreme changes in weather and diet and overwhelmed by grief, countless Tibetans perished in those early years in exile.

With courage and resilience inspired by the leadership of His Holiness, the Tibetans as a people have persevered, and to this day, continue to keep their culture alive. They have rebuilt homes, schools, monasteries, and vibrant communities. Three generations have since been born, raised, and educated in exile.

Meanwhile in Tibet, under the Chinese communist regime's systematic policy of population transfer, Tibetans have effectively been reduced to be a minority in their own homeland. Their way of life has been dramatically altered with limited opportunity for higher education and economic advancement. Tibet's precious resources, untouched for centuries, have been exploited; minerals and raw materials mined excessively and ancient forests have been cut down. These destructive actions continue to cause visible climate change and environmental damage. Moreover, repression continues, and religious freedom—something that is essential for all Tibetans—is closely monitored.

Yet the unrelenting thirst for freedom cannot be quenched, and Tibetans, now living all over the world, continue to strive for self-determination.

Sweet Beginnings

I was born in Guangzhou (Canton), China after the civil war between the Communists under the leadership of Mao Zedong, and the Nationalists led by Chiang Kai-shek. My family hailed from the Toisan district in the south. My mom was from a middle-class family; she was well educated, and before the war, served as a municipal judge in Canton. Her father was a merchant who ran an inter-coastal shipping company, but lost his fortune due to the political upheavals. My dad descended from a modest background and was a soldier in China's battle with Japan between 1937 and 1945. His post-traumatic stress was so severe that it haunted him his entire life. Before my birth, he immigrated to Canada following in the footsteps of my paternal grandfather.

When I was still a toddler, my mom relocated us to Kowloon, Hong Kong. Until she joined my dad in Canada, we lived there in the densely populated housing projects of the Mongkok District. My parents' passage to the West was sponsored by a prominent Canadian family who owned a whiskey company. Dad worked as their chef; Mom as their domestic. They were amongst the early Chinese immigrants to settle in British Columbia after the Chinese Exclusion Act was repealed in 1947.

Marya with mother (in suit) and grandmothers at the Hong Kong Airport when mother left for Canada, circa 1957

After my mom left, I continued to live in Mongkok with my maternal grandmother for two years, in a cramped closet-size walk-up. My parents sent for me when I was seven years old. By then, they had parted ways with their employers to try their luck with their own business. They opened small coffee shops in the Marpole and Gastown areas of Vancouver before succeeding with Dean's Café. It was not a Chinese restaurant; rather, it served Canadian food and catered to longshoremen and working-class folks. Its retro vinyl-covered counter stools and booths were usually packed with hungry men at noon and during dinner time. During lunch breaks and after class, I went to Dean's to help my parents—waiting on tables, cooking, and washing dishes.

Marya in Gastown, Vancouver, British Columbia, circa 1960

My siblings—both born in Vancouver, B.C.—and I grew up in a working-class area in the East End. In addition to our Chinese names, we were given the names Maria, Anthony, and Sylvia, befitting the Italian neighborhood in which we lived. We spoke Chinese at home, although our Toisan-country dialect was considered uncultured by the educated. When vocalized, the sounds were expressed in thunderous statements, not unlike an explosive argument.

My parents were extremely strict and had a strong immigrant work ethic. Dean's Café was a block from our home—a two-bedroom, one bath, two-story stucco house with a basement built in the early 1900s. It was across the street from an elementary school and within walking distance of the high school.

After high school, I went to a community college for a semester, but I felt a longing to travel and find a deeper meaning of life. In 1972, Vancouver was a spiritual haven for Eastern philosophy with visiting gurus from India and other parts of Asia. I attended talks given by various teachers—a Tibetan lama, a Zen scholar, and a Hindu swami in Kitsilano, the "it" scene for the counterculture of the 70s. When an opportunity came up to go to Mexico with a group of friends, I took it as a sign to leave Canada.

Within a week of my arrival in Mexico, I met Michael from Portland, Oregon. We spotted each other in the crowded fruit stands at the Oaxaca market. We exchanged shy smiles. He was very cute, with a wispy beard and braided hair and dressed in a t-shirt and denim overalls. A day later, we met again at the beach in Puerto Angel; we have been inseparable ever since.

I was twenty, naïve and impressionable. He was three years older and had traveled extensively in the States, Europe, and parts of Africa. His father was an attorney and the German Consul for the West Coast. Michael had attended a private prep school in Portland. Later, he studied at Washington University in St. Louis, Missouri for two years, before dropping out for reasons similar to mine.

For nearly a year, we lived in a dirt-floor hut near the Zapotec temple ruins in Mitla, Oaxaca. The Mexicans called him Miguel, so I did also; he has had this nickname ever since.

When we returned home to the States, the cold damp weather of the Northwest no longer suited us. "I think that you kids would like Hawai'i," Miguel's grandmother said. At Florence's suggestion, we flew to the islands with one-way tickets and our backpacks. We stayed in Holualoa, above Kailua-Kona on the Big Island. For a year, we enjoyed leisure in the sun, planted an organic garden, and had few responsibilities. We were drawn to a spiritual life and followed a simple routine of self-taught yoga and meditation.

Miguel and I became involved with Buddhism in 1974. At that time, little was known about the religion in the West. One day, while shopping at a natural foods store, we spotted a sepia poster with a silhouette of a man seated cross-legged by a window. The poster announced that a Tibetan lama, Kalu Rinpoche, would be on the island to give a public talk in Hilo.

I recognized him immediately and told Miguel, "Before we met, I went to one of his lectures in Vancouver."

"Let's go see him!" I eagerly suggested.

We made our way to Hilo, but since we had no car, it took all day to hitchhike from Kona. The venue for the evening program was at the Hilo Meishoin, a Japanese Buddhist temple. We arrived just in time to learn that a weekend retreat was soon scheduled in the Kaʻu District. Naturally, we wanted to attend.

An offering would be appropriate, we thought. So, I created a batik of a symbol etched in stone that I had seen in the pages of National Geographic. Though we didn't know its meaning, it captivated my interest. I painted the bold vertical strokes that resembled letters on a square yard of silk twill, giving it a background of indigo blue and creating the image in a light sky shade. We later learned that this was the Kalachakra "power of ten" symbol in Sanskrit, a mantra that represents a balance of the elements in our physical bodies and the planet. Kalachakra[7] is an Anuttarayoga Tantra, one of the most profound among esoteric Buddhist practices.

With our gift in hand, we arrived on the outskirts of the sleepy plantation town of Pahala at sunset and were picked up by Matthew in a lemon-yellow Volkswagen beetle. As we drove up the country road, our bearded, shaggy-haired driver told us, "You know you have to take Refuge; the retreat started yesterday, and all of us took part in that ceremony already."

Neither Miguel nor I knew what Refuge was. However, by the sound of Matt's serious tone, we surmised that it was something official. We glanced at each other. In that unspoken code, we shook our heads skeptically, as if to say, "Uh, uh, not us. We have already taken "refuge" in our own way, in our hearts."

---

7.   As of January 2017, H.H. the 14th Dalai Lama has bestowed thirty-four Kalachakra empowerments dedicated to world peace. The first was given in May 1954 at Norbu Lingka in Lhasa, Tibet; the most recent one was in Bodhgaya, India.

We drove miles uphill on a paved road lined on both sides with towering fields of rustling sugar cane. There was not a person or house in sight. We were in the middle of nowhere! Where were we being taken? After crossing multiple bridges and gulch crossings, we turned into a wooded area. There, nestled in a grove of sky-high eucalyptus trees, was a building elevated upon a slight hill. It was a classic Japanese temple impeccably designed with pillared verandas on three sides, double-hung windows facing the east and west, and carved smiling elephants. I felt as if we had been transported to Japan or somewhere in the Far East.

Waiting through the open doors, sat a serene, bald-headed lama on a simple dais draped with hand-woven textiles. He was reed-thin with delicate features, personifying the mystique of a far-off land.

"Go up to the front," we were told by several of the devotees who sat cross-legged on the wooden floor. "You have to take Refuge before we can continue." Before we could object, we were ushered into the front row, directly in the presence of the lama.

"Repeat these verses after Rinpoche," the Caucasian translator instructed us. We listened to the strange sounding words. Although we didn't understand their meaning, without resistance, we mumbled the phrases in unison with the others and crossed the threshold onto the path of Buddhism. Later, we learned that we had taken Refuge in the Three Jewels: the Buddha (symbol of enlightenment), Dharma (teachings and path), and Sangha (spiritual community).

The weekend was a blur. We were initiated into the practice of Avalokiteshvara (Tibetan: Chenrezig) the manifestation of all-seeing compassion, and were taught visualization and the recitation of a mantra. We were told that the six syllables "Om Mani Padme Hung" symbolized the cultivation of loving-kindness for all living beings. It was all new and exotic, yet remarkably familiar.

At the close of the program, Jesse, one of the coordinators, stood up to announce that in the spring of the following year, a lama named Nechung Rinpoche was expected to come and live at the temple for a year. That pronouncement ignited a fervor in my mind—an inexplicable sense of excitement. It was as if bells rang in my ears. We had to meet this teacher!

Instantly, we decided to help with whatever was necessary to prepare for Nechung Rinpoche's arrival. The fact that he would not just be passing through but actually living here was compelling. It meant we would be able to study with a qualified master.

Within two months, in early 1975, Miguel and I had moved into a rambling plantation house owned by a native Hawaiian family in lower Pahala. Shortly thereafter, we were living at the temple, which was built in 1902 as the first Nichiren Mission in Hawai'i. It was located in Kapapala at the entrance to Wood Valley.

It took longer than anticipated for Rinpoche to leave India, due to previous commitments and bureaucratic delays. Meanwhile, he corresponded with us via post and sent written prayers for good fortune. He also instructed us to recite the verses daily for auspiciousness and to invoke the presence of enlightened beings. Before his arrival, Rinpoche aptly named his future home Shing Lung Gonpa or Wood Valley Temple. He would later give the sanctuary the prestigious name of Nechung Dorje Drayang Ling or Small Immutable Island of Melodious Sound, after his monasteries in Tibet and India.

In October of 1975, Nechung Rinpoche finally arrived in Hawai'i after finishing his contract at Vishesh Kendriya Vidyalaya, a Central School in Delhi where he taught Tibetan to students from the Himalayan regions of India. He traveled from India with a Tibetan named Ngodrup Paljor who had a scholarship at the East West Center at the University of Hawai'i in Honolulu. Paljor would act as our translator on occasion.

Initially, communication was a challenge, since Rinpoche spoke not a word of English and we had no comprehension of Tibetan. He brought with him an English-Tibetan picture dictionary that had basic colloquial words and sentences. Whenever he needed to get a message across that did not transmit through sign language, he would pull out this small book and point to a word or the black/white line drawing next to it. Such was the case when he opened to the pages with pictures of noodles and meat to convey that our vegan, mostly raw-food diet did not suit his tastes.

"You need to learn Tibetan," Rinpoche advised us. "There will be many lamas in the future who will be elderly and will not speak English. Besides, it is important for you to learn the Dharma straight from the source."

He loved teaching Tibetan, starting with the alphabet to grammar, writing and reading of the scriptures, as well as the spoken language—both colloquial and honorific terms.

"Tibetan is a language that expresses the subtlety and profundity of the Buddha Dharma," he said. "It will be of great benefit to you in the future." How prophetic and correct that statement would turn out to be.

The moment we met Nechung Rinpoche, he said, "You take charge of the management and finances, and I will teach you the Dharma." That he did, from the basic principles of Buddhism to the nature of the mind and phenomena as well as the highest yoga Tantras and Dzogchen. Rinpoche covered in depth, subjects that spanned the entire spectrum of Buddhism: from mind training, the stages to enlightenment, common and uncommon preliminary practices, to the symbolism of Buddhist deities and Secret Mantra. What we experienced during the formative years that followed—living, studying, and working with Rinpoche would lie at the core of our lives and principles. Our innocent minds were receptive to the purity of the Buddhist teachings, and we embraced the philosophy with ease. His love, kindness, and exceptional blessings penetrated the depths of our minds and have inspired us through the decades.

Rinpoche having tea on the temple lawn, circa 1979

We studied day and night; it was constant and continuous immersion in Tibetan culture. There were scheduled Saturday afternoon classes that a dozen or so students attended. Rinpoche taught the great classics of the sages of ancient India such as *Entering into a Bodhisattva's Way of Life* (*Bodhicaryavatara*) written by Shantideva and *Letter to a Friend* (*Shetring*) by Nagarjuna. He also taught the inspired writings of the founders of Buddhism in Tibet such as *Words of My Perfect Teacher* (*Kunzang Lama'i Zhalung*) by Patrul Rinpoche and *Jewel Ornament of Liberation* (*Dakpa Targyen*) by Gampopa. Each of these courses of study often lasted a year.

Rinpoche performing one of many fire rituals on the temple property

Rinpoche was exceptionally skilled at putting the most profound views into perspective and encapsulating lengthy teachings into a concise discourse. When he explained the interdependence of all phenomena and the wisdom of emptiness, it was natural and relaxed. Nechung Rinpoche was a tantric master, fully trained in all levels of Secret Mantra.[8] Yet, he conducted rituals and gave commentary on esoteric subjects without pretense or fanfare.

Nechung Rinpoche palms in prayer, circa 1979

8.   *Mantra means protection of mind from ordinary perception and view. In this practice, one trains to pierce through the illusory veil of existence and view the world and sentient beings in its natural, pristine state.*

His Holiness the Dalai Lama made his first visit to the United States of America in 1979, so we accompanied Rinpoche to see him in Los Angeles. Rinpoche's humility and genuine respect for His Holiness are etched in my memory forever. During our audience, he bowed low from the waist and spoke barely above a whisper using the honorific terms distinctive of the finest Lhasa dialect. As we sat on the floor in His Holiness' suite at the Beverly Wilshire, Rinpoche extended an invitation to him to visit and teach at Nechung Dorje Drayang Ling in Wood Valley.

"Most certainly," His Holiness responded. He kept his promise, and in the spring of 1980, we were informed that he would be coming that October. We would have the honor of hosting a three-day visit, as the last stop on his second tour of North America. We were advised of his plans during the early phases of renovating a second building on the temple property. It was a place of worship in the Japanese Shingon tradition—a plantation-era house with a recessed shrine we had moved from Pahala—being revamped into a two-story retreat center. We worked around the clock with a volunteer staff to prepare for His Holiness' arrival.

Our training during those months leading up to the visit went beyond theoretical aspiration. We put into practice the principles of giving, patience, diligence, concentration, and other Buddhist concepts. Miguel focused on building and landscaping, managing the crew and the multitude of details associated with construction using reused wood and other materials, plumbing, painting, and so forth. I worked with federal, state and county officials on logistics and public relations, and all the planning that goes with hosting such an esteemed guest.

The entire visit was private and magical. His Holiness arrived on the evening of October 27, to bestow a grace for the temple—a gentle benevolence and keen wisdom which can still be felt today.

The next day, we hosted a casual luncheon attended by island ministers and dignitaries on the lawn. The chefs were volunteers from the island Vietnamese community.

In the afternoon, His Holiness inaugurated the temple that had been freshly painted in brilliant primary colors chosen by Rinpoche. Then he sat on a burgundy dragon rug on the floor and delivered one of his first talks "Religion and the Importance of Practice" in English. There were about two hundred guests, here by invitation, filling the temple, and overflowing onto the veranda, stairs, and grounds. Afterwards, His Holiness held a press conference with journalists from the local newspapers and television stations on the lawn in front of the temple.

*Rinpoche offering flower leis to His Holiness and entourage
at the luncheon, October 28, 1980.*

*Rinpoche delivering the welcome address at luncheon with Marya, Reverend and
Mrs. Dwight Nakamura from the Hilo Meishoin.*

His Holiness in contemplative thought at the press conference.

His Holiness and his entourage stayed in the rustic quarters at the temple. We saw him frequently. In the mornings, he relaxed on the open veranda bedecked with orchids and enjoyed the warmth of the Hawaiian sun. At night, the brilliance of the full moon lit the grounds, and the scent of tuberose and night blooming jasmine permeated the air.

His Holiness relaxing on the temple veranda.

It was a leisurely trip. He toured Hawai'i Volcanoes National Park and took a stroll on the barren pahoehoe lava fields. There, he remarked that this must be like the formation of a new universe as described in the Buddha's teaching. Afterwards, he even enjoyed a picnic at Kamoamoa Beach Park, under swaying palm trees.

His Holiness at Kilauea Caldera, Hawai'i Volcanoes National Park, October 29, 1980.

His Holiness at Kamoamoa Beach Park, October 29, 1980

The eight years with Rinpoche flew by swiftly. We studied day and night. It was an extremely rare opportunity to study with a master of such high caliber and to be accepted into his household. Our lifestyle was a pure assimilation of language and Dharma. Many of our lessons were impromptu; we learned over tea, meals, handicraft projects, chopping wood, and building bonfires. Of course, there were the scheduled weekend classes for which I translated, when I learned Tibetan along with Buddhism, all the while sitting on the hot seat, converting the deeply philosophical concepts from Tibetan into comprehensible English.

Rinpoche making meditation cushions with Marya, circa 1980

Rinpoche was not concerned about size or numbers, nor was he interested in starting numerous centers. For him, success was not measured by quantity; rather, the sincere dedication of a few serious students was what mattered. "A small stove with a hot blazing fire is far more effective than a large hearth with a weak, insubstantial one," he would say.

He taught us well, impressing upon us the value of laying a realistic groundwork for the Dharma. "A strong foundation is critical in the construction of a building," he would say. "In the same manner, you need to establish a solid understanding of the Dharma and lead a life that benefits others. The mind is the source of all thought, speech, and action. If the mind is pure, then the actions and path that ensue will be positive. If the mind is self-centered, then the actions and path that ensue will be negative. Eliminate afflictive emotions and cultivate altruistic intentions and deeds."

Rinpoche with Miguel, circa 1980

Nechung Rinpoche, circa 1981

There is a Tibetan saying that even if an ordinary tree branch were tossed into a grove of fragrant sandalwood, over time that nondescript wood, too, would absorb the essence. For those of us who had the good fortune to study with Nechung Rinpoche, that training has been the inspiration for every aspect of our lives. Our conviction in the tenets of Buddhism has remained steadfast, and our gratitude and respect for our root and lineage lamas, beginning with His Holiness the Dalai Lama, have no limit.

Nechung—the Oracle, Medium, Lama, and Monastery

After His Holiness' visit, a number of Taiwanese students living in Honolulu and the mainland United States became increasingly interested in studying Buddhism with Rinpoche. They visited the temple, and occasionally Rinpoche would teach in Honolulu. In December 1982 and January 1983, Rinpoche made a tour to teach some of the Chinese supporters in California and New York. Although Rinpoche had shown no prior signs of sickness, it was during this trip that we noticed his declining health and loss of weight. Upon returning to Hawai'i, we were made aware of his terminal illness.

A few months later, in May, Miguel and I accompanied Nechung Rinpoche on the gruesome journey from Wood Valley back to Dharamsala. Rinpoche was weak, and there were multiple layovers en route, plus a reprieve in New Delhi where some monks offered prayers in a ritual ceremony. After Rinpoche passed away at his monastery in Dharamsala in August 1983, Miguel and I stayed in India, to grieve and contemplate the transitory nature of life. We spent most of our year-long sabbatical at Nechung Monastery in Dharamsala. There, we personally observed what Rinpoche and a few senior monks had accomplished in exile.

Nechung Monastery plays a significant role in Tibetan history and culture dating back to the eighth century. Padmasambhava, fondly known as Guru Rinpoche, was an Indian master whom the Dharma King Trisong Deutsen had invited to join in the momentous task of building Samye, the first monastery in Tibet. Construction of Samye did not come easily. Due to obstructive primal forces, walls and structures erected during the day were mysteriously razed to the ground at night. With his supernatural powers, Padmasambhava subdued the harmful spirits hindering the endeavors, and converted them to beneficent guardians. At Hebori, a hill close to Samye—Pehar, a powerful entity, was "bound to oath" as the chief protector of the Dharma. The first eight monks in Tibet were ordained at Samye, and steadily the tenets of the Buddhist philosophy took root.

Samye became known as Nechen (large place), and would serve as the abode for Pehar. Later Nechung (small place) was established below Drepung Monastery, to become the new home of Pehar. Subsequently, Drepung became the largest monastic institution in Tibet before 1959 with seven colleges. The first monks of Nechung Monastery came from the Deyang College of Drepung. Since then, Pehar became prevalently known as Nechung Choekyong, or simply Nechung, in reference to the name of the monastery.

Nechung Choekyong manifests as the "Five Kings," who are considered to be emanations of the Five Wisdom Buddhas. The entity that communicates through the human medium—the Nechung Kuten—is Dorje Drakden, the "Renowned Immutable One," emissary of the King of Speech. Unlike reincarnate lamas, who are generally found when they are children, the Nechung Kuten is said to be chosen by the Protector. There are distinct signs when this occurs and a methodic process is conducted to unmistakably recognize the person as the pure vessel. During a trance, the Kuten is the medium or conduit who verbalizes the message of Dorje Drakden in our earthly realm. As such, Dorje Drakden is often called the Nechung Oracle or Nechung Choekyong, Protector of Dharma.

The Nechung Choekyong is closely connected to the succession of Dalai Lamas and their activities. Nechung and Palden Lhamo are the two principal protectors of the Dalai Lamas and the Tibetan people. Periodically each year, His Holiness the Dalai Lama, the Tibetan government, prominent lamas, and monastic institutions consult with the Nechung Oracle on vital matters of religion and state.

Lobsang Jigme became the Sixteenth Nechung Kuten in 1945 when he was fifteen years old. He served in this capacity until his passing in 1984. His tenure as the channel for the Oracle was during a pivotal period of Tibet's history. He voiced predictions that were instrumental in major decisions, such as the Dalai Lama escaping into exile in 1959.

In India, the Nechung monks initially found themselves in transitional housing. While searching for a more permanent location, the key factor was to be in close proximity to His Holiness the Dalai Lama. When the Indian government granted land to His Holiness in Dharamsala, a former British hill station in Himachal Pradesh, he took residence and established his government-in-exile there. Therefore, it was logical for Nechung to be situated close by, so the monastery and Oracle could serve in the same capacity as it had in Tibet.

A small farmhouse in lower Dharamsala, a short distance from Kotwali Bazaar, served as the temporary quarters for Nechung for sixteen years. Among the eight monks who escaped Tibet were Nechung Rinpoche, Kuten Lobsang Jigme, Kushog Thupten Phuntsok, and his disciple Kushog Wangyal. Although few in number, their combined skills were ample in providing the groundwork for a fresh start in exile. A new wave of novices was admitted and began the rigorous training under the tutorship of the senior monks. Those early days were full of challenges such as financial difficulties, poor nutrition, health issues, and substandard living conditions.

Undeterred by hardship, they persevered, with the determination to reconstruct the institution and preserve its unique tradition. Nechung Rinpoche imparted the initiations, oral transmissions, and commentaries of the monastery's rituals, recitations, and practices. The Nechung Medium performed his duties whenever called upon by His Holiness the Dalai Lama or the various government agencies.

Kushog Thupten Phuntsok had a photographic memory. In addition to teaching, he passed on the transmissions for the sacred arts—techniques to create sand mandalas, ritual thread crosses, and embroidered appliqué thangkas of the images of enlightenment.

Kushog Wangyal became the administrator and supervised the construction and laborers. He was always gracious in welcoming eminent lamas, abbots, and monks who constantly visited Nechung to request prayers and blessings.

Eventually, a small plot of land was given to Nechung Monastery by the Tibetan Administration. It sat below the Library of Tibetan Works and Archives in Gangchen Kyishong, the seat of the Tibetan Government-in-Exile in the central part of Dharamsala. From there, a brisk walk up a steep, windy hill led to the main temple of Thekchen Choling and the private office and residence of His Holiness the Dalai Lama. The first phase of the monastery included living quarters for the monks; it was complete and in use by 1981.

In the 1980s, Dharamsala was a small town with few cars, a scattering of old buildings, and remnants of the British hill station. Most Tibetans lived in tiny shacks in McLeod Ganj, the upper area of Dharamsala. Some supported themselves by opening small restaurants and shops selling handicrafts and tourist paraphernalia. Life was simple back then. Few people, minimal security, and ample quality time all defined a sparse lifestyle.

During the late winter and early spring months, His Holiness gave lengthy discourses lasting two to three weeks at Thekchen Choling after Losar (Tibetan New Year). Miguel and I would make the journey to Dharamsala yearly for the priceless opportunity to see him and receive his teachings. We always secured an excellent seat on the side veranda or inside the temple hall by the opened windows within eye contact of His Holiness. During the morning and afternoon sessions when His Holiness scanned the hall for familiar faces, he would frequently flash one of his radiant smiles, sometimes accompanied by a chuckle. That itself would be worth traveling the thousands of miles from Hawai'i!

On the first day of Losar, we were often invited to join His Holiness, his staff, the Tibetan Cabinet, and some senior monks for ceremonial prayers. This took place on the main temple rooftop in the early morning hours. It was an intimate setting with only a few dozen people; we would sit in the freezing temperatures close to His Holiness, mesmerized by the chanting that penetrated the silence into celestial realms. As the first light of another dawn rose over the mountain ridges, dedication for the well-being of living beings and peace in the world would resonate into all directions to bring in the new year.

Audiences with His Holiness were relaxed and personal. His personal secretary always obliged our requests to see him. So, we were fortunate to consistently meet with him during every one of our visits. On each occasion, our discussions covered a wide variety of subjects, including Buddhist philosophy, Tibet's struggles, and projects for which we could volunteer. The conversation would invariably turn to Nechung Rinpoche's reincarnation. His Holiness would nod his head contemplatively. "Yes, yes," he would say, eyes deep in thought. "I will think about it," and then it would be time to thank him and leave.

Nechung Monastery became our second home and its monks our extended family. In the foothills of the Himalayas, with the snow-lined Dhauladhar mountain range to the east and the vista of the Kangra Valley below, we felt familiar and at ease within the confines of austere monastic life. Our one-room studio at the monastery, on the second story of a building with a view of the main prayer hall and courtyard, proved to be the perfect spot to observe the constant comings and goings of the monastics and visitors.

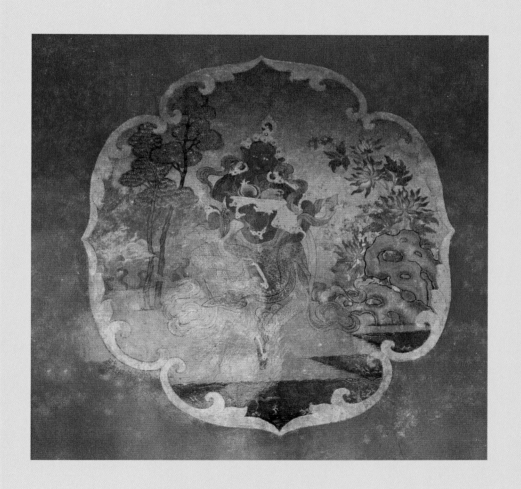

Offering goddess mural in Lhasa temple

THE FIRST JOURNEY:
Summer 1987

Our Search Party

Through divination and his special insight, His Holiness the Dalai Lama can identify the true reincarnations of distinguished lamas. After Nechung Rinpoche's
passing in 1983, we waited patiently, certain that the day would come when he would
apprise us of our lama's rebirth. Yearly the administrators at Nechung in Dharamsala
sent a formal letter seeking His Holiness' advice regarding Rinpoche's reincarnation.
They did this on behalf of the Nechung monasteries in Tibet and India, as well as
our temple in Hawai'i which was the only affiliate center in America at the time.

In 1987, we received the news that we had long anticipated—His Holiness had
determined that Nechung Rinpoche had reincarnated in Tibet, specifically in the
east side of Lhasa, and advised the monastery as such. With His Holiness' blessing, Nechung Choekyong's prediction, and the monastery's support, Miguel and I
made plans to go to Tibet that summer to be part of the search party. In addition to
us, our team included the other two members of Rinpoche's household—Lobzang
Toldan and Thupten.

Lobzang Toldan, known by his nickname Tiapala ("the man from Tia"), had
been Nechung Rinpoche's attendant in Tibet and India. He was born in Tia, Ladakh
in the Jammu Kashmir district of northern India. When he was a boy, Tiapala had
some recollections of his previous life—his name had been Paltup and he had died
prematurely. He remembered his family's house and the surrounding countryside.
To everyone's surprise, when Tiapala led them there, the details of his descriptions

proved to be accurate. Tiapala joined Likir Monastery in Leh, Ladakh in his early teens. At the age of eighteen, he journeyed to Lhasa and was admitted into the Likir-Spituk Fraternity of Loseling College at Drepung Monastery, which was a short distance up the hill from Nechung. Spituk monks customarily served as temple custodians at Nechung. Thus, Tiapala became a caretaker for one of the monastery's chapels and graduated to become a junior assistant to Rinpoche. Tiapala stayed in Tibet until 1961 when he left for India at Nechung Rinpoche's behest. As an Indian citizen, there were no restrictions on his departure. He reunited with Rinpoche in 1962 and served as his attendant until Rinpoche came to Hawaiʻi. In 1984, we invited him to be the resident monk at the temple.

Thupten had been our close friend since 1983, during our year sabbatical at Nechung in Dharamsala. Each evening after the prayer session, he would knock at our door, and over tea, we would stay up late into the night discussing politics, philosophy, or whatever was on his mind. He was extremely bright, quick-witted, and highly respected by all the monastics. The elders considered him to be the reincarnation of an influential Nechung monk known to all as Lopon Gyeu, or Bearded Ritual Master. When Thupten was seven, Rinpoche visited Ladakh and overnighted with his family. Thupten insisted that he wanted to be a monk and to go with the lama. Rinpoche, although impressed with the boy's precociousness, was unprepared to take the child with him. Not to be dissuaded, early the next morning, Thupten went out to Rinpoche's car and ensconced himself in a seat refusing to budge unless Rinpoche agreed to take him. Consequently, at the time, he became the youngest boy admitted to Nechung.

China had recently opened Tibet's borders so it was a favorable time to visit. We had no expectations of finding Rinpoche since His Holiness had forewarned us that our chances of finding him on this trip were improbable. Besides, "The boy should not leave his mother at such a tender age," he said, "and you certainly don't want to be surrogate parents!" He suggested that we go to Central Tibet to familiarize ourselves with the territory and people in preparation for the actual time when it was opportune to find Rinpoche and bring him out.

This mystical land encircled by snow mountains was the source of the philosophy and practice to which Miguel and I were so karmically linked. The Buddha's teachings and commentaries from India had been translated from the original Sanskrit and preserved in their entirety in Tibet. Due to the country's isolation for centuries, the lineages and transmissions of the various paths—Theravadin, Mahayana, and Vajrayana[9]—were preserved, unsullied, and passed from teacher to disciple, generation after generation. Tibet no longer would be a faraway realm high above the clouds, we were soon to be there ourselves!

The trip's logistics came together effortlessly. Our main concern was the visa. Tibet was a new destination and we had no prior experience with Chinese government travel regulations. Tiapala, being an Indian national, was convinced it would be easier to get his visa in Nepal. Miguel and I decided to apply in Hong Kong since we were somewhat familiar with the city. En route to India, we had often stopped in Hong Kong to see my maternal grandmother, who still lived in the projects of Mongkok in Kowloon. The layovers gave us a chance to acclimate to the sweltering heat and the massive populations of Asia. Besides, it was fun to feast in the restaurants, window-shop, and check out the newest electronics and fashion.

We had heard that select travel agencies in Hong Kong could issue tourist visas to Westerners. Our first attempt was a large travel office in a high-rise on the waterfront. We were turned away. "Sorry, you have to join an escorted tour," the agent said, "no visas are ever issued to foreign independent travelers (FITs)."

Fortunately, we stumbled upon a tiny China Travel Service close to the Prince Edward subway station next door to Miguel's favorite ginseng store. A bored clerk was pleased to process the paperwork for us as FITs, overnight with no questions asked. Miguel and I quickly filled out the applications, paid for two visas with multiple entries, and returned the next day to reclaim our documents.

We met up with Thupten in India and flew together to Kathmandu, Nepal where we stayed in an inexpensive guesthouse in Thamel, a bustling area where rich ancient cultures, Western materialism, and tourism converged. Centuries-old Hindu temples and buildings created an exotic backdrop for a diverse cast of characters. There were the hippies, some with youthful gaits and others, the weathered remnants of the 1960s. Adorned with flowing tresses, dressed in vibrant attire and beaded jewelry, they were walking mannequins for the shops around Thamel. Trekkers, sporting outdoor gear, stayed in town only long enough to organize their excursions into the mountains with supplies, guides, and porters. There were also the shopkeepers,

9. *Theravadin is a practice through which the practitioner seeks self-liberation. This practice includes the precepts of ordination. Mahayana, or the great path, focuses on altruism and benefiting others—both in thought and action. Vajrayana is the tantric, secret mantra path. This path has many techniques to accumulate merit and wisdom to attain transcendental awareness.*

money changers, beggars, and rickshaw drivers, all trying to make a rupee or two off of the wealthier folk. Everyone played their role beautifully. Intoxicated with the richness of the vast array of sights, sounds, and scents, they traipsed and weaved through the Thamel streets to the Indian music blasting from storefronts.

We were roaming down one of those lanes when someone called, "Marya! Miguel!"

"Oh my god!" I groaned and rolled my eyes jokingly. Even in this congested bazaar, we ran into people whom we knew. They were friends from Hawai'i, Noriko, her husband Scott, and their two young daughters. Noriko had attended a thangka[10] painting class at our temple with an artist who had trained in Nepal during the heyday of the 1970s.

"We heard that you were coming!" she said. "We're going to get some dinner. Please join us."

We ducked into a café and sat in a booth near large windows where we chatted while watching the constant colorful street theater. Scooters and three-wheeled bicycles decorated with metallic tinsel maneuvered passed pedestrians; though there were no sidewalks, everyone managed to steer clear of one another. "Rickshaw?" they would call out while tooting their horns, "Madam! Sir! Where you going?"

Before long, we recognized Peter, an old-timer from Dharamsala. Many a tale had circulated about his larger-than-life persona—his travels to Tibet, his aid to the Khampa guerrillas who fought on the eastern frontier against Communist China, and his honorary membership in the Four Rivers–Six Mountains political organization. The rumor was that he had made a small fortune by exporting hand-loomed Tibetan carpets to New York, and that he had invested the profits in a hotel-cum-restaurant with a well-known lama. We had often seen Peter in Dharamsala, mostly as he raced by on his motorcycle. We were just acquaintances, but somehow, here in Nepal, it was like running into an old friend. He waved and we motioned for him to join us.

"There'll be a crackdown soon," he cautioned with the latest news, having just returned from Tibet. "The border's closing in a week, so if you're planning to go in, you better do it soon—like, in the next few days. You have all your visas, right?"

His words resonated with urgency. We could not linger in Kathmandu, but Tiapala didn't have a visa and there was an unforeseen glitch.

---

10. *Thangkas are scrolled paintings or hand-sewn, embroidered appliqués. This sacred-art features images of Buddhas, spiritual teachers, and deities.*

While citizens of India did not need visas for travel to Nepal, not having a stamp showing entry into Nepal meant that a visa to Tibet could only be procured in the country of origin. So Tiapala had to return to India to apply for his visa at the Chinese Embassy in Delhi. We would have to reconnect with him in Lhasa.

Thupten had no official permit to Nepal either. He could have carried an Indian passport but chose to travel with an Identity Certificate (IC) issued to Tibetan refugees by the Indian government. When we had first discussed paperwork, he declared, "I'm Tibetan, and will not get a visa from the Chinese Embassy! I refuse to go to Tibet under the guise of an overseas Chinese. That would be admitting that we Tibetans are Chinese!" He was a patriotic twenty-one-year-old and adamant about not needing Chinese authorization to go to Tibet.

Into Tibet

Fresh mountain air filled our lungs as we drove into the wide-open spaces of the Nepalese countryside. Heading to the border, we gazed out at the endless fields of swaying grain and terraced lands. We passed an occasional ox cart loaded with hay, sacks of grain, and riders hitching a lift. We witnessed processions of villagers, living a simple life, headed to market. Men dressed in plain cotton shirts and loose pajama-style pants and women in long tunics over full, drawstring bottoms. These were the national uniforms. A woman's individuality was differentiated by the choice of fabric, pattern, and colors. Buses and the occasional truck passed by, honking, as passengers stretched their heads out of unwashed windows to stare at us in our unmarked taxicab. Occasionally some schoolgirls would wave merrily and called out greetings with joyous laughter.

Soon we reached Kodari, the entryway to Tibet on the Nepalese border. An unpretentious wooden structure resembling a rustic cabin functioned as the immigration station. Two officers sat indoors in an unlit room, hovering over their journals, logging names, passport information, and visa numbers of travelers.

Surprisingly, we encountered no problems, and Miguel and I got through passport control quickly. Since Thupten had opted to not get a visa, there would be no evidence of his admittance into Tibet. Thankfully, there were no other agents guarding the boundary to check for valid entry. Dozens of men milled around outside. Some drank glasses of caramel tinted sugar tea; others stood and gawked at me, joking and nudging each other. Having spent considerable time in India, I had gotten used to certain men's fixation with Western and Asian women, and it no longer bothered me. In fact, the pandemonium was a welcomed diversion.

Porters positioned themselves for work, clustering around the foreigners and their belongings. It was late in the day and few opportunities remained for them to compete for precious tourist rupees. We had left the task of negotiating to Thupten, who had remained outdoors. The bargaining started; it was loud and aggressive, and continued until a deal was reached.

The three of us walked with our porters over the guardrail toward Tibet. It was unbelievable that we were about to make our entrance into this mysterious, enchanted land. Conscious of every step, we marched straight ahead on a narrow stretch of concrete interestingly named the Friendship Bridge that crossed a rushing river. We had arrived in Tibet.

A government truck transported us further up a long hill, then abruptly dropped us off at the edge of a huge landslide. We were on our own with our three porters. Dynamite blasts sounded off at regular intervals from above as massive boulders and debris tumbled down to find their resting place on the trail that lay before us. Following the lead of our helpers who seemed to know the drill, we dashed in spurts between explosions, taking shelter behind shrubs and any object large enough to grant some superficial protection. Later we learned that the explosions were from the construction of a new mountain road, and workers were often killed in that danger zone that we had maneuvered.

Upon safely reaching the other side, we faced a rugged cliff with a craggy trail winding its way up the hill. It was rush hour on the mountain, yet everyone was courteous in allowing others to pass on the congested track. The hike, while moderately strenuous, was merely a warmup to what was ahead. As we headed higher, the defined route had crumbled and ceased to exist altogether.

Monsoon rains had come early that year and pathways that previous travelers had followed had all but disappeared. What remained were muddy trails, slippery waterways, pits, and hollows. We scrambled to move forward and upward. At times we were on our hands and knees, gripping overhanging branches, exposed tree roots, and even to mother earth herself, clawing ourselves uphill. Our destination was Zhangmu, more commonly known as Dram, the border town on the Tibetan frontier.

Thupten and Marya with border crossers climbing the hill to Dram

It was dusk when we arrived, exhausted and drenched with sweat. Perspiration glistened on our cheeks and dripped from our brows. Our jeans were caked with mud, tees torn, and jackets stained. Yet the fulfillment of having arrived greatly outweighed our fatigue.

Once they collected their fees, which seemed insignificant for their burden, our dutiful porters disappeared to find a place to settle before dark. Alone and unsure of the new territory, we decided to stay put until daybreak. Nearby, a Tibetan road crew had convened around a campfire to stay warm. They offered to share a minimal meal with us, washed down afterwards with salty black tea.

"Vehicles going to Lhasa have all left for the day," they informed us in their native Tibetan dialect. "Sometimes there are buses, but that's uncertain. It all depends if there are enough passengers. Perhaps one will leave tomorrow."

We had no expectations for specific comfort, hence were not disappointed to spend our first night in a makeshift shelter. After all, besides searching for our reincarnate lama in Tibet, we wanted to meet her people and learn about their lives. We discovered an open bus parked a short distance away and crawled into the back seat to rest our weary bodies.

That same bus would transport us onwards the next day. The narrow road out of Dram wound its way up the mountain through tropical terrain and rainforests shrouded in mist, past dramatic landscapes—precipitous cliffs, rushing waterfalls, and rapid torrents—unlike what one imagines of Tibet. We climbed higher and higher until the topography gradually transformed into the panorama of the Tibetan Plateau.

Army barracks provided lodging on our second night. The accommodations were sparse; we had a roof over our heads in a hall with wall-to-wall wooden platforms. Meals were dished out in the mess hall where workers served us heaping portions of pork and rice for dinner and breakfast. Leaving our plates cautiously untouched, Miguel and I opted for handfuls of nuts and dried fruit from our survival kit. Thupten, however, was famished and ate everything in sight. He royally paid for it with diarrhea and severe stomach cramps for the rest of our trip to Lhasa.

During our two-day journey overland to Lhasa, I lost count of the exhilarating ascents required to reach the mountain passes. Each was crowned with hundreds of colorful, wind-blown, and tattered prayer flags along with makeshift altars created from heaps of stones contributed by countless pilgrims.

Nechung Monastery in Lhasa

We walked up a stone stairway to a large courtyard where two ferocious looking stone lions guarded the entrance of the main temple halls. There was not a person in sight.

"I'll go find one of the monks," Thupten said, leaving Miguel and me to sit in silent wonderment. Before long, he returned with a tall, toothless monk (I guessed) in his mid-fifties who welcomed us with "Tashi Delek!" and then unraveled two long white silky scarves and draped them around our necks.

His name was Tsewang, and he had been one of the younger monastics in the 1950s. "Most of our monks are in Lhasa," he told us over tea. He was happy to meet Thupten, whose reputation had preceded him, adding, "They will be here shortly. First you must rest. I'll prepare a room for you."

Prior to 1959, Nechung Monastery housed 115 monks. Now, there were only sixteen, most of them had been ordained before the uprising. Since then, due to restricted enrollment imposed by the Chinese authorities, only a few novices had joined the congregation.

The customary uniform for monastics under the communist regime was shirts and loose trousers in shades of blue, gray, and black. Monks rarely wore their monastic robes, except during prayer ceremonies. They were encouraged to work in the fields and engage in other mundane activities, rather than studying and meditating. For their labor, they were paid with kilos of grain and *tsampa*—parched barley ground into flour that was a Tibetan food staple high in protein and vitamins. The study monks, as they were called, had to find support from private sources or sponsors.

Most of the Nechung monks roomed in town, but they still considered the monastery their true home. The psychological damage from the war and the ensuing hardships were etched deeply into their faces and further reflected in their physical carriage. They had survived but still seemed haunted by the brutality of the atrocities.

The monastery offered Miguel and me a place to stay—a cottage behind Nechung Rinpoche's house that was built by one of his previous assistants, Lobsang Dawa who had married after 1959 and had parented three daughters. Due to his connection with Rinpoche, the Chinese soldiers had tortured him so cruelly that he tried to commit suicide several times. Once he jumped off a cliff into the rushing rapids of the Tsangpo River. Since he couldn't swim, he thought his demise was certain. But the currents kept him afloat and carried him to the opposite shore! After that he gave up trying to die and accepted his fate.

Lobsang Dawa became our standup comedian. "I am the best cook in Lhasa," he would brag, pointing his index finger to the tip of his nose. "I can prepare twenty-course meals for the Chinese generals and all the important people in Lhasa. When they have banquets, they come to me, Lobsang Dawa! I've done everything, even tried to kill myself! I'm just not supposed to go yet." Even the stories of his suicide attempts made us laugh. His arrogance was animated and he spoke with swagger and thumped his chest. We enjoyed his company and soon knew every one of his stories by heart.

He and his daughters lived in the house that had been Rinpoche's residence. Rigzin the oldest, was the workhorse; she did all the chores, took care of the animals, milked the cows, and cooked for the family. She was very shy, but always flashed a gold-capped toothy smile each time she saw us. Another daughter had special needs, placing added responsibility on Rigzin. We never met the third girl who was away at school.

Our cottage was a twenty-by-thirty-foot building with two single beds. The cabinets were painted with Tibetan good-luck symbols and Chinese longevity motifs such as cranes, peaches, and long-life gods. Sets of ceramic bowls, plates, and teacups, plus cotton bedcovers and shams, all made in China, filled the shelves. We found carved wooden bowls filled with dried apricots and hard candies in the cupboards, as well as baskets of deep-fried cookies coated with powdered sugar that were left over from Losar.

Outside our house shimmered two trees laden with sweet juicy peaches. Every morning, we stretched our hands out the window and plucked the bite-size fruits to our hearts' delight. They melted in our mouths and tasted like nectar from the gods.

Lobsang Dawa was a good host. He often brought us creamy milk, thick yogurt, and fertile eggs. We welcomed the protein and the home deliveries. This gave Dawa the opportunity to talk about himself to a captive audience—foreigners fluent in Tibetan, no less. Eventually, the repetitive tales bored me, but Miguel, true to character, engaged him time after time, as if listening to each story anew.

We had brought a small kitchen with us from Hawai'i, including a camp stove that ran on almost anything, an aluminum pot, and utensils for two. We lived on scrambled eggs, miniature potatoes from the market, and canned duck and noodles from the Chinese stores. With the excess milk and eggs from Lobsang Dawa's livestock, we made delicious custard in a pressure cooker purchased in Lhasa.

I remember the quirks of our idyllic home that summer very clearly. One involved Dawa's wild beast of a dog with white, ghostly eyes and the most threatening bark. He guarded the entrance to our house and we named him White Eyes. It hated everyone except its owner and Rigzin, and though chained, it thrashed about so ferociously that I had no doubt it could break loose and attack us. Somehow,

Miguel worked his charm on this hound. I'm not sure how, but I think the greasy sauce and bones from the canned duck that he tossed at it day after day led White Eyes to literally eat out of his hands. I remained terrified of this creature and continued to creep past it with the utmost caution.

The other inconveniences were the lack of indoor plumbing, particularly a toilet, and no running water. We carried water in buckets from a well, then boiled it on our little stove for drinking and sponge baths. It was a luxury to have hot water, and we would often scent it with aromatherapy oils such as lavender, pennyroyal, and eucalyptus. The "lavatory" was open air, accessible by walking through the courtyard gate, running past White Eyes, going out of the main entrance through gnarly brush, sliding down a small ledge to the white sandy bottom of a dry riverbed, and crouching out of sight from bands of feral dogs.

Townspeople often dropped off litters of puppies at the monastery. As the pups grew into mangy mutts, they formed packs and roamed the territory in survival mode. During the day, and especially in the stillness of night, we would hear the yelps and squeals of dogs eating one another. Sadly, in modern Tibet, the metaphor of a "dog-eat-dog world" was true.

Aside from this day-to-day living, we noticed something controversial happening at the monastery. A three-story complex adjacent to the main temple halls, once auxiliary chapels and monastic quarters for Nechung, had been converted into a dialectic institute and dormitory, administered by the Chinese authorities.[11] This effort was intended to impress upon Tibetans as well as the foreign press that freedom of religion was still alive and well in Tibet. Indeed, dozens of young men attended the classes at the school.

The government officials had arbitrarily appointed a headmaster for the institute who had no ties with any monastic tradition. They installed him as the Ganden Tripa, throne holder of Je Tsongkhapa, the founder of the Gelug Lineage. This acclaimed position was customarily achieved through a lifetime of training in Buddhist philosophy and practice, but now the selected person had been coerced into playing a role. As a consequence, he received no respect from the Tibetan community, who aptly nicknamed him the Fake Tripa.

This situation was a mere fraction of the tragedy that befell Tibet since 1949. Nearly all her monasteries were demolished during the Cultural Revolution (1966 to 1976), and their irreplaceable religious treasures looted and hauled away. Like-

---

11. *The institute has since closed, and the buildings are back under the auspices of Nechung Monastery.*

wise, frescoes that remained to grace what temples were left were defaced. Statues were disfigured or destroyed, and bronzes melted down and made into ammunition.

Tibetans were prohibited from keeping anything associated with the Buddha Dharma[12] in their homes. Texts, statues, and paintings of the Buddha and meditation deities, photos of lamas, especially those of the Dalai Lama, were forbidden or confiscated. They were forced to throw manuscripts of spiritual writings and commentaries into roaring bonfires in city squares or toss them into the river torrents. Some people buried their possessions with hopes of retrieving them in the future. Unfortunately, in their haste, most of these sites were unmarked, and those precious heirlooms never resurfaced again.

Miguel and I witnessed the results of nearly thirty years of cultural genocide during our summer visit. When touring the Potala Palace, the legendary home of the Dalai Lamas, we were escorted to one of the dark, dusty upper floors. It was filled with heaps of random pieces from desecrated Buddha statues, every component and body part imaginable. Not one part matched another in this cavernous space. Statues had been torched, crushed, smashed, broken, and scattered. The rage and hatred that fueled these senseless acts was palpable. Why would anyone want to disfigure objects of such beauty and destroy these symbols of peace and enlightenment?

Saddened as we were by these sights, the truth in the Buddhist teachings came to mind. Unlike animals that seek out their prey and kill for food or physical defense, humans have the immense capacity to think and reason to choose actions that benefit the world. Contrarily, they can pursue paths of personal gain, revenge, and corruption. Others, out of ignorance, follow orders with no sensitivity or consideration of the negativity and harm their actions bring.

A famous master once said that although happiness is desired, actions arising out of ignorance destroy happiness as if it were the adversary; and while the wish exists to eradicate suffering, ignorant deeds chase one back into the path of misery itself. It moved us to tears, realizing that these principles taught over 2,500 years ago by Shakyamuni Buddha, were still so relevant in the present day.

Despite these dismal conditions, we felt blessed to have a refuge at Nechung Monastery where the buildings remained intact, although as with other institutions, its religious artifacts also had been destroyed. The monks were very hospitable and

---

12. *Buddha is symbolic of awakening from the sleep of ignorance and having full omniscience. Dharma represents the transformation of mind, based on teachings and practices that lead to that state of pristine awareness.*

enthusiastically engaged Thupten in conversation whenever the opportunity arose. He was the first representative from Nechung in India to visit, and they were eager to learn more about His Holiness the Dalai Lama and life in exile. Miguel and I sponsored several services and were gratified to see the halls vibrate with activity, and to sit with our monastic brothers as they belted out prayers for the benefit of all living beings in baritone voices and melodic chords.

Nechung monks in prayer assembly at Nechung Monastery, Lhasa, Tibet

Tiapala and Thupten making offerings to the Nechung monks

In the mid-1980s, when the ban on Buddhism had been lifted to a small degree, those affiliated with Nechung Monastery coordinated their efforts to restore and replace some of the monastery's sacred images. Loyal supporters of Nechung, former monks and laypeople alike, selflessly offered their labor and skills. Others gave monetarily and donated what remained of their heirlooms and religious reliquaries. The central figure was a spectacular statue of Guru Padmasambhava that rose to a dramatic three stories in height to the crowning rooftop. Golden and resplendent, inlaid with antique turquoise, coral, amber, and mythical *dzi*[13] stones, the statue stood as a symbol of the resilience and commitment of the people of Tibet. It had been consecrated with all the special substances and scriptures merited by such a monumental undertaking. The collective inspiration and wishes of all those who contributed were dedicated toward the fulfillment of His Holiness the Dalai Lama's altruistic aspirations, and for the Tibetan people to regain self-determination and happiness.

Guru Padmasambhava statue at Nechung Monastery in Lhasa

13. *Natural dzi stones are believed to have fallen from the heavens and to possess mystical attributes such as protection from physical and psychic harms, and to bestow good fortune and health. They are antique treasures— jewel heirlooms passed down through the generations.*

First Public Tsok Ceremony

Before we left Dharamsala for Tibet, His Holiness had given Thupten an assignment. He was to organize a Guru Padmasambhava Bum Tsok,[14] a ritual honoring the patron saint of Tibetan Buddhism, enlightened masters, tutelary deities, and protectors.

The only area in Lhasa that was still wholly Tibetan was the historic Barkhor area built around the Jokhang, the holiest temple in Tibet. Thus, the Jokhang was the perfect venue for the momentous occasion. It would be no easy task to stage the event there, or anywhere for that matter, since such a public ceremony had not occurred in Tibet since 1959.

Thupten was undaunted, and shortly after we arrived in Lhasa, he contacted leading activists in the political underground to help with the Bum Tsok. Among them was a charismatic man by the name of Amdo Lungdok, whose activities were well known to the Lhasa police. Despite being detained and imprisoned on numerous occasions, he never deviated from his beliefs and the pursuit of an independent Tibet.

We had managed to smuggle in a large quantity of booklets published by the Information and Security Office of the Tibetan Government-in-Exile. These materials chronicled historical facts, PLA atrocities, lists of missing persons, photos of dead prisoners, and descriptions of torture methods implemented by the Chinese government. Thupten had promptly dropped them off at covert resistance cells in Lhasa, so that people in Tibet could be aware of the efforts of their compatriots in exile.

Amdo Lungdok and Thupten began to plan for the Tsok that was to last five days, beginning on the sixth of the fifth lunar month, and concluding on the tenth. Remarkably, after approaching the few remaining lamas in Lhasa, they secured commitments from teachers of all four lineages who were keen to attend.

A senior Nyingma lama named Gyalsay Rinpoche agreed to preside over the ceremonies as ritual master. He was a frail, elderly man, nearly deaf from the brutal beatings by the Red Guard. He had been a contemporary of Nechung Rinpoche; indeed, Rinpoche had gifted his entire library to him before his escape in 1962.

Dordrak Rigzin Chenmo, the principal lama of Dorje Drak Monastery, was another high-profile person who accepted the invitation. Now married, he worked

---

14. *The term Bum (One Hundred Thousand) Tsok (Feast Offering) indicates that the offering verses are recited a combined one hundred thousand times by the attendees.*

in the Office of Religious Affairs, which was under the auspices of the People's Republic of China.

Illustrious figures of the Kagyu lineage also wanted to participate. These included Drikung Chungtsang Rinpoche, one of the two heads of Drikung Kagyu, renowned throughout Tibet for Phowa—the transference of consciousness at the time of death. His counterpart, Drikung Chetsang Rinpoche, had escaped from Tibet and had since reestablished a monastery in northern India. Before his flight, Chetsang Rinpoche had been a key player on a national soccer team and was a celebrated athlete. His successful breakaway was a major loss and public embarrassment for the Chinese government.

Another was Gyalsap Rinpoche, a close disciple of the Sixteenth Karmapa from the Karma Kagyu lineage who happened to be visiting from India. We suspected that he may have been in Tibet on a discovery mission similar to ours, since the Karmapa had passed away in the late 1970s.

Scholars and abbots from various monasteries around Lhasa represented the other traditions. The consensus was that only lamas and the monastics would be seated to chant the liturgies with the exception of Miguel and me, who were given the honor of joining the assembly.

Numerous people wanted to be there, and there was no shortage of supporters, but it was prudent to limit the number of participants. Being the first gathering of this magnitude—nothing like that had been attempted for almost thirty years—taking the utmost precaution was not to be understated. If there were any political repercussions, the potential of incarceration and investigation of everyone involved was an undeniable reality. The coordinators decided that one hundred people, more or less, would be a safe number and sufficient to accumulate the 100,000 repetitions for the Tsok ceremony.

In the early phases of preparation, we were not certain if the formalities should be held in such a public venue as the Jokhang. Since our intentions were pure, we believed the energy generated from the Tsok would be beneficial no matter how many people were involved or where the ceremony was held. So perhaps it was wise to be discreet.

A small chapel dedicated to the chief female protectress, Palden Lhamo, was located above the main Jokhang shrine. That room was a consideration, and after Thupten discussed this option with the temple custodians, he felt confident that permission would be granted. However, everyone felt an irrepressible desire to openly exercise the religious freedom that the Chinese government had declared was the right of all Tibetans. A public prayer ceremony would be a perfect opportunity to put that to the test.

Thupten defiantly secured the use of the central courtyard inside the Jokhang gates which would provide ample room for the assembly as well as for interested observers.

Amdo Lungdok and Dordrak Rikzin Chenmo's wife were assigned to form a committee in charge of donations and food. They had to organize a crew to accept both monetary and edible offerings and were responsible for preparing tea and meals for the attendees. Their team was to record the income and present daily honorariums to the clergy. At the completion of the event, they were to distribute the balance of funds to monasteries and community organizations.

No one was prepared for the overwhelming response and fervor. Hundreds of enthusiastic worshippers congregated for the prayer sessions daily. They wanted to contribute to the ritual, make offerings, and jointly share in the wealth of goodness and merit. And that they did, with immense generosity. Daily, there was an abundance of donations—cash, mounds of butter, sacks of dried cheese, blocks of brown sugar, meat, dried and seasonal fruits.

A hill of tsampa, offerings for the Bum Tsok at Jokhang

Volunteers preparing the tsampa for tormas

Each day so much *tsampa* amassed in the center of Jokhang's courtyard, shovels were needed to separate this roasted barley flour into smaller heaps. The *tsampa* was combined with butter, sugar, and dried fruit, and formed into *tormas* (molded ritual "cakes") then offered and blessed during the prayer recitations.

Tibetans making torma "bricks"

Red brick torma "wall"

A large percentage of the volunteers at the ceremonies were nuns. They were from Shugsep, a respected nunnery across the river from Lhasa, renowned for Chod, a meditative practice for the realization of the wisdom of selflessness and the removal of karmic debt. Chod consisted of hauntingly beautiful melodies sung to the beat of a large hand drum. Before the Chinese invasion, an extraordinary woman named Shugsep Jetsun Rinpoche lived at the nunnery. She was revered by laypeople and monastics alike, and was considered to be one of Tibet's greatest female masters. Nechung Rinpoche and many of the monks at his monastery had studied with her. Over the years, we had heard many stories about her great skill in teaching, her insight, and natural wisdom. She was said to have the angelic voice of a young girl and her songs drew one magically into a state of meditative absorption.

A disciple of Shugsep Jetsun Rinpoche came to the Bum Tsok. She had long, graying hair rolled up in a knot and the melodious voice of accomplished Chod practitioners. I felt a strong kinship with her, and we bonded during the meditation sessions as we chanted together in harmony.

Somehow, the news had circulated to Tibetan communities abroad that a Bum Tsok would be performed at the Jokhang per the wishes of His Holiness the Dalai Lama. Not only did the gathering manifest in the heart of Lhasa, but Tibetans around the world did the same practice and recitations on the exact dates.

Lamas in prayer assembly at Bum Tsok

The five-day Bum Tsok unfolded as a tremendous, once-in-a-lifetime experience, and we were humbled to be included in such an auspicious occasion. For ten hours every day, we sang and prayed, savoring every minute of the experience. "How fortunate," I thought, "to be sitting here doing this practice with the Nechung and Namgyal[15] monks at the Jokhang. Who could ever have dreamed?"

At the Jokhang, Tibetans from the city and from every region of the country came to observe and listen over the course of those few days. Proud were the Khampas from Eastern Tibet, men known for their courage, women for their beauty.

---

15. *Namgyal Monastery is connected to H.H. the Dalai Lama. Namgyal monks assist him in prayer and ritual.*

The men stood tall, noticeable from afar, with colorful red string woven into their long, braided hair. Cords strung with red coral and *dzi* stones dangled from their necks to accentuate broad shoulders and muscular builds. On the street, clustered in groups with exposed daggers on their hips, these Khampas were intimidating, but here at the Tsok, they came to pay their respects like everyone else.

Tibetan worshippers gathered around the shrine at Jokhang

Everyone stood in solidarity. The Khampas towered over the villagers, who brushed shoulders with the nomads. They appeared to be unfazed by the mid-summer heat, even though many were dressed in dark woolen *chubas* over layers of undergarments. Some pilgrims had prostrated, trekked, and traveled for days, weeks, even months, from the countryside to reach the holy city.

All were there to receive the blessings of the enlightened ones, whose collective presence was invoked to emerge from their divine pure-lands and bestow pristine qualities of body, speech, and mind upon sentient beings. The worshippers held their palms together at the heart, with eyes full of devotion, and lips slightly ajar with whispers of mantra and prayers.

The voices of the assembly recited melodic verses to graceful, symbolic mudras,[16] hands holding vajras (Tibetan: *dorje*)—spiritual implements that symbolize the absolute nature of mind and skillful means—and bells (Tibetan: *drilbu*) to signify primordial wisdom. The deep reverberation of long horns and clash of cymbals would occasionally sound to the beat of the large floor drums, signaling precise stages of the ritual that culminated with dedicating the accumulation of virtue for the welfare of all beings.

Daily, the excitement of the crowd increased as the ceremonies moved toward their conclusion. The weight of the multitudes' bodies pressed upon one another, moving ever closer toward the roped barricades. All were familiar with the sequence of the prayers and knew that the distribution of the *tormas* and food offerings was imminent. As the assistants sliced the *tormas*, opened biscuit packages, and divided heaps of candies and fruits, the spirit of the crowd intensified with anticipation. Outreached hands stretched over the barricades, clamoring around and under each other. The volume of fervent voices grew louder by the second. The servers added to the chaos by shouting out, "Get back! Move! Wait your turn! You'll get a share!" Then they reiterated, "Get back, get back…" All the Tsok offerings were apportioned eventually, appeasing the throngs of devotees and pleasing the celestial beings.

Plainclothes Chinese officers who were easy to spot were in the audience. They had overtly set cameras on tripods smack in the middle of the hall and videotaped hours of the proceedings. Occasionally they snapped photos of the assembly, cross sections of the crowd, and persons of interest.

The "secret" police appeared to be confused about Miguel and me. During the rituals, when looking into the crowds, we caught them scrutinizing us with perplexed expressions. I could only guess what they were thinking: "Who are they? Why do they have permission to sit with these lamas and monks? They're not Tibetan and not dressed in ordination robes; yet they're reading the folios of the Tibetan scriptures and chanting the language with ease. He's a white man… is he from America or Europe? The Asian woman…is she Chinese? From what country?" It gave me great satisfaction to watch their consternation.

On the second day, several of them confronted us during the lunch break. In aggressive voices, they rattled off Chinese verbiage that sounded like a series of

---

16. *Mudras are symbolic hand gestures while making offerings, invocations, etc.*

questions. People who had lingered behind gathered around to listen. The situation was tense, and although we were apprehensive, I felt no fear.

Tibetan is an Indo-Burmese language derived from Sanskrit and distinctly different from Chinese. So, although we were fluent in Tibetan, we were unable to engage them in even the simplest dialogue. Looking back, I wish that I had become more proficient in Chinese and its many dialects. To have had the ability to communicate within Western, Tibetan, and Chinese cultures would have been a great asset in our work.

But in the temple courtyard, under the watchful eyes of these agents, not knowing the language was a bonus. We stared wide-eyed, looking perplexed. Miguel made some wise cracks and laughed, which they did not comprehend. Finally, with mock courtesy, we shrugged our shoulders and walked away. It was time to reconvene the afternoon prayer session; the lamas and worshippers were waiting. Frustrated and powerless, the plainclothes men returned to their cameras and avoided us for the remaining days of Tsok festivities.

Nevertheless, Miguel and I remained somewhat prepared for the situation to worsen. In case of violence, Miguel had devised an escape route. We would go behind the cushioned area where the assembly sat; then, go through the back of the courtyard, past the prayer wheels, and into Meru Nyingpo. This was the Nechung shrine in town that was situated behind Jokhang. However, there was no need to enact the getaway. The Bum Tsok came to an splendid conclusion without further interference.

The Way to the Visionary Lake

Weeks had passed and Tiapala still had not arrived. Having completed the Bum Tsok, we began to make plans without him for the anticipated excursion to Lhamo Latso, the visionary lake and abode of the protectress Palden Lhamo, high in the mountains southeast of Lhasa.

Thupten, Miguel and I would travel with three other companions. Our expedition group included Tsering and Drolma, who were the parents of Kalsang Dawa, one of our monks at Nechung in Dharamsala. Their two-room apartment was where we would go whenever we were hungry or needed a place to strategize. Drolma, a jolly, plump, talkative woman would invariably cook up something tasty and nutritious. Tsering was a former Nechung monk, and somewhat of an introvert, contemplative and philosophic on every matter.

The sixth person on our team, "Drikung" (Thupten's nickname for him) was a short, stocky monk with an unusual alignment of his eyes. He was an acquaintance of Thupten's from Drikung Monastery in northern India and had come to Lhasa as the advance person for Drikung Chetsang Rinpoche's visit. When the lama didn't arrive for the Bum Tsok, "Drikung" decided to join us on the adventure to Lhamo Latso.

Transportation was a challenge. It was particularly problematic in our situation since Lhamo Latso was located close to the border, in a zone prohibited to foreigners. A friend of Thupten came to our rescue by loaning us an official jeep. We just had to make our way to Tsethang, where the vehicle and its designated driver would wait for us.

Tsethang was a garrison town filled with bases for the Chinese military at the crossroads of the highway to the border. India and China had had a boundary dispute since warring in 1962, and they were positioning themselves to plunge into conflict again. The streets were lined with army trucks and crawling with soldiers. We had ventured into hostile territory, but no one noticed us amidst the bustle.

We spent the first night in Tsethang in a hostel with all six of us crammed into a frigid cell. The walls were streaked with tea splatter, the floors filthy. Bathrooms and the stained toilets, from whence emitted a putrid stench, were down the hall. Printed bed covers, soiled and slept on by many previous tenants, could not disguise the hardness of the beds. I was thankful that we had brought our own bedding and relieved when the management declared that Westerners were not allowed to room there. Miguel proposed to pay for an upgrade at a better hotel where the driver picked us up the next morning.

Lhamo Latso was in a restricted area, distant from civilization and unspoiled by human activity. All roads leading to that locality were patrolled with checkpoints at junctions to inspect vehicles and passengers. If apprehended, it was likely we would be deported back to India. We would *never* have reached our destination had we not been riding in a jeep with the required legitimate registration and markings of an authorized vehicle. It so happened that our road trip coincided with a policemen's gala and other festivities in Lhasa. So, most of the police force in the Tsethang district had gone to the city, leaving the roadways with minimal security. Our guardian angels appeared to be watching over us.

We passed dozens of nondescript communities with guard posts, a shop or two, and hole-in-the-wall eateries, where villagers peered at us from their simple shacks. At several minor inspection stations, and one major one, we were stopped by armed guards who searched our jeep, questioned the driver, and scrutinized us through the windows. Since our driver had no idea where we were heading, nor the whereabouts of the lake, he could honestly answer that he was taking his passengers on a sightseeing tour. He had a current license and permit to drive in the district, and the registration of the vehicle clearly indicated that it belonged to a government agency. All the paperwork was valid, and with no more than a nod and a wave of hand, we were sent on our way.

Our driver was a shy, quiet fellow, but that didn't keep us from befriending him. As we traveled into the restricted territory through multiple checkpoints, it was critical that he become part of our team. Miguel had bought a case of beer and kept it on the floor behind the front seats. "Chinese beer at room temperature is tolerable up here in the Tibetan Plateau," he would say. The alcohol and Thupten's relentless teasing kept our chain-smoking driver oblivious of the distance we had covered on our quest to find the visionary lake.

Gradually the terrain changed. We left the dusty roads and villages behind us. The path became narrower, the surroundings greener—hillsides filled with high-elevation pines, grassy meadows with saffron and lavender wildflowers. A rushing river with crystalline rapids flowed to our right as we drove into the valley. Soon we were no longer on a road but merely following the course of the river on a bumpy uphill trail etched by trickling water. Mist enveloped us. Now and then, we spotted a nomad on the distant slopes herding longhair yaks. We breathed in tranquility as we slipped farther and farther away from the civilized world into what might well be the pure-land of Shangri-La.

As we climbed higher into the mountains, the vegetation morphed into clipped grasslands. Rolling foothills seemed to extend into the reaches of space, and gradually the landscape became vast panoramas beneath open skies. Hours passed, yet I was unaware of time, completely mesmerized by our surroundings.

Suddenly, the dark shapes of a cluster of buildings loomed into view. We had arrived at our destination. These were the remains of a grand monastery called Chokhor Gyal, now mostly rubble from bombings and war demolition. In the midst of the ruins and half-standing stone walls were some intact structures that the current residents, few that there were, had managed to reconstruct from debris and salvaged materials. Although the Chinese army had dynamited the buildings, painted murals of guardian protectors remained visible at the entrance, boldly defiant of the Red Army's attempts at complete destruction.

We sensed that our personal protectors had journeyed with us when Drolma recognized the manager of Chokhor Gyal to be her cousin. He welcomed us wholeheartedly and was most hospitable. "There's not much here anymore but we do have a vacant building. Please stay as long as you wish," he offered.

The dark hut, lit by a single opening in the rock wall, was heated by burning yak dung in a makeshift pit that also served as a stove. Ventilation was nonexistent. Each time we made a fire, the entire room filled with thick, heavy smoke, causing my eyes to sting and tear. At those elevations and freezing temperatures, there was no choice but to keep the fire stoked even if it caused everyone to choke and cough incessantly.

Miguel and I were given the opportunity to sleep off the floor on a five-by-two-foot platform next to the window. It was barely large enough for one person, let alone two, and our communal living conditions were much too public to snuggle together. So, we set our sleeping bags side by side and laid ourselves head to foot.

What was the price I paid for sleeping on such a "deluxe" cot, while everyone else slept on the earthen floor? Body lice and unbearable itching were made worse by an allergic reaction.

I gave in to my urge to scratch, and dug into the welts with my sharp, jagged nails, long overdue for a manicure. The vigorous scratching provided temporary gratification but caused scabs that lasted for weeks. For relief, we soaked towels in boiled water and applied steaming compresses to my irritated sores—the hotter the better. These treatments brought momentary comfort and pleasure. The lice favored the tender flesh around my waist, upper thighs, underarms, and breasts. They laid their eggs, clear gelatinous forms with dark centers, into the waistbands of my jeans and seams of my T-shirts. We did our laundry in boiling water just to ease my mind that the little crawlers were eliminated.

Word traveled fast in the valley that strangers had arrived, including two monks with sacks of blessings from His Holiness the Dalai Lama. Dozens of people showed up at our door with gifts of eggs, milk, cheese, and dried meat—all commodities that were never sold, merely shared and bartered. In return, Thupten and Drikung gave them color photos of His Holiness, blessing "pills" consecrated with mantra and prayer, and knotted red protection cords.

Thupten giving blessings to Tibetans at Chokhor Gyal

Chokhor Gyal lies at the confluence of three valleys surrounded by three mountains. A wide, shallow creek flowed by the monastery, its water from glacier runoffs was sparkly, icy cold, and pure. On the opposite shore, ruins of the Second and Third Dalai Lamas' retreats could be seen on the ridges of the two closest hillsides overlooking the valley.

Drolma's cousin sent a guide to accompany us and let us borrow Tibetan ponies for our excursions up to the lake. It was convenient to have an escort on the first trip, and the animals were advantageous to have, although I felt tinges of guilt that they had to labor to give us ease. Initially we followed well-defined trails, then continued straight up the mountain until we reached an alpine meadow where we saw indications of former habitation—partial walls and the foundation of a dwelling.

Miguel on a Tibetan pony on the way to Lhamo Latso

Lhamo Latso

Prayer flags in primary colors, inscribed with symbols and mantras, flew fiercely in the brisk wind on a hilltop as if summoning us to ascend to pay homage to the goddess of the lake. We scrambled on the loose stones and boulders up to a narrow, snowy ridge and gazed down into a vast, glassy amphitheater. The oval lake was a reflective mirror at the bottom of a basin, protected by steep, curved walls. We were lone observers sitting on the ledge encompassed by a tranquil silence. All was still but for the frosty kiss of the gusty breeze.

Lhamo Latso, the Visionary Lake

Our entire team had come on this initial trip. Alongside the existing flags, we quickly hung those that had been carried all the way from India. Imbued with blessings from many a high lama, the gauzy cloths, emblazoned with wind horses and victory banners, soared through the air, carrying prayers into all directions.

Miguel making a smoke offering at the ridge overlooking the visionary lake

Monks and Marya raising prayer flags on the ridge overlooking Lhamo Latso

The current Dalai Lama Tenzin Gyatso had been recognized at the age of two with signs of his whereabouts seen at Lhamo Latso. Images in the visionary lake included Tibetan letters pointing to the Amdo region and Kumbum, a landmark monastery. Outside a nearby farmhouse, the vision reflected a small boy with a spotted dog. Thereafter, a search party, disguised as common folk, found the actual place as envisioned in the lake. The young boy knew the delegation members by name and correctly identified the personal possessions of his predecessor. After a series of tests—inner, outer, and secret—were completed, he was recognized as the indisputable reincarnation of the Thirteenth Dalai Lama, Thupten Gyatso, and enthroned as the Fourteenth Dalai Lama.

Lhamo Latso at about 17,400 feet, was everything we imagined it to be. I could sense that the lake held a mystery only those with the wisdom eye might hope to decipher. We sat enthralled, gazing into the lake for the longest time, but nothing of significance was revealed on that first day.

In the following days, Thupten, Drikung, Miguel, and I made subsequent journeys without Tsering and Drolma who were content to rest at the monastery. For our final trip, we were motivated to spend the night so that we could begin our vision quest at daybreak. We packed overnight gear, warm clothing, some provisions, and our well-used camp stove.

We arrived late in the day and set up camp within some crumbling stone walls that gave an illusion of shelter. Miguel prepared a steaming duck soba soup that everyone consumed with gusto. After dinner, we stretched a waterproof tarp over the platform, set the ponies out to graze, and retired to bed, anticipating an early morning.

Marya and Miguel with Thupten and Drikung in the makeshift tent at Lhamo Latso

Miguel and I had cozy down-filled bags while the monks, being the young braves that they were, had nothing more than wool blankets. Sometime during the night, we awakened to a snowstorm and discovered that everything had been completely covered with drifts of freshly fallen snow. The blizzard was so heavy that we couldn't see beyond the boundaries of our makeshift shelter.

The only thing visible in the beam of our flashlights was the redness of Thupten's parched face and the multiple cold sores on his lips. Having dismissed the use of sunscreen, he was badly burned and peeling from the intense high-altitude sun and wind.

We pulled the covers over our heads and managed to stay warm. Despite the freezing temperatures, the four of us in the small space created enough body heat to be quite comfortable. We slept soundly until daybreak.

At dawn, Miguel fired up the stove, brewed the remainder of our Hawaiian organic coffee and cooked a full pot of oatmeal. We were ready. Still in the clouds, we made footprints on the pure white carpet as we hiked up to our perch and waited for the lake to appear. I deeply longed for a vision. So with wholehearted aspiration, I prayed for some clues to guide us to Rinpoche's reincarnation.

Just as vapor dissipates off a mirror, the lake slowly made its appearance. We sat, bundled in our layers of wool and down, and peered single pointedly into its mystical surface. It felt as if I was in a trance. My eyes burned and my skin smarted from the cold, but it did not matter—I was under the hypnotic spell of the reflective mirror.

Jokingly, Miguel muttered one of his sarcasms from beneath his wool scarf. "This is how Tibetans get high. Fast on water, starve yourself on little food, hike as quickly as possible uphill at twenty thousand feet, then look into the lake and hallucinate!" This acute observation caused me to laugh aloud, sending echoes in all ten directions.

As I gazed into the goddess' sphere, I saw the elegant script of Tibetan calligraphy and a simple house set in green pastures and wildflowers. What did these symbols represent? Was it a clue for the quest to find our reincarnate lama? Did anyone else see these same images—or anything at all? I glanced over and saw that my companions were in different stages of concentration. One was huddled under his blanket, head nodding in a blissful nap. Another looked dull and rather bored. The third was staring unblinkingly into the lake, trying his hardest to have a vision as well. No one spoke, since the experience was beyond words; we simply reveled in the peace of the moment.

Around noon, we intuitively knew that it was time to head back to base camp. Our time at Chokhor Gyal Monastery was coming to a close. Our driver was anxious about getting back to work. After all, he had only been given permission for a short leave. We agreed to depart within two days.

The Elusive Chamseng Latso

Thupten and Drikung were full of energy and decided to make one more jaunt up the mountain, this time to a lake called "Chamseng Latso," the abode of a ferocious protector. It was in such a secluded area that it was rarely visited. They left before sunrise and returned by midday, breathless and exhilarated.

"You must all go!" Thupten exclaimed. "It's really different from Lhamo Latso. You will be able to sit at the shore of the lake. It's awesome!" His enthusiasm was infectious.

"How far is it, and how will we find it?" Miguel asked.

Thupten slapped Miguel on the back as if to convince him: "It's *really* close. Look how fast we got back today. Don't worry, I'll give you directions!"

Of course, we couldn't resist. Early the next morning, well-rested Tsering and Drolma joined Miguel and me, and we started our trek. The first part was a pleasant and gradual incline through fertile green hillsides covered with tiny flowers. Soon we met up with some locals. Most of them were on their hands and knees, as if searching for something in the grass. We couldn't fathom what was going on, so we stopped.

"What are you doing?" I inquired. "Are you looking for something?"

They all glanced up but no one spoke. Finally, one of them replied, "We're looking for Yar-tsa Gun-bu."

"What's that?" Miguel asked, full of curiosity.

Drolma knew and spoke up, "The meaning is in the name," she explained. "Yar-tsa—plant in the summer; Gun-bu—insect in the winter."

It still didn't make sense, so Miguel and I got down on our hands and knees to join the party. It didn't take long to focus on the object of the hunt. There it was—a tiny chameleon-like root that blended in perfectly with the reeds.

"Chinese doctors and pharmacies pay us good money for these. They're considered to be medicinal, said to cure back pains, kidney ailments, and purify blood," they told us. "They're in high demand due to their scarcity. Only in the summer, up at these altitudes, can you find them. As winter approaches, these roots will metamorphose into a worm-like being."

"Strange," I thought, but then, in the world of phenomenal existence, anything was possible.

"Can we buy some from you?" I asked. "What are these things worth?"

This was a chance to support the local economy, so we settled for the asking price and were given our pick of the crop. Having scored a precious supply of Yar-tsa Gunbu, we continued on our hike to Chamseng Latso with our newfound friends.

Marya with the root hunters on the way to Chamseng Latso

As we climbed, the terrain became rocky, the trail steep and merciless. Before long, the four of us started to lag behind. Our companions charged ahead effortlessly while we stopped and gasped for breath every few steps. My heart raced and I felt it pounding in my chest and eardrums.

"At this rate, we'll never get there," I said, feeling slightly discouraged.

Tsering and Drolma weren't doing much better. At twelve thousand feet, Lhasa was in the lowlands compared to this. "I've heard about Chamseng Latso my entire life," Tsering commented. "Travelers' heads split open in pain, noses bleed profusely, and hearts stop while hiking to this lake. The patron deity of Chamseng Latso is so wrathful that it manifests in any weakness of the physical body. Not many people attempt this journey, and even fewer reach the lake."

Yet, we had come too far to turn back. The route was like an obstacle course; several areas resembled wide riverbeds where we stumbled on rocks, scrambled over boulders, and clambered up the opposite banks. Around each bend on the trail, up every crest of a hill, and at each false summit, we expected to see the lake. Every time we looked up with anticipation, there was nothing, just more of the same terrain. With sheer willpower, we heaved our weary bodies forward. Before long, our steps turned into a trudge. The midday sun was beating down upon us as we dragged one heavy foot ahead of the other.

Every few yards, Miguel and I had to pause to inhale deeply, trying to capture all the oxygen we could in each gulp of thin air. We didn't have the strength to speak. I didn't know whether to laugh or cry. All that we could muster was to roll our eyes and shake our heads in dismay. This had to be a monk's practical joke: There was *no* lake!

Still, we pushed forward. After what seemed like an eternity, as we turned one last corner, our half-closed eyes, squinting from fatigue, caught sight of a mirage-like body of water shimmering in the near distance. With faster steps, we shuffled forward down the narrow slope to the lake. There we joined the root hunters, lounging by the shore.

The reward of surviving the ordeal and reaching our destination did not seem to compensate for the hardship that we had endured to get there. The lake appeared to be no larger than a fishpond—shallow and diminutive. At least that was how it seemed from my mundane perspective. Very likely, it was a grand celestial palace filled with divine beings and infinite goodness reaching into the sky.

Perhaps it was the tremendous effort it took to get there and the sheer relief of arriving, or the massive blessings that penetrated the core of our being, but we all fell asleep the moment our exhausted bodies sank into the ground at the edge of Chamseng Latso. In our daze, cradled by the warmth of the sun and the sweet whistle of the wind, whatever visions we may have had were solely registered in our daydreams.

Upon awakening, we felt uplifted with no hint of weariness. The glacier lake seemed to have transformed as well, and for a magnificent interminable instant, we were graced by its luminous tranquility.

Sacred Pilgrimage Sites

The return trek was swift, and it was still light when we entered the monastic grounds. We prepared to leave Chokhor Gyal before nightfall. There were still several pilgrimage sites on our wish list before we returned to Lhasa. One was a visit to Machig Labdron's meditation cave. I had long been interested in the life of this female adept, responsible for the transmission of the Chod practice, and I wanted to visit the site where she had gained realization of wisdom and nature of mind.

The jeep had begun to show signs of abuse shortly after leaving the remote monastery. It rattled and sputtered as black smoke spewed from the exhaust. Even so, we arrived without incident and were soon hiking up to the cave which had been encased within stone walls. It had the semblance of a citadel, humbly perched atop a hill overlooking lush green fields with yellow mustard flowers in full bloom that stretched into the vastness of Yarlung Valley. I felt a surge of gratitude for all the remarkable masters who had tread the path before us, thankful for their sacrifices and the legacies they left behind. This heartfelt feeling infused me with tenderness and devotion.

Everyone concurred that the next stop should be Cholung, where Je Tsongkhapa, often called Je Rinpoche, spent long periods in retreat to engage in practices such as physical prostrations for purification and the accumulation of merit.

Our driver had to return to his job and could chauffeur no longer. He had been a good sport, polite, obliging, and never once complained. We parted ways at the crossroads to Cholung and the highway back to Lhasa—thanking him and waving good-bye until he disappeared into the distance.

Left to fend for ourselves, we strolled down to the river crossing and shared a snack on the grassy knoll next to a ramp. There, we waited for the daily ferry that was pulled mechanically by an overhead cable from shore to shore.

Once on the other side, the monks hitched a ride for us in the back of a truck that dropped us off by a warehouse occupied by some villagers. We hired the only transportation available for the next leg, a tractor-trailer, which was a common form of conveyance in Tibet. The motorized forepart had a single seat for the operator; this towed an open cart for transporting miscellaneous commodities—in this case, passengers.

"Cholung is up there," the driver told us after a bouncy ride. He pointed to a rocky cliff. "You can't miss it."

"Have him come back to get us," Miguel whispered to Thupten.

"We'll stay two nights," Thupten said, "can you come back for us?"

"Yeah, sure," the driver agreed, looking away.

I looked skeptically at Miguel who glanced back at me with raised eyebrows.

"You know, I heard that the oldest Nechung monk, Jampa Soepa-la, is at Cholung," Tsering said. "He has students whom he teaches, and they attend to his needs. This place gives him solace away from government and politics."

Indeed, we did find Jampa Soepa-la, a frail man in his late seventies, who resembled a saintly hermit. He seemed to be content in this austere setting with minimal material possessions. We were greeted like extended family and offered food and accommodations.

During our candid conversation with the elder, everyone encouraged him to return to Lhasa. "Nechung desperately needs you," Thupten pleaded. "The novices, few as there are, deserve a teacher from the old days who has knowledge to guide and inspire them. The situation is dire and complicated, but it is essential that the senior monks work together to rebuild the strength of the monastery. Please consider our suggestion!"

Jampa Soepa-la acknowledged the veracity of Thupten's words with a slight nod; but he remained silent and gave no assurance that he would heed the request. Some years later, we heard that the old monk did return to Nechung Monastery and became the head teacher until he passed away.

Je Tsongkhapa's meditation room was Miguel's and my temporary lodging. This was an unexpected privilege since individuals seldom slept there. We laid next to where Je Rinpoche had accumulated his 100,000 full body prostrations. An impression of his body could be seen on the smooth stone slab of granite from the countless repetitions. Though it had been over 500 years since he had practiced there, the profundity of his experience and the timeless blessing were palpable.

In the Tibetan tradition, there are two methods of doing prostrations. In both instances, practitioners begin in a standing position and place their hands on the crown of the head, at the forehead, throat, and heart. This represents eliminating negativity—physical, verbal or mental—and attaining enlightened qualities of body, speech, and mind. With the five-pointed prostration, the person kneels down and touches his or her forehead, two palms and two knees on the ground, thus a "five-pointed" prostration. This symbolizes the purification of the five afflictions—desire, anger, ignorance, pride, and jealousy. This is usually done thrice upon entering temples or in the presence of lamas and holy images to pay respect.

The full body prostration is more of an accumulative practice. Here, the practitioner also begins as described above, but instead of the five points touching the ground, he or she bends forward and slides their hands until the entire body is stretched out on the ground or platform. This symbolizes purifying all the beings in the ground below oneself. Upon rising, one imagines raising beings out of unfortunate lower states to a higher consciousness. The number of prostrations counted is a personal choice. One of the practices in the "*ngondro*" or preliminaries is the accumulation of 100,000 full prostrations.

Despite Cholung's wondrous history, nothing extraordinary happened; no major revelations or visionary dreams, nothing to guide us to our reincarnate lama, just a restful interlude. Soon it was time to move on.

Unfortunately, Drikung, our accompanying monk, had developed a bad case of dysentery from some rancid pork that Drolma had fed him. It was so severe that he was bleeding.

"Ha, I never get stomach problems," Drolma boasted, scoffing at the ailing Drikung. "I love pork, the older the better. No matter how much I eat, I never get sick!"

Drikung was weak and could hardly stand up. It was serious enough that Thupten had to piggyback him down the mountain. As we had predicted, no one came to meet us at the bottom of the hill—no tractor-trailer, no driver. We made our way to a granary and spent the night in the empty building, hoping that someone would come the next day. By mid-morning, it was clear that we had to get moving. Thankfully, Drikung had improved somewhat and could walk without assistance.

Along the way we met two people and negotiated a lift back to the river crossing that we had traversed three days earlier. This time however, I sensed an uneasiness in the air. We were told that during our time at Cholung, police had scoured the entire region looking for foreigners who had reportedly entered the restricted area. Truck drivers were threatened with sizable fines, confiscation of their licenses, and potential jail sentences should they be caught with a foreigner in their vehicle. No doubt they were searching for us. Still, we needed to solicit a ride, given how far we were from our next stop, Samye Monastery. Finally, a Tibetan driver, albeit with great hesitancy, consented to take the risk.

"You guys and those two (pointing to Tsering and Drolma) can get in now and come across the river with me," he directed Thupten and Drikung. "The foreigners should go on the ferry and pretend they're traveling alone. When we reach the other side, I'll drive up to the guardrail and go through the security check. Your Western friends should head up to the highway and meet us there."

Miguel and I did as instructed. Once again, circumstances favored us. The guards had stepped away for a tea break, leaving their post deserted. We jumped onto the flatbed of the waiting vehicle and were off, undetected.

To reach Samye, we had to cross the Tsangpo River in an antiquated yak-skin boat along with a few other passengers. As we steered across the river, I recalled the metaphor of the ferryman who navigates his vessel across a waterway with his passengers. This metaphor symbolizes someone who strives for liberation by traveling together with others on the path to attain simultaneous enlightenment.

Reaching the opposite shore, we were treated to a spectacular view—dunes as far as the eye could see. It was as though the entire universe were covered with fine grains of sand. In the sweltering afternoon heat, with barely a breeze and the sun's rays beating down upon us, all we saw was blinding whiteness.

Two former Nechung monks with whom Thupten was acquainted were at the water's edge, as if waiting to greet us. How fortuitous! They were expecting a ride to the monastery; as anticipated, a truck soon showed up. We were invited to jump in the back, sparing us the long march to Samye. We rode for miles, wind blowing through my hair, sand prickling my eyes, and limitless space all around. For a moment, I drifted in a free Tibet.

It wasn't long before a sharp needle pierced my illusory bubble. Setting foot on the Samye Monastery grounds, we stood with palms clasped, admiring the newly renovated entrance. Suddenly several Tibetan men rushed toward us. In harsh voices, they shouted vehemently, "Hey you, foreigners, pay your entry fees! Pay and get out of the way!"

Their attitude outraged Miguel. "What are you doing! Are you Tibetans or Chinese hacks? You should be ashamed of yourselves. We're on pilgrimage and you're demanding money." He threw some cash at them. "We intended to give more than the admission fee. Take your renminbi. Is that enough, or do you want more?"

Taken aback by a white man uttering honest words in their native tongue, the gate-keepers were dumbfounded. At a loss for words, their eyes darted back and forth between the members of our group. A small crowd had congregated to gawk and listen to the altercation. To avoid further awkwardness, they ushered us hastily through the gates.

The men from Nechung were trained artists commissioned to head the restoration of the murals at Samye. They were doing a superb job on the frescoes covering the walls, masterpieces detailing the dissemination of Buddhism in Tibet, how Samye was established, and the numerous great lamas in Tibet's glorious past. Freshly painted, the scenes were vibrant and dynamic, gilded with golden highlights, their evocative figures seemed to reenact Tibet's ancient history with animation.

We spent a memorable week at the monastery where we ambled through the halls and visited chapels, including those dedicated to the Protector Pehar from the days when it was his prime abode before the migration to Nechung.

One day, we took a short hike to Hebori, a hill close to Samye where Pehar was "bound to oath" by Padmasambhava to protect Tibet, her people, and the teachings and practitioners of Buddhism. Perched on the peak was a small temple to commemorate this occasion that occurred in the eighth century. The view from Hebori was breathtaking. We could gaze far into the four directions and beyond.

Thupten at Hebori Hill with Samye Monastery in the background

On another occasion, we traveled by horseback to Chimpu, a mountain where we explored a series of caves carved into the cliffside. There, countless meditators once dwelled in search of the spirit of enlightenment. Some caves were tiny, with room only for the mendicant to sit cross-legged. Others were spacious, where one could stand up straight, stretch, and prostrate. Some even had a hearth to prepare simple meals and extra room for a fellow hermit. The place was magical. We felt as if we had gone back in time to an age when peace prevailed and beings had the leisure and endowment to practice.

Drikung Monastery

W hen we returned to Lhasa, we linked up with Tiapala. He had arrived during the three weeks we were away. He was staying in one of the rooftop rooms at Nechung Monastery, happily chatting with old acquaintances, drinking butter tea, and reminiscing about the past. Although Tiapala was enjoying his visit, the political situation in Lhasa had deteriorated. Several lamas, including Gyalsay Rinpoche, who had presided at the Bum Tsok ceremonies, advised us to leave Tibet expeditiously. Our allies in the underground had been forewarned that a public strike from the Chinese police was imminent. They also warned us that Thupten had been marked as an activist, and naturally, Miguel and I were viewed as accomplices. Indeed, our lives may be in danger.

The message was clear. We were not to find the reincarnation of Nechung Rinpoche on this journey.

"When the time is right, you will receive the assistance required to find your lama and bring him to safety," we were advised by seers and trusted their words implicitly.

Despite the potential risk of delaying our departure, Miguel and I wanted to visit Drikung Monastery before leaving. It was east of Lhasa, and by all accounts, it fit the description of my "vision" at the sacred lake of Lhamo Latso. It was wishful thinking, but perhaps Drikung held clues to the mystery of Rinpoche's birthplace. Only Thupten, Drikung, Miguel, and I would make the trip to the monastery.

Another friend of Thupten solved our transportation dilemma this time. He offered to drive us in his company's SUV; so once again, we traveled in style. As we made our approach to the monastery, we saw tractor-trailers moving in the same direction. In the trailers were solid heaps of something wrapped in fabric. "Those are corpses in there," the monk Drikung told us. "They're being taken to Drikung

Monastery for Phowa, that powerful ritual to transfer the consciousness of the deceased to a pure realm. Many people bring their loved ones here for prayer and final sky burials."

At the monastery, the administrator put our team in the unoccupied apartments reserved for their head lamas (Drikung Chetsang and Chungtsang). Chungtsang Rinpoche lived mostly in Lhasa. Coincidently, Chetsang Rinpoche was visiting our Nechung Temple in Hawaiʻi at the same moment we were at Drikung. The monastics at Drikung were still expecting Chetsang Rinpoche's impending arrival, although it seemed less and less likely as the weeks passed. We heard later that the lama never made it back to Tibet because the Chinese government had denied him a visa.

Drikung proved to be an intriguing place. In the mornings, we sauntered on the narrow, winding path to the lookout over the monastery entrance. Each time we saw corpses wrapped in cloth, often in seated positions. Sometimes they were still in the trailer or truck that had delivered them. Occasionally, the bundles were tossed on the ground. Monks would perform the rites of passage, chanting deep melodic prayers accompanied by hand mudras holding vajras and bells. Billows of smoke scented with juniper, pine, and incense drifted from an urn. The purpose of the ritual was to assist the consciousness with a smooth passage through the bardo, or intermediate state—a transitional stage between death and rebirth.

Cremation, a method reserved for high lamas, was not common in Tibet. There wasn't much wood for fuel, and the Tibetans were environmentally conscious. Ordinary people might be cremated if a plague had caused their deaths or if the individual had died from a communicable disease. The sky burial grounds were in the opposite direction from the monastery gates. Vultures soared and hovered above constantly. These giant carrion eaters would swoop down to play their role in disposing of the remains of physical bodies left behind after the consciousness had departed.

Below our quarters was a small shack where the man responsible for conducting sky burials lived. One day we met him on the footpath at sunrise. I instantly knew who this wild, wide-eyed, long-haired "yogi" was. He was returning from a job, surprisingly relaxed, and gave us a big toothless grin while holding out his palms in greeting. Miguel laughingly reciprocated, shaking his hand with no concern for the dualities of clean and unclean. Certain that there was no tap with running water at the burial site, I winced and veered off the path, leaving a safe distance between myself and those hands that had severed many a cadaver.

At Drikung we met two holy men. Palchung Rinpoche was a lama who survived on minute portions of yogurt. He meditated day and night and had no need for sleep. His body was sheer rainbow light. In his presence, we felt the luminescence of his meditative absorption. When we sat at his feet in a small meditation hut, he generously shared his yogurt with us, and the tiny portion aroused delight to our senses.

We also met a yogi with long, matted hair wound up on his crown like a beehive. Isolated in a cave for years, his window to the outside world had been a two-by-two-foot opening sealed with rocks. Benefactors placed food and provisions on an outer ledge. Periodically, he would remove the mosaic of stones and reach for some morsels of food.

Having just completed a long, solitary retreat, we were among the first to meet him. His acute awareness was pure and unadulterated, and his mind clear as the cloudless Tibetan sky. He wept openly when Thupten spoke of the compassion and humanitarian activities of His Holiness the Dalai Lama. In simple, candid words, he articulated how the self and the phenomenal world around us truly exist and the way they appear to exist to the ordinary mind. This realization shattered the illusory premise of how most people view reality.

Soon after our acquaintance, he left his sanctuary and fled Tibet for India. In exile, he became known as Drubwang Rinpoche or the Precious Powerful Accomplished One. He would spend time in seclusion as well as teach those who sought his wisdom.

To the Tibetan Border

It was time to leave Tibet. We dashed around Lhasa getting our affairs in order and arranging transportation. It was complicated since there was a shortage of jeeps for hire and public transportation was infrequent and unpredictable. So, we decided to charter our own bus with a driver from the army barracks. It was old and decrepit but was the only thing available. We were confident that we could pay for its cost with other travelers like ourselves, so we posted notices on bulletin boards in the downtown hostels, and within a week, there were enough people to fill the small bus, mostly from Europe and America.

This time Tiapala would travel with us and bring along his childhood friend Lobzang Jamspal, who happened to be vacationing in Lhasa. In the mid-1950s, Tiapala and Jamspal had trekked from Ladakh to Central Tibet. Tiapala became a monk at Drepung and Jamspal had entered Tashi Lhungpo Monastery. Tiapala now lived in Hawai'i with us while Jamspal had moved to New York, where he earned a doctorate and taught classical Tibetan at Columbia University. The two were like brothers.

Jamspal, older than Tiapala by several years, was health conscious. He preferred raw foods, brisk strolls, invigorating cold showers—even an icy dip in a lake at the crack of dawn. Tiapala, although in excellent physical condition, enjoyed an ample amount of meat, butterfat, and caffeine. Usually after a couple of days together, they would playfully debate and quibble over nutrition and fitness.

The monsoon season had been unrelenting. Consecutive storms and torrential rains had damaged forty-seven kilometers of road on the Nepalese side of the border. The steep hillside from Dram to the Friendship Bridge was now inundated by a massive mudslide. Blood-sucking leeches waited in the drenched trees, ready to feast on unsuspecting hikers. Gulches and rushing rivers ran where roads existed previously. The paths were narrow and slippery, and ravines steep and treacherous. We heard harrowing stories of brave porters with heavy loads slipping and plunging to their deaths. Daily, the reports sounded more and more horrific.

Then another serious problem surfaced. Thupten might not be able to leave the country. The Nepalese government mandated that travelers leaving Tibet have valid visas. Since Thupten had rejected getting visas for Tibet or Nepal, there was no proof in his travel document of admittance into either country. Consequently, the Nepalese embassy in Lhasa would not issue an exit permit from Tibet nor an entry visa for Nepal.

"Please help us; you have to give him a visa!" I pleaded, trying feminine charm on the clerks behind the glass counter. When that failed, Miguel used the tried-and-true baksheesh method, a "gift" with denominations of Chinese bills slipped into Thupten's IC.

"Madam, sir, it is not possible!" they said, shrugging their shoulders helplessly, pushing the IC back at us. "There is no evidence of entry into Tibet, so how can we give him a stamp to leave?"

"Well, what are we supposed to do?" I cried in frustration.

"Go to the border and see what happens," one of them suggested. "Perhaps you'll be able to just walk through."

"That may be a viable solution," I thought, reminded of the chaos at the border. Besides, it was our only recourse, so we had to take our chances.

We left our hotel before daybreak. From the army barracks, the bus made its way downtown to pick up the Westerners at the Banak Shol Hotel. There we directed the driver to swing by another guest house to pick up Tiapala, Jamspal, and Thupten. When the driver, a Chinese soldier, saw our three friends, his mouth gaped open in surprise.

"Hey, you didn't mention that Tibetans are coming on this trip!" he shouted, staring incredulously at the trio. "I cannot take them. They must get off this bus right now, otherwise I'm not driving anywhere!"

We were outraged at this blatant racism. Miguel and several of our fellow passengers burst into a rapid dialogue with the soldier.

"The Tibetans are coming with us! They have every right to be on this bus that we hired and paid for," Miguel insisted. "You will drive all of us to the border!" Others piped in with the same sentiment.

The driver gave some pathetic excuses to defend his position but it was a weak attempt, and eventually he conceded and we were on our way.

The morning light filtered through the windows as we traversed the open expanse of the Tibetan Plateau. The mood was merry. While loud Chinese music blared in the background, everyone talked and shared stories about their experiences in Tibet.

I closed my eyes and took some deep breaths of the cool air as the warmth of the sun kissed my skin, giving rise to a blissful sensation. In this vast sphere of mother earth, with panoramas of open space and sky, I felt at one with the elements. Within the noise, there was voidness, interrupted only by the ever-moving river of thoughts echoing the true nature of mind.

From where do these thoughts arise? Where do they go? And for the time that they command our attention, where do they abide? Are they laced with positive or negative emotions? And how tangible are these feelings? What about actions that stem from these thoughts and their results?

For centuries, in this holy land, high in the Himalayas far away from the distractions of the material world, countless great masters, yogis, and yoginis have explored the mysteries of existence and realized the ultimate truth of reality.

Suddenly the old bus lurched, jerking me back from my contemplation. The driver revved the engine, moving the vehicle forward a few more hundred feet, but it soon chugged to a full stop. After failing to fix the problem, our driver and his assistant hitched a ride to the nearest town for help.

We had been traveling for some hours and the sun was now directly overhead. Wispy clouds floated in the distant blue. Basking outdoors, we looked yonder at rolling hills while sitting in a grassy alpine meadow. All in all, it was a lovely place to get stuck. We decided to enjoy our last day in Tibet by having a picnic. There were plenty of snacks to share—pastries, cheese, fresh fruit, dried apricots, and cashews. We played Tibetan folk music and rock and roll, feeling perfectly at home in this faraway land.

Poor Jamspal was the only person not having a good time. He had a gastrointestinal ailment contracted from the unsanitary toilets in his hotel. To make his condition worse, he and Tiapala had indulged in *momos* at a going-away party. The dumplings had been filled with spoiled yak meat. Tiapala had an iron-clad stomach and was not affected in the least, but Jamspal was pale and vomiting. Every so often he ran across the road and concealed himself behind a large boulder.

Hours later, after the sun had inched its way across the sky, the drivers returned with the necessary parts and repaired the bus. Long after nightfall, we arrived at the army base, the same overnight camp where we had stayed three months earlier.

Summer had passed so quickly. Everything was now just a memory filed away for recollection. As I laid awake on the wooden plank in the barracks, the illusory nature of time struck me, how the past and future exist, dependent upon a split second in the present moment. Innumerable instants are strung together in the span of a lifetime, when our actions are moved by the impulses of attraction, repulsion or indifference to the objects of our senses. These give rise to positive, negative, or neutral deeds of body, speech, and mind. These, in turn, imprint patterns into our consciousness and propel our mental continuum in the cycles of existence.

In minute degrees, one moment continues on to the next until we wake up one day and notice how we have aged. The ravages of time that cannot be erased—those fine lines that turned to etched wrinkles and weathered skin; a random white hair, then another, until the whole head becomes gray, silver, or bald. Ultimately, father time may be illusory, yet we are caught in its conventional web.

Hopefully, we would gain some wisdom during our short time on this planet, become less self-centered, genuinely care about others, as well as engage in positive activities that benefit humankind and make the world a better place. After all, we are only guests, *temporary* guests, passing through time.

Border to Kathmandu

Along the stretch of road to the border, we stopped for Tiapala and Thupten to raise a pole of prayer flags high on a pass, with mountains gleaming in the distance. There were two checkpoints between Lhasa and Dram—a single guard station situated close to the Everest turnoff, and the next was the security post at Dram. Thupten stayed out of sight at both places. For the rest of us on the bus, the inspections were perfunctory.

It was impossible to carry all of our luggage, so upon disembarking at Dram, we hired porters to assist us again. Thupten had most of the weight, having amassed a stockpile of rare collections of Buddhist texts, antique bronze statues, and other religious artifacts. Monks and laypeople had entrusted him with these priceless possessions, requesting that they be offered to His Holiness the Dalai Lama and the Office of Religion and Cultural Affairs. There were also care packages of sentimental value, such as photos and letters to be hand-delivered to relatives or children at boarding schools and monasteries. Miguel and I had accumulated a few extra kilos ourselves, but not in body weight; we were remarkably trim, having hiked the long distances and eating sparingly for months. Our extra duffel contained finely illustrated manuals on Tibetan medicine and sacred art.

The porters, five in all, were so overloaded that they resembled human pack animals burdened with cargo, but these lean, almost bony men, seemed unfazed by the task. I wanted to hire a few more helpers to distribute the weight, but they protested, insisting they do the job themselves. Understandably, fewer laborers meant more cash for each of them.

Jamspal and Tiapala carried very little. Jamspal was still sick, so he only had a daypack and an umbrella. Tiapala figured that we had porters to do the grunt work, so all he had was a monk's bag and a new, empty Chinese thermos. Miguel and I could not allow our helpers to do all the work, so we hoisted our matching packs onto our backs and slung the smaller bags over our shoulders messenger style.

True to rumor, the storms had been cataclysmic. Conditions getting to the Friendship Bridge had worsened since our entry earlier in the summer. The hillside had become a sludgy landslide with water coursing down in muddy streams. We had to navigate through deep ditches carved by the excessive runoff. Forced

Tiapala and Thupten raising a flagpole on the way to the Tibetan border

to glide in our boots, slide on our butts, and brace ourselves with our hands, we made it down the mountain and somehow managed to avoid the leeches.

When we arrived at Kodari at the Nepalese border, the immigration station was bustling with people and animals. It felt like déjà vu, a replay of the same scenario from a few months ago. Vying for the attention of prospective customers, dozens of porters pushed, shoved, and called out, hustling for work. Cows chewed their cud, giving an occasional moo for sound effect.

We strode into a full room where everyone was talking at once. It looked like the same two immigration officers seated behind the pockmarked table. Tour guides stretched out their arms, holding stacks of passports for their groups. Lone travelers did the same. People butted into line. Money for visas was tossed back and forth. Our companions from the bus added to this maddening crowd.

A group of men stood around the table gaping wide-eyed at everyone, their heads bobbing with curiosity. "These guys aren't travelers!" I said, shaking my head in dismay. "They're not going anywhere! Don't these people have anything better to do?" I clutched my handbag with the money and documents ever closer.

Miguel went over to Thupten, who was lingering at the entrance. "Just go!" he whispered. "Don't bother showing your IC or talking to anyone in here. It's a madhouse. Go! We'll be right behind you."

Our prayers for frenzied confusion at the Nepalese border had been answered. If this were a typical immigration checkpoint, Thupten would wait in line to show his IC, only to reveal he had no stamped visas. In all probability, he would be refused entry, leaving us in a quandary.

It was forty-seven kilometers, about thirty miles, to the place where we could catch a bus to Kathmandu. We had to hike in soaring temperatures on waterlogged, makeshift trails at the edge of steep precipices overlooking swollen rushing torrents. Our ever-present porters soldiered on, with towering double loads strapped to their backs and bags dangling off each shoulder. They balanced some baggage on their heads with one hand and clutched parcels close to their chests with the other. It reminded me of the overloaded trucks in India that topple over from the weight. The entire scene was surreal.

Between the danger zones and the fragmented, damaged roads, large sections of the pavement remained intact. Here and there, we walked on solid ground, sometimes through small villages, markets, and clusters of dwellings. We took turns keeping a watchful eye on our porters who in the short-term, were in possession of most of our belongings and treasures.

There were six checkpoints that also served as toll booths. At each of these stops, a bamboo pole stretched over the width of the crossing to block the road. These makeshift "gates" were hoisted up with ropes and pulleys when the guards felt satisfied with the documents proffered, or just as likely, persuaded by a hefty bribe.

Thupten stayed within sight slightly ahead of us. At the final checkpoint, we created a diversion to distract the guards when we noticed them eyeing him suspiciously. Speaking loudly to capture their attention, we dropped our bags and rummaged through them frantically as though we had lost something. The men watched our little drama with amusement and forgot about Thupten, who quickly disappeared around the next bend.

We spent the night in a quaint guest house in one of the villages. It was a typical Nepalese building with a brightly lit shop at the ground level, and a narrow, steep stairway that led to a second floor where we shared a room with wooden shuttered windows. A bare lightbulb hanging from the ceiling provided dim lighting until the entire town blacked out. Thupten had vanished after the last checkpoint, so Tiapala ran around in the dark trying to find him. He returned with dinner—dahl and chapatis—but no Thupten. We ate our fill of the spicy lentils and flatbreads by candlelight, and exhausted, fell asleep to the blare of the music, barking dogs, and street noise.

The next morning, we dragged our tired, achy bodies out of bed and continued toward our destination. During those last kilometers, my fatigue became almost unbearable. At this lower elevation with more oxygen, the exertion was not as excruciating as the trek to Chamseng Latso, but our reserves were depleted and the goal seemed unreachable. Heat, exhaustion, and dehydration had begun to take their toll.

Finally, we caught sight of some buildings, a small market, a bus, *and* Thupten. I let out a sigh of tremendous relief and my mind automatically erased the pain from my throbbing limbs and muscles. We picked up our pace and veritably bounded down the home stretch.

After several rounds of ice-cold sodas, the porters were paid their well-deserved earnings plus a tip. By now, many of our companions from the Lhasa bus had joined us. We were all happy to sit and unwind, having nothing to do but wait for the bus to leave.

Everyone except Thupten. He was agitated.

"What's wrong?" I inquired. "Relax!"

"I have to go back," Thupten declared.

"Why? We just got here!" Miguel exclaimed with disbelief. "Where do you need to go?"

That was when we learned that Thupten had been entrusted with the vestments worn by the Nechung Mediums during official trances in Tibet. These vintage garments were not only museum worthy, they were a token of our monastery's ancient history, and were to be taken to Nechung in India for safekeeping. To our bewilderment, Thupten had passed them to Martin, one of the passengers on the bus from Lhasa.

Miguel had engaged with Martin who had claimed to be an antique dealer of collectibles from Asia. He boasted of his abilities and the treasure troves that he had found on his recent trips to China and Tibet. We were unimpressed, but Thupten's naiveté had prompted him to trust Martin with the irreplaceable ceremonial robes.

What we observed was that Martin bargained with his porters ruthlessly. "You don't have to pay them much," he told us. "These guys are desperate for work. They'll take whatever you give them!" We disagreed; rupees were negligible when the exchange rate was calculated. The occupation of these laborers was extremely onerous. I couldn't imagine being in their shoes and living a life of toil as they did. It was unethical to exploit them and to not give them a fair wage, but we didn't interfere since it was Martin's business.

Now we were involved. Somewhere along the forty-seven kilometers, possibly after the town where we overnighted, one of Martin's porters disappeared and with him, Thupten's parcel.

Martin who was close by, began to curse, "That *#*#* took off with my stuff! I had priceless antiques in those bundles. Damn!"

He continued ranting: "Now I have to go back and try to find him! I'll retrace our footsteps and track him down! Don't worry, Thupten. Go with your friends. I'll meet up with you guys in Kathmandu."

"Well," I thought to myself, "if you had given your helper a decent amount of money, he probably wouldn't have run off with your stuff. Surely he'd rather have cash than things he needs to sell."

Still, I was glad that Martin had offered to take care of the mishap. Thupten had sailed past the guards without complications, and we weren't about to chance that he could do it again. We knew that it was improbable to locate the porter in the unfamiliar countryside, and true to our assumption, we never saw Martin or the vestments again.

Before nightfall, we arrived in Kathmandu. It was there that we heard demonstrations had broken out in Lhasa the day after our departure. The rallies were initially peaceful but quickly turned violent when Chinese soldiers began beating and arresting protestors. Tibetans, out of desperation, threw rocks at government buildings and torched the police station. They were gunned down. Many Tibetans died, and countless more sustained injuries. Similar marches, followed by further oppression, would recur in the ensuing years.

We returned to Dharamsala and met with His Holiness the Dalai Lama. We gave him our report about the situation in Tibet, the Bum Tsok, Lhamo Latso, and our delegation's attempts to find Nechung Rinpoche's reincarnation. His Holiness reiterated that the boy was young, and still needed his mother's care. He reassured us that when the time was right, he would help us find Rinpoche.

Although we had not found our beloved lama, the three-month sojourn had been invaluable. We had made vital contacts in Lhasa and the experience gave us a deeper insider's perspective of the prevailing culture of Chinese-occupied Tibet. This gave us the confidence and preparation for a future mission.

Offering goddess mural in Lhasa temple

THE SECOND ATTEMPT:
Summer 1993

The Long-Awaited News

Nearly six years after our journey to Tibet, we received a phone call from Thupten with the exciting message we had long anticipated. His Holiness the Dalai Lama had notified the Nechung monks in Dharamsala that it was time to find Nechung Rinpoche's reincarnation. This news would set into motion a journey that would test the limits of our ingenuity and courage well beyond anything we had ever encountered.

"What *exactly* did His Holiness say?" I asked. "*When* did...?"

"We just heard today," Thupten replied. "I called you immediately!"

I could hear the exhilaration in his voice. His Holiness had revealed the names of both of Rinpoche's parents, and the boy's year of birth as 1985—the Year of the Earth Bull. He further confirmed that Rinpoche was in Lhasa.

"So, if his parents are willing to part with him, we'll bring him to India." Thupten continued in his quick-witted way, "He can be educated as a monk at the monastery."

I was overjoyed. After waiting patiently all these years, His Holiness had finally given the signal to go ahead. "What incredibly great news! The timing is perfect!" I said breathlessly. "Miguel and I are planning a trip to China with students from the University of Hawai'i. We have our plane tickets already and will leave for Beijing in a few weeks."

"Once there, we don't have to stay with the tour group for long. We will meet up with you as soon as possible," I told Thupten, expressing our wish to be involved. "We'll go to Tibet together!"

But Thupten had no intention of waiting for us.

"I'm leaving for Delhi tonight," he informed me. "One of the kids already went to the bazaar and bought me a bus ticket. *This* time I *will* apply for a visa at the Chinese Consulate. Then I'll fly to Kathmandu and catch another flight to Lhasa."

Thupten's response was predictable—his zealousness was one of his endearing attributes. At heart, I was opposed to him going alone and felt compelled to tell him so. Certainly, I had an urge to jump on the next plane and head straight for Lhasa too, but a well-planned strategy was necessary. The undertaking was too sensitive to rush, and the stakes were too high to fail.

"The three of us should go in as a team. *Please* wait for us," I insisted. "We're dealing with a precarious situation, and there's safety in numbers."

By now, Miguel and Tiapala had joined me in the office, listening keenly to the loud conversation. Thupten and I were speaking at full volume as a vestige from "the old days" in India, when static in the landlines often caused a breakdown in communication. In addition, we were talking with each other across oceans about a matter very dear to us. This only added to the intensity.

"No, I'm not postponing my trip," Thupten declared stubbornly. "I'll be in Tibet within a week." His plan was to collect a list of boys' names born in the Year of the Earth Bull to present to His Holiness for consideration.

"If His Holiness identifies one of the boys to be Rinpoche's reincarnation," Thupten declared, "I may even have the boy in India before you guys are ready to come to Lhasa!"

Thupten gave me the phone number of the place where he would be staying. "Call me when you get to Beijing," he said.

We had no choice but to acquiesce.

"Be careful," Miguel warned, "danger lies ahead!"

Visit of Khenpo Jigme Phuntsok

Our departure for China was scheduled for July 4th, but first, we were to host another momentous program. The temple had committed to host the Hawaiʻi visit of Khenpo Jigme Phuntsok Rinpoche, the incarnation of Lerab Lingpa who was a historically renowned teacher. Khenpo Jigme Phuntsok was considered to be one of the greatest contemporary Buddhist masters in recent memory. He was responsible for training a young generation of lamas in Eastern Tibet where he had established Larung Gar, a thriving monastic community which grew to house over 10,000 Chinese and Tibetan monks and nuns.

The Chinese government had granted him a one-time leave with the stipulation that he would not speak about politics. Khenpo Jigme Phuntsok was to come to the United States after he met with His Holiness the Dalai Lama in India.

We had first heard about this lama from Nechung Rinpoche who referred to him as Terton Sogyal. Rinpoche spoke of him with such esteem that it instilled a strong wish in us to meet him. So we were thrilled to hear that he had inquired about Nechung in Hawai'i and articulated an interest in visiting the temple.

Nechung Rinpoche's relationship with Terton Sogyal was from his previous life. The Thirteenth Dalai Lama had sent Rinpoche's predecessor to Eastern Tibet to retrieve the esoteric texts of the Vajrakilaya Tantra, a *terma* revealed by Lerab Lingpa. A *terma* is a Dharma "treasure" concealed or hidden by enlightened masters, to be revealed or discovered by persons with an interconnection, at a later time when it would be of benefit to living beings. Since Vajrakilaya is a powerful practice known for removing outer, inner, and secret hindrances, the Thirteenth Dalai Lama had the foresight that this tantra and its rituals could help to avert potential calamities in Tibet's future. It was widely believed that this spiritual intervention alleviated the potency of the challenges that Tibet faced and delayed the onset of adversities.

Khenpo Jigme Phuntsok's visit began with welcoming him and his entourage at the Honolulu Airport. Miguel and I waited outside the international arrival gate seemingly for hours. One after another, travelers filtered through the exit until the very last passengers from their flight had come through the sliding doors, but there was no sign of the lama or his assistants.

Baffled, I turned to Miguel. "This is really strange. Do we have the right date and flight number?"

Eventually, several people resembling our guests from Tibet ambled through the gates but no head lama. He was still inside, we were told, being interrogated by Immigration and Customs.

What possibly could they suspect in an elderly lama?

Finally, a maroon-robed lama wearing old-fashioned Tibetan felt boots came into view. It was Khenpo Jigme Phuntsok! With amusement, he explained why he had been delayed. In his luggage were several kilos of *tsampa* he had brought from Tibet, since it was his diet staple, and a commodity not easily acquired in America. Due to the light color and fine powdery consistency of the barley flour, comprehensive screening tests were done to rule out that the substance was not a narcotic.

Khenpo Jigme Phuntsok had a formidable presence and a personality so magnetic that people came from across the islands to be near him and to receive the nectar of his teachings. Rainbows arched in the sky above him when he sat in the lava fields at Kilauea, the volcano abode of Madam Pele, the fire goddess of Hawai'i.

He bestowed the initiation of Vajrakilaya Gurghukma, one of the *terma* treasures that he had discovered. It was an abbreviated practice of the lengthier text that his predecessor revealed. Another profound teaching that he gave was "Buddha in the Palm of Your Hand." His voice was distinct like a lion's roar. He spoke in Golok, a vernacular so foreign from the Central Tibetan dialect that was familiar to us; it was virtually incomprehensible to me, except on a subconscious level.

We apprised him of our upcoming trip to China and our mission to find Nechung Rinpoche's reincarnation in Tibet.

"In China, you must go to Riwo Tse Nga, the Five Peak Mountain of Manjushri—the manifestation of enlightened wisdom," he advised. "I went there myself with some students on pilgrimage. Manjushri manifested to me vividly when I meditated at the peak. It is a very sacred site."

The lama graced us with prayers for success—his visit offered a prelude to what was ahead.

Summer in Beijing

With Khenpo Jigme Phuntsok's blessings, we departed for Beijing, the first leg of our journey. Asia had been on our travel agenda since the late 1980s. At that time, we had undertaken an outreach project to publish information on Buddhism as well as on Tibet and her history and had distributed the printed materials to the extended Chinese community in Taiwan. Miguel and I were curious about the extent of religious freedom and the standard of living for working-class people in

China. We also wanted to know how newly emerged materialism and consumerism had affected the masses under the communist regime. These questions were best answered by firsthand experience.

Our trip was coordinated by a professor at the University of Hawaiʻi in Hilo who had negotiated a student exchange program with the University of Beijing. Although we had never traveled with a group before and would be confined to the parameters of an organized tour, the opportunity provided us with the ideal pretext to be in the country.

Housing was at the university campus in one of the newer dormitories where the sparse quarters echoed with voices and music from the stairways and other rooms. Bathrooms and shower stalls were down the hall where hot water was available for two hours a day. The rooms had two standard single beds with firm mattresses draped in candy-pink bedspreads. Basic amenities included light comforters, a metal thermos, tin cups, and enamel washbasins. An overhead ceiling fan that served as the cooling unit ran constantly to relieve the unbearable humidity, though all it did was circulate the same stale hot air. Miguel broke out in a heat rash with tiny, red itchy blisters throughout his entire back. Frequent cold showers were the only respite from the irritation, washing off the dust and sweat of summer in the city.

Our meals were taken in the cafeteria which had a daily set menu of rice and vegetables. Whenever we got bored with the monotonous fare, we went to a nearby restaurant. Although the dishes we ordered were vegan, they were still fried in lard that the Chinese people loved to use. Ordering food was awkward indeed, as was all verbal communication, since my colloquial Mandarin, the official dialect for modern China, was negligible. Whenever we ventured off campus, even the simple exercise of conveying an address to taxi drivers was problematic. Everywhere we went, Chinese people spoke to me expecting me to be fluent and were perplexed when I looked at them with incomprehension. It was a humbling experience.

Our stay in China, so long anticipated, had taken on a whole new meaning, now that we were committed to a more significant goal. We had to go to Tibet, meet up with Thupten, find Nechung Rinpoche's reincarnation, and conceivably escort the boy safely to India. For two non-Tibetans to be involved in this type of search was truly unprecedented.

It was propitious that we had the guidance of His Holiness. We now knew the year of Rinpoche's birth, the names of his mother and father, and that he was in the east side of Lhasa. Still, in an area with a population as large as Tibet's capital city, engulfed in the mire of the Chinese communist police state, the search would be a challenge!

To keep abreast of our temple's business in Hawai'i, we routinely called Tiapala from the university student center. Whenever we spoke with him, concerned that the phone lines were tapped, we kept the dialogue cryptic, avoiding key words such as Dalai Lama, Tibet, and Rinpoche. It was with joyful disbelief during one such conversation that we learned that Rinchen Dharlo, His Holiness' representative at the Office of Tibet in New York had called with the news that His Holiness would visit the temple the following year.

I couldn't believe my ears. "Are you sure?" I kept repeating. "Next year? 1994?"

Miguel, who was in the tiny phone booth with me, sensed my exhilaration. "What?" he asked. "What's Tiapala saying? What's going on?"

"His Holiness is coming to Drayang Ling next April!" I whispered. "Oh, my god, how incredible is that?"

"You should contact Mr. Dharlo," Tiapala suggested.

"Yes, yes," I assured him, "but it's too risky to do it while in China, we'll get in touch with His Holiness' secretary when we get to India."

What a time to hear this news! How much more excitement could we take?

Thupten's Mysterious Disappearance

Based on the estimated time for us to make a gracious departure from our tour, make travel arrangements, and get from Beijing to Lhasa, our plan was to connect with Thupten in August.

We knew a person in Beijing named Joanne, a British woman whom we had met at a Tibet Support Group Conference some years ago. She was the assistant manager at a hotel that catered to foreigners. On one of our outings, we found the establishment and made contact with her. Joanne confirmed that phone lines in the city were wiretapped to monitor voice and fax communications. Everything was sent through a central government system. A way to bypass this surveillance was to use the public telephones in the five-star-hotel lobbies. AT&T had been expanding its worldwide network that year and had made its commercial debut in China—a country with enormous consumer potential. The new technology allowed customers to access operators in various countries with the push of a button. Nevertheless, the phone wires ran from the public phones to offices where hotel security could listen in. Joanne apprised us of the break and shift patterns of workers, so we could avoid scrutiny.

We frequented these hotels whenever we needed to make a phone call. They were the best spots to enjoy a refreshing drink and alternative cuisine, while luxuriating in the air-conditioned premises. Being quite at ease in such surroundings, we would saunter through the grand lobbies with their sparkling crystal chandeliers and shiny marble floors, then discreetly edge our way to the phones in a private corner.

This is how we called Thupten in Lhasa. A woman picked up the phone on the second ring.

"Wei," she greeted us cautiously in Chinese.

"Is Thupten there?" I asked in Tibetan.

An awkward silence. Perhaps she didn't understand my Tibetan. I inquired again.

"Who are you?" she asked suspiciously.

"I'm a friend of Thupten. He told me to call him when we got to Beijing." I articulated the words in my best Lhasa dialect.

"Thupten is no longer here. He returned to India." Her response was blunt and had a tone of distress.

"What? Why? When did he leave?" I was astonished. "We were supposed to come to meet him in Lhasa. Did he finish what he set out to do?"

The woman would not give me any answers. "He left two or three weeks ago. You can call him in India," she said and then hung up abruptly. The exchange left me feeling perturbed, and I sensed that something unexpected had happened.

Thupten was like our younger brother. We knew him well and appreciated his intelligence, sense of humor, competence, and charisma. He could also be boldly fearless and occasionally impulsive—a dangerous combination for a political activist in a country under authoritarian rule.

Repeatedly, we attempted to reach him in India to no avail. Even with the sophisticated satellite systems in tourist hotels, we couldn't get a stable line to our monastery in Dharamsala. The two times that someone answered, we lost the connection within seconds. We had no clue where Thupten was, if he was safe, and what could have caused him to deviate from the plan and his sudden departure from Lhasa.

We decided to stay on course and get to Tibet as soon as our obligation with the cultural exchange was fulfilled.

Five Peak Mountain

Weekly flights were available to Lhasa from Chengdu, the gateway from China to Tibet. The only problem was that the Chinese government preferred organized groups that were more profitable and easier to monitor. This policy discouraged foreign individual travelers (FITs), so it was nearly impossible to find travel agencies who sold tickets to FITs. Rumor was that FIT reservations and tickets were available at the China Travel Service (CTS) in Beijing. After making painstaking efforts to get to CTS, we were informed that all travel arrangements from Chengdu to Lhasa had to be made *in* Chengdu and nowhere else.

After Beijing, we were scheduled to visit Riwo Tse Nga—the Five Peak Mountain, then Xian, renowned for the archaeological excavation of thousands of life-sized terra-cotta warriors. The city of Shanghai would be the last stop. Our tour package with the University of Hawai'i included our domestic travel and accommodations.

"We need to go to Riwo Tse Nga just as Khenpo Jigme Phuntsok advised," Miguel said, "and since everything has been prearranged and paid for already, we should go with the group to Xian. That'll get us closer to Chengdu."

So, we stayed. In the mornings, we attended classes at the university. Since the curriculum was sanctioned by the government, the lectures lacked creativity and had a definite Chinese bias. Afternoons were filled with tours to the Great Wall, the Forbidden City, and other famous sites. Shopping trips to the biggest Chinatown in the world were available, for those who wanted to purchase silk shirts, cloisonné, and other bargains.

The early 1990s marked a transition for China—the onset of transnational corporations making investments in the country. Cheap Chinese goods were already a commodity abroad. With China's growing wealth, a thriving domestic market had also developed. New retail shops and fast-food restaurants such as McDonald's were springing up everywhere. We witnessed the avid consumerism whenever we pounded the pavement of the packed streets swarming with people and vendors hawking their wares.

We visited old temples—they were impressive, well-maintained buildings filled with icons and statues, but somehow felt hollow and devoid of spiritual energy. Custodians stood around guarding the facilities, and on occasion, we saw men dressed in monks' robes engage in prayer ceremonies.

It was at one of these temples that an incident took place. We were standing at the base of a very tall Buddha statue flanked by "No Photos Allowed" signs. Miguel, mischievous as usual, decided to take a couple of souvenir snapshots with his Nikon, which was strapped beneath his jean jacket. The lighting was so dim that he needed to use the flash, which alerted the temple keepers who scanned the crowd of tourists but couldn't spot the culprit.

One of the college students with us, Matthew, wanted a memento too, and since Miguel made it look so easy, he pulled out his camera and snapped a photo. Instantly, several guards descended upon him. They yelled with incomprehensible exclamations, yanking at his camera and demanding the film. When Matthew refused to cooperate, the guards became increasingly animated and belligerent. We didn't need language skills to understand that police involvement was imminent. Straining their necks to see the cause of the disturbance, an assemblage of curious people had congregated as the situation intensified.

"Give them the film. It isn't worth getting thrown in jail," Miguel advised. "The statue is so tall that without a special lens and lighting, all you're going to have is a poor shot anyway. You can have a copy of mine, if it comes out."

Without further hesitation, Matthew tossed the roll of film at the guards who were determined to take a detainee into custody and firmly gripped his arm. "Leave him alone!" Miguel shouted, waving his arms, signaling the guards to withdraw. "You got your film, we're leaving!"

The guards continued to pursue us with threatening gestures and sounds. We dashed to our bus, waiting with the motor running, and jumped on board to the cheers of our fellow group members.

After weeks in the city, we were eager to leave. The divinities of Riwo Tse Nga[17]— the Five Peak Mountain were calling…

Traveling by rail gave us a slow-moving vista of China's extensive countryside. The scenery was splendid, like the flawless images portrayed in many an artist's painting of the ancient empire. That is, if one could ignore the inescapable truth—that the country was plagued by uncontrolled pollution from its dependence on coal. Billows of black exhaust emitting from innumerable smokestacks smothered the atmosphere with heavy gray smog. It was even more dramatic at night when the silhouette of the dark shadows could be seen against the massive glow of crimson embers from burning coal.

17. *Wu Tai Shan in Chinese*

Wu Tai Shan, the town with trinket shops, open canteens, and tented markets on unpaved streets, resembled any other tourist trap in a developing country. Our group was booked in one of the better hotels for two nights.

We had come with two specific goals. The first was to meet with the administrators of Wu Tai Shan's Buddhist Association to discuss the likelihood of establishing exchange programs between Buddhists in the Chinese and Tibetan traditions. This prospect was dismal. The officials were not keen on the Tibetan angle. However, they did express an interest in America.

The second goal of course, was to pilgrimage to the mountain summit where Jigme Phuntsok Rinpoche had encouraged us to visit. The mountain range was a holy Buddhist site, considered to be the earthly abode of the Bodhisattva[18] Manjushri. Just as the Dalai Lamas of Tibet are revered as the embodiment of Avalokiteshvara, the Bodhisattva of Compassion; the early emperors of China were considered to be manifestations of Manjushri, the Bodhisattva of Wisdom.

Manjushri has five aspects: Golden Manjushri, Youthful Manjushri, White Manjushri, Blue Manjushri, and Manjushri Seated upon a Lion. All depicted images of each of these aspects wield a sword in the right hand, symbolic of cutting through the veils of ignorance to see everything as it truly exists. The left hand holds a scripture, the *Prajnaparamita* (*Perfection of Wisdom*) that focuses on the realization of primordial wisdom.

We hired a car and driver to take us up to the eastern peak of the mountain. The vehicle arrived hours before dawn. It was pitch black, so we paid no attention to the car's condition. We drove out of town on empty, lonely streets and began to climb the hillside's gradual incline. At times, the road and mountain merged into one broad track. As we ascended, the car began to sputter and stall, its small engine signaling that it was not suited for the task.

"Let's just hike the rest of the way," Miguel proposed. "Anyway, it's more appropriate to put in the extra effort. We'll still be up there before dawn."

We jumped out and headed toward the summit, breaking our own trail, walking briskly to keep warm in the early morning chill. It was before daybreak, so we circumambulated in a clockwise direction around the temple with the pilgrims who had arrived before us. The shrine room was compact, the altar simple, yet it felt more hallowed than all the places that we had visited in the capital. We prostrated,

---

18. *Bodhisattvas are motivated to achieve enlightenment for the sake of benefiting all living beings.*

offered incense, and prayed for peace and happiness for all beings. Outdoors, we sat to watch the radiant hues of sunrise at the top of the world and recited verses for the success of our mission in Tibet.

City of the Gods

Xian would be our last stop on the tour. There, we purchased our tickets to Chengdu; this would be our entryway to Lhasa, the City of the Gods. We traveled to Chengdu in a vintage 1950s Russian turbo-prop. The plane flew at low altitudes, allowing us to survey the peaceful seclusion of the mountain ranges of Western China that bordered Tibet.

In Chengdu, we found moderately priced accommodations to spend the night. Here too, as we had experienced in other parts of China, the smog was so thick that we could not see across the street from our window. Having done our homework in Beijing, we had the name and address of a travel agency that dealt with foreigners like us. It was within walking distance on the second floor of a nearby hotel. The lobby was decorated with polished rosewood armchairs cushioned in gold silk brocade. Black lacquer folding screens with oriental motifs were randomly placed to give the room dimension. To further the stereotype associated with Chinese culture, red good-luck symbols were everywhere.

"Very ethnic," Miguel commented dryly, "it's so Chinese."

"What do you expect?" I said. "We're in China."

We walked up a short flight of stairs to a cluttered office furnished with shelves crammed with books, a couple of desks, and two chairs for prospective clients. The travel agents spoke English and were genuinely helpful. We counted out Chinese renminbi for our tickets, plus a gratuity for their trouble. The men politely refused the tip, which I thought was very decent. We were told to return the next morning to retrieve our passes for a flight in the afternoon. The transaction had been unexpectedly easy.

The Air China flight to Lhasa was booked solid; we must have gotten the last two seats. The passengers were predominantly Chinese settlers returning to their new homes in Lhasa with purchases and supplies from Chengdu. The few Tibetans on the plane dressed and behaved like Westerners. "They must live in America or Europe and just going to Tibet for a visit," Miguel surmised.

Here we were, in Tibet again, with a formidable task and much uncertainty ahead of us. My heart beat rapidly while we waited in a long line to clear immigration. "It must be the altitude," I whispered to Miguel, "but I'm feeling light-headed and really nervous."

Since Lhasa was officially in China, we passed inspection with no hassles. To play it safe, we had acquired multiple-entry visas before leaving the United States. The area around the airport terminal was heavily guarded. We were ushered into buses headed for Lhasa proper. There was no other choice of transportation—no taxis, no shuttles—only government-controlled vehicles. At any other airport in the world, friends and relatives would be joyfully greeting loved ones. Not so in communist-occupied Tibet.

Lhasa had changed since our last visit and the transformation was appalling. The celestial deities seemed to have abandoned the City of the Gods. In 1987, the increased rate of Chinese immigration was already a problem. In 1993, it had grown into an epidemic. Tibetans were rapidly becoming a minority in their own homeland. China had effectively enticed thousands of its citizens to migrate to the Tibetan mountain plateau by giving them low-interest business loans and irresistible tax cuts. Though most Chinese had difficulty living at high altitudes so distant from their native soil, the material benefits of moving to Tibet were just too lucrative to pass up. They now owned restaurants, bakeries, storefronts, and other enterprises. The only area still under Tibetan tenancy was the Barkhor.

Furthermore, pool halls, bars, night clubs, and brothels had sprung up all over Lhasa. It was heartbreaking to see these venues frequented by young Tibetans. With few jobs available and little hope to prosper, they were trapped in a culture simply struggling to survive.

We contacted some trusted friends whom we had met in 1987—one family in particular. The woman, Yudron, was the niece of a senior Nechung monk and had a small shop in the Barkhor. Her husband Khenrab, was a scholar and a radical in his youth. The couple had children who held middle management positions with the Chinese government and financial institutions. We saw them often in '87, and were aware that their family was put at risk each time we walked into their housing complex. They, too, had been conscious of this but never once showed a hint of annoyance. Whenever we surfaced, they gladly served us salty butter tea, candies, and biscuits. Sometimes, if we arrived at the right time, we would be treated to home cooking—a bowl of steaming noodle soup with root vegetables.

Khenrab had been somewhat of a mentor to Thupten, and they often discussed politics during our visits. These folks were our confidants, the locals with their fingers on the pulse of the community. Certainly, if anyone knew about Thupten, they would.

"What happened to Thupten?" I asked Khenrab upon setting foot in their apartment.

He stared at us, poker-faced.

His wife poured tea into Chinese porcelain cups.

Silence.

Then, in a hushed voice, Khenrab replied, "He was arrested by the Lhasa secret police. They detained him for several days and then let him go. Thupten gathered his belongings and left town hurriedly. I don't believe that he was hurt, but we have no other information."

Now we were more anxious than ever. How could we contact Thupten? What had gone wrong? Was he in danger? Had the police learned of our search for Nechung Rinpoche? We had a hundred questions and no answers.

Nevertheless, we took some time to relax but deliberately avoided seeing anyone else. We didn't even visit Nechung Monastery, knowing that the monks would be curious as to why we were back. They would undoubtedly inquire if His Holiness had given clues on the whereabouts of Rinpoche's reincarnation. It would be safer if they were uninformed. That way they would not be implicated; if interrogated by the Chinese police, they would honestly have nothing to disclose.

We stayed at the Sunlight Hotel, the only available lodging on the east side of the city. It was inexpensive, had low occupancy, and was in the direction of Lhasa where His Holiness had indicated Rinpoche would be found. Sometimes, we shared the dining room at lunch or dinner with employees from the government offices nearby. The clientele was a friendly mix of Chinese and Tibetans who seemed comfortable in each other's company. They shared meals and drinks as coworkers would do anywhere in the world. We observed them from our corner table, watching their body language and listening to their spirited conversations.

Our room was large but dark, with heavy curtains shielding the window that faced the entry courtyard. It was a perfect setup to enact our imaginary roles as secret agents. We would turn off the lights, and from behind the velvet shades, watched people come and go.

Daily, like clockwork, we saw truckloads of Tibetans pass by the crossroads close to the hotel. They were being transported, we were later told, to a prison on the outskirts of Lhasa.

Miguel and I stayed in Lhasa for a week. During that interval, we reacquainted ourselves with the city. We explored the east side, went downtown, walked the main streets, window-shopped, and retraced the back alleys around the Barkhor. Once again, we were "at home" in the City of the Gods. Although we enjoyed the interlude, it was all too brief; we had to continue on to India to find Thupten, and that meant we had to get to Nepal first.

Potala Palace, view from Barkhor 1993

Travel in India

There were now three weekly flights between Lhasa and Kathmandu. These did not exist in 1987, and we were grateful to be spared the grueling overland journey. Delhi was our next stop after Kathmandu. We took another plane, our most expedient option. Time was precious. We had to find Thupten.

His Holiness happened to be in Delhi giving a lecture on the day we arrived, so we took the opportunity to see him at the event. The hall was packed with attendees—Tibetans, Indians, and a few Westerners. In the sea of people, we spotted Thupten with other maroon-robed monks close to the stage. We managed to contain ourselves for the duration of the talk, then hurriedly pushed our way through the crowd afterwards so as not to lose him again. As we approached, he turned around as if knowing we were there. I grabbed his bare arm and there we were, face-to-face with our intrepid monk! He looked fine, relaxed and unscathed.

"What happened to you?" I asked earnestly. "Why did you leave Lhasa in such a rush?"

Thupten wasn't about to appease our curiosity, not a word. "I'll tell you later. Not here, okay?" Rather, he asked about our plans, "when are you going to Dharamsala? I'm leaving tomorrow. So I'll meet you guys there, and we'll talk at leisure!"

Next came that horrendous overnight road trip to Dharamsala, a route with which we were all too familiar. Leaving after dark, our "deluxe" bus chugged down the highway through the bustling towns that comprise the endless suburbs of Delhi. Before reaching Chandigarh, which is about halfway from Delhi to Dharamsala, there's a stretch of highway we jokingly call "Death Row"—the hazardous, grand-trunk highway that stretches across northern India. This road is backed up 24/7 with endless traffic and the deafening honks of what sounds like a thousand horns.

In this vast country, the modes of transportation included anything and everything that one can imagine. We sank back in our seats to watch the spectacle through the soiled windows. Vehicles weaved wildly in and out of traffic, managing to avoid the lounging cows occupying the road, trying to arrive at their destination a little faster. King of the road were flatbeds transporting goods heaped in towering mounds of overfilled burlap sacks. The trucks teetering on undersized tires, jostled with ox-driven carts that were also overloaded, sometimes with people hanging onto each other. Buses, jam-packed with passengers inside carried more riders and freight on their roofs. Seven or eight people squeezed into cars suitable for four persons. Scooters and bicycles balanced as many as four people on their tiny frames, including toddlers and young children with no safety helmets. The occasional camel, elephant, or horse-pulled buggy with riders trundling along with the mob, all added local spice.

The first stop was around midnight to grab a cheap meal at a roadside stand. Seating consisted of picnic-style benches on dirt floors. The menu was chapatis, dahl, and sabji (mixed vegetables). Ordinarily we avoid eating or drinking much liquid on these trips, preferring to peel a tangerine or banana. On this occasion, we munched on a couple of whole wheat chapatis. The choice seemed to be a safe bet compared to the spicy options. Too often greasy food caused nausea on the winding roads to Dharamsala, evident from the streams of yellow slime streaking the sides of the unwashed buses.

Since there are no toilets on Indian buses, we took a quick bathroom break. That meant finding a private spot in an open field behind a village shack. There would be only one other pit stop before we reached Dharamsala.

We sat awake as the bus continued down the road in the night. The muted drone of the conductor's chatter and storytelling to keep the driver awake was interrupted by the intermittent snores and heavy breathing of sleeping passengers.

At last we reached Chandigarh, nestled between the great northern desert and the breadbasket of the Punjab. Considered to be a modern city, it was built as the capital of that region and designed with streets similar to British roundabouts. From Chandigarh, the highway narrowed and wound its way through hilly terrain.

Sunrise, another day was dawning, and we were on the last leg to Dharamsala. Traffic noticeably decreased, and buildings and populations became sparse, as we climbed higher into the mountains. An occasional vehicle or motorcycle honked as they whizzed by on the blind curves. Buses and trucks overloaded with people and goods showed an uncanny ability to maneuver past each other on this precarious road. Dangerously steep precipices looked down into deep ravines, rushing rivers, and terraced fields. Covered with wildflowers and the harvest of late summer, the topography was lovely indeed.

It was comforting to be back in Dharamsala, our hill station refuge at the foothills of the Dhauladhar Mountains. The cool air was refreshing and the Tibetan community familiar. We were heartened to see Thupten at the monastery, and in the privacy of our room, learned what had happened to him in Tibet.

The Secret Police

"Shortly after I arrived in Lhasa, the Chinese secret police arrested me," Thupten took a deep breath before continuing. "They dragged me into a car, threw a hood over my head, and drove a long way out of the city into the countryside."

"For three days they interrogated me through the night," he winced, recalling the ordeal. "During the day they brought some inedible food, gave me very little water, and told me to sleep."

He shook his head, "That was impossible."

Thupten described typical torture techniques where prisoners are deprived of sleep, kept hungry, and dehydrated. The ensuing fatigue weakens resistance.

"What?!? Why were they on to you in the first place?" I asked in disbelief.

"Well…" he said sheepishly, "I had bags filled with booklets and other things from the Information Office to deliver to various people in the underground, and I was distributing them to people around Lhasa who seemed interested. I guess the word got out."

"You've got to be more discreet!" Miguel was perplexed. "Why draw attention like that and put yourself in harm's way?"

"How can I not? You know how unreasonable the Chinese government can be!" Thupten defended his actions.

"Remember the ban on Dalai Lama photos? How they arrested and tortured Tibetans who treasured their images of His Holiness? It's all so stupid! It's ludicrous! They're so afraid of His Holiness' influence on Tibetans, and they continue to try, in every way possible, to undermine it." He crossed his arms defiantly, "I can't sit back and do nothing!"

It was pointless to debate him. "Better to move on," I thought, wanting to hear the rest of the story. "Well, then, what happened?" I asked impatiently. "Did they threaten you or hurt you?"

"After the initial fear, I realized that they weren't going to harm me." Thupten paused, "They just wanted information about His Holiness and my personal involvement." There was some truth to what he said. The Chinese government had a desire for intelligence, but since it refused to have an open dialogue with the Tibetan Government-in-Exile, it effectively closed all channels for credible information and news.

"So, I just acted like myself and talked openly. I had nothing to hide." Thupten continued, "In fact, I even taught them basic Buddhism and mind training. Those poor Chinese soldiers and policemen have had nothing but communist indoctrination their whole lives."

"And what else did you tell them?" I prodded. In the course of our conversation, Thupten had pivoted from relaying a dangerous incident to making light of it.

Thupten grinned. "I told them that I wasn't an agent for the Tibetan Government-in-Exile. I had no such agenda and that…," he stopped for a suspenseful few seconds, "…that I was in Lhasa to find the reincarnation of my lama, Nechung Rinpoche."

"You said what!!" I exclaimed, my eyes bulging.

"No, you didn't!" Miguel balked.

We could not believe our ears and didn't know whether to feel relief over Thupten's safe getaway or panic over the exposed mission.

Over the years, we had heard enough troubling accounts on how the undercover police handled espionage matters in Tibet. There was zero tolerance for suspected traitors. If someone was a potential spy or mole, he or she would be executed without a fair trial. For that, we were thankful that Thupten had not been tortured and was released. But to expose our mission!

Thupten wasn't concerned. "Don't worry!" he assured us. "The Chinese government isn't interested in reincarnate lamas.[19] To further support his assertion, he said, "Sure, now that the Seventeenth Karmapa has been found, they're attentive to him, but that's because he's the head of the Karma Kagyu lineage—well-known and a great showpiece." His point was well taken. The Karmapa did give daily blessings to pilgrims and tourists at his Tsurpu Monastery, and the government accrued a tidy sum from his orchestrated performances.

"As long as the Chinese government maintains a positive public facade, people who don't know better will think that Tibetans have religious freedom. Karmapa is trapped under the domination of the Chinese authorities. He'll soon long for a safe escape to India."[20]

He continued to present his case, "Otherwise, the communist government has no official policy about reincarnate lamas. They don't believe in reincarnation, they

19. *Two and a half decades later, the Chinese Government has become interested in the subject of reincarnation. Involving itself deeper into the religious and cultural affairs of the Tibetan people, the communist administration now claims to be the only entity authorized to recognize reincarnate lamas or "living buddhas."*

20. *The Seventeenth Karmapa safely escaped from Tibet in early 2000.*

don't care about lamas or the Buddhist doctrine, and they know nothing about our tradition of finding and recognizing a lama."

"They didn't question you about Rinpoche?" Miguel asked.

"No. When they realized that I was politically harmless, they let me go. I was never in danger, but, hey, I wanted to get out of Lhasa. Besides..."

"Any breakthroughs or clues about who Rinpoche is?" I interrupted, "or where he is?"

"Oh, yes!" Thupten declared enthusiastically. "Since His Holiness had provided us with the names of Rinpoche's parents and the year of his birth, I sought out a person from the Office of Vital Statistics and solicited her assistance. This woman kept track of the birth and death records in Lhasa, so I asked her to check for boys born in the Earth Bull Year. She generated a substantial list, but only one child had the exact parents' names as given by His Holiness."

"I felt that having this list of children born in the same lunar year as well as the name of this specific boy may be enough to ask His Holiness for a confirmation. The particulars have already been submitted to him, and we're just waiting for a response. He's really busy. So if you guys get the opportunity to ask him personally, we may speed up the process."

"We have to be skillful though," Thupten cautioned. "We don't want Rinpoche to end up like the Karmapa. If the Chinese government catches on, they could ensconce him at Nechung and stage another tourist show. We must move fast!"

Miguel and I were pleased to hear Thupten acknowledge the need for vigilance. We called Tenzin Geyche, His Holiness' dedicated secretary, and requested an audience. We didn't have to wait long; a slot of time was found within a few days for us to see him.

We arrived early and showed our passports at the gate guarded by personnel assigned by the Indian government to protect the Dalai Lama. Inside, the compound housed offices, reception rooms, staff quarters, and His Holiness' personal residence. The reception room was by the entrance—a simple, unpretentious space with padded benches along the walls. We signed into a bound logbook, confirmed our appointment, and sat next to the other Westerners and Tibetans who were also waiting to see His Holiness.

After a while, we were called outdoors and directed to separate areas for men and women. I was acquainted with the Indian policewoman on duty from our previous stays in Dharamsala. She had been at the job for years and was always the one charged with this task. She smiled broadly, as did I, happy to see her. As usual, she was amiable and quickly rummaged through my purse and gave me a cursory pat-down. We exchanged pleasantries, I spoke in English, she in Hindi, neither of us understood the meaning of the other's words, just gestures of friendly interaction.

Miguel and I walked up a slight hill and stairs to a larger reception room lined with cabinets displaying Tibetan antiquities and memorabilia. Here too, the seating arrangement consisted of benches lining the walls, each covered in colorful wool rugs with Tibetan motifs. We sat and waited patiently knowing that someone would come soon to usher us into the inner sanctum to see His Holiness. I had butterflies in my stomach…

His Holiness was welcoming and greeted us with outreached hands. He wrapped his arms around each of us as he led us toward the Western-style sofa chairs. As always, he was warm and engaging and immediately put us at ease.

"My Chinese friend!" he teased me with that infectious laugh. Back then, you could count the number of Asians[21] at his discourses on one hand. I, in turn, giggled demurely.

Before sitting down, we moved to prostrate, as is customarily done when meeting a high lama. "No, no, not necessary," His Holiness said, but we continued anyway and completed our three prostrations.

We shared some highlights of our recent trip to China and Lhasa with His Holiness. He listened intently, keenly inquiring about the living conditions of the Chinese people and the state of religious affairs. When the subject of Tibet came up, and we told him about the radical changes in Lhasa, his eyes misted over, his gaze was deep and penetrating, as if he perceived and shared the pain of his Tibetan brothers and sisters. He reflected upon the matter in silence, it was a compassion beyond words. Then…

"What about Nechung Rinpoche's reincarnation?" he asked. "Did you find anything?"

Miguel nodded, saying, "Thupten has a list of boys' names born in the Year of the Earth Bull that he has given to your office. When you have time, will you please do a divination as to which one is the true reincarnation?"

"Yes, yes. My staff told me about the list. I'll get to your request."

Then he added pensively, "I heard about Thupten's troubles in Tibet. He's very patriotic and committed."

"If you determine that one of the boys on the list is Rinpoche's reincarnation, should we go with Thupten to find him?" I asked, seeking clarity on the next move.

---

21. It recent years, His Holiness the Dalai Lama gives annual discourses at Thekchen Choling, the main temple in Dharamsala, at the request of Asian people from Taiwan, Korea and Southeast Asia.

Confident as we were, and as much as we desired to be the ones to find Rinpoche and bring him out of Tibet, we sought His Holiness' affirmation that we were the best people for the job. After all, there were dozens of monks at Nechung Monastery. Perhaps it would be better if some of them went instead.

Perturbed about Thupten, I added: "Is it even safe for Thupten to return to Tibet?"

After a contemplative pause, His Holiness replied, "You are Westerners. That could be a disadvantage, but it could also work in your favor. With American passports, you have more freedom in Tibet than our own people. I will do a *mo*."[22]

His Holiness stood up and motioned to an assistant who was quietly standing in the back of the room. The signal was an ever-so-slight movement of his head, but the monk knew exactly what to do. He handed His Holiness two rolled-up silk *katas*. After His Holiness unfurled them, we leaned forward, bowed our heads, and he blessed us by draping the long white scarves over our necks. Our audience had reached a natural closure.

His Holiness determined that the boy Tenzin Losel, born in the Earth Bull Year, was the indisputable choice. His parents were the ones he had identified earlier.

The senior monks gave Miguel and me their approval to go on the expedition. "You are one of us," Kushog Phuntsok said. "We trust you implicitly. The two of you and Thupten are Rinpoche's closest students and part of his household. It's auspicious that the three of you go together to find Rinpoche. For our part, we will recite daily prayers for your rapid success!"

These words of love and encouragement brought tears to our eyes. Although we realized that we were part of the monastery, to be entrusted with this critical mission was validation of their full acceptance.

We intended to leave at once but had to delay our departure because Thupten and I had caught nasty colds, probably provoked by fatigue and changes in weather and elevation.

Leaving a few days later, Kushog Wangyal presented us with the customary *katas*. "You two are just like our own monks, and Thupten is one of our bright hopes for the future."

"We have complete trust in you," he reiterated. "Take care of yourselves and be careful. Have a safe journey!"

With these assurances and blessings, we were on our way back to Lhasa.

---

22. *A mo is a divination performed using various methods.*

One Step at a Time

The heat was unbearable in Delhi, so we stayed only long enough to rest and purchase our airplane tickets to Nepal. In Kathmandu, we circumambulated the Bodhanath Stupa and by chance met Khamtrul Rinpoche, one of our dear teachers. He was with his wife and two senior monks from Namgyal Monastery. They had recently returned from a trip to Mustang, a border region between Nepal and Tibet. We promptly shared the exciting news with Khamtrul Rinpoche. He was equally exuberant and offered prayers for our success.

"What a great start!" I said to Miguel. "How auspicious to see Rinpoche at such a holy site."

"Yeah, it really was a good sign!" he agreed.

As expected, making travel arrangements to Lhasa required some effort; it wasn't easy being FITs. Thupten had befriended two Nepalese women who worked for the airlines and charmed them into selling us three one-way tickets. It was pointless to buy return tickets since we had no idea how long we might be in Tibet.

The truth was we had a multitude of questions. First and foremost, how were we to find this boy? Where would we start? Even with the names of the child, mother and father, it was still a challenge. What were Rinpoche's parents like? Did they have faith in the Buddha Dharma and the Dalai Lama, or had they been indoctrinated into the Communist Party? What would their reactions be? Would they allow us to take their child to India? Moreover, what about the young boy—would he leave his parents to go with total strangers and join a monastery?

We were embarking on the journey simply with a signed letter from His Holiness the Dalai Lama stating that Tenzin Losel was the bona fide reincarnation of Nechung Rinpoche. As for a comprehensive strategy to bring him out of Tibet, we had none. Not yet, anyway.

When a delegation approaches parents with the announcement that their child has been recognized as the reincarnation of a lama, the tradition is to present them with a bounty of gifts. Kathmandu was the perfect place to shop—a city teeming with people, narrow streets, restaurants, and stores. We substituted the rich cuisine that we had savored in India with a vast array of gastronomic delights. Here, one can feast on anything from quiche, pizza, and pasta, to sushi and triple layer chocolate cakes.

We integrated ourselves into the local population and roamed the marketplaces—admiring Nepalese hand-loomed carpets, colorful cotton clothing, sterling silver and semiprecious gemstone jewelry. Excellent selections of statues, each uniquely crafted in the lost-wax method, competed with contemporary goods. Stockpiled in multistory malls, modern items included name brand appliances, electronics, jeans, and cosmetics. Thupten knew exactly what was appropriate to offer to the lama's family, and we chose items for the young Rinpoche.

While in Kathmandu, Thupten introduced us to a friend—a Tibetan entrepreneur in his mid-thirties named Kunzang Lama. Lama is a common Nepalese surname. It doesn't refer to a spiritual teacher with exceptional qualities and insights. This particular "Lama" was a successful businessman who sold Toyota SUVs and luxury cars—new and used—to the Chinese government and its related agencies.

Kunzang Lama was an affable fellow, extending his assistance to us without hesitation. "So, I understand you're all going to Tibet. I'll be in Lhasa myself in the next couple of weeks for business," he said. "Let me know if I can be of any help."

Thupten told us afterwards that Lama frequently delivered fleets of jeeps and cars to Tibet and China. "He has many contacts in the government. He is very knowledgeable about the conditions in Lhasa and the border crossings," he gushed. "Lama can help us get Rinpoche out of Tibet."

Miguel and I were surprised at this utterance. Thupten obviously had great respect for Lama, but we had no preconception that anyone besides ourselves would be handling the assignment.

Idealistic and impressionable, Thupten made a case for his recommendation. He seemingly had it all figured out. "Listen," he said, "we'll go to Tibet together as planned, meet the boy and his parents, and present them with the gifts. By then, Lama will have arrived in Lhasa and we will decide what to do."

"It'll be really easy. Don't worry!" he declared. "You guys can fly back to Kathmandu and rest in a guesthouse," he continued. "You can wait there for Lama and me to bring Rinpoche out of Tibet. That way, you'll avoid the arduous two-day dusty road trip from Lhasa to the Tibetan border. Why endure that journey when you don't have to? You can fly instead!"

We were speechless and slightly offended. After all, why would we go all the way to Tibet, just to fly back to Kathmandu and wait in a hotel? How could we pass the responsibility for such a crucial undertaking to a person whom we knew nothing about?

While Thupten was competent and persuasive, at 27, he was still fairly naïve, and occasionally lacked the judgment to make clear, mature decisions. I recalled our 1987 Tibet trip with him, as well as his recent detainment in Lhasa.

No, we would never agree to his ill-conceived plan. How the next sequence of events would unfold was anyone's guess. We were resolute that the three of us had to stay together and work as a team on the entire process. His Holiness' smiling face and words of support came to mind. I was reminded of his insight on how we could be of value to the mission.

We made no attempt to debate but acknowledged that we heard him by saying, "Let's see what happens. It's hard to predict what's going to happen from here. We can only go one step at a time."

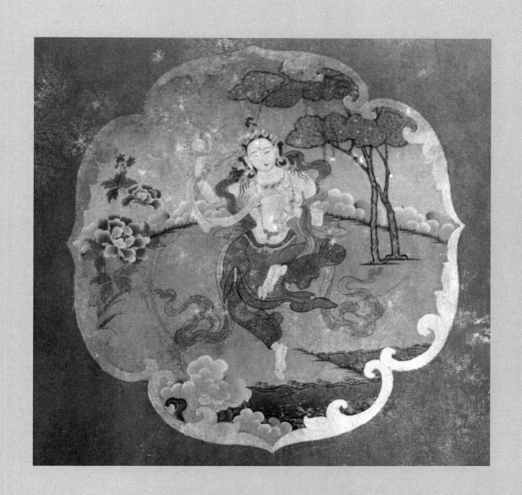

Offering goddess mural in Lhasa temple

THE DISCOVERY:
September 1993

Lhasa Encounters

I t was early September when Thupten, Miguel and I arrived back in Lhasa. The city was quiet and felt strangely deserted. We were later told that dignitaries and the police force had gone to Shigatse for the dedication of a stupa[23] commemorating the Panchen Lama who had passed away in 1992.

Our first course of action was to find accommodations for Miguel and myself. During our 1987 trip, we had occasionally stayed at the Lhasa Hotel whenever we wanted modern amenities. It was *the* place for foreign tourists; the only other large hotel in the area was patronized by Chinese visitors. The rooms were clean with private bathrooms and the luxury of hot water around the clock. We would request a room in the economy wing, which was not only less costly, but supposedly more secure. A friend of Thupten, who had installed most of the hotel's electrical wiring, had informed us that units in the rest of the hotel were electronically tapped.

Before leaving Tibet in 1987, our room at the Lhasa Hotel doubled as a rendezvous point for the political underground and distribution center for information provided by the Security Office of the Tibetan Government-in-Exile. In addition, Thupten gave away hundreds of photographs of His Holiness, protection cords blessed by him, and assorted prayer books.

We opted for the Lhasa again. With the precariousness of our current venture, we wanted comfort and familiarity, and this hotel was the sensible choice.

"Our cash reserves are starting to run low," I told Miguel. "Since it's September and the tourist groups have thinned out, maybe I can make a deal for a cheaper rate."

23. *A monument that is symbolic of the mind of enlightenment*

As I negotiated with the receptionist for a discount, two attractive Tibetan women walked by. "Thuuup-ten!" they called excitedly.

"Oh my god," I mumbled under my breath. "Someone's already spotted us!"

We knew that keeping a low profile was never easy for Thupten since he was so outgoing and personable. But we had just arrived!

They were Thupten's friends Pema and Dawa, two "it" girls in the Lhasa scene. Generally, most Tibetans were too intimidated to walk past the gates of the hotel's imposing edifice, but for the younger generation with Chinese jobs, the Lhasa Hotel was the hot place to hang out. We had met Pema in 1987 when she was a teenager and she had blossomed into a poised young woman.

"You remember Pema, right?" Thupten said, making the introductions. "She works as a TV broadcaster now and this is Dawa."

The girls were well dressed, favoring the contemporary Lhasa fashion—trousers in dark shades, tailored blouses and jackets, accessorized with Chinese-made shoes and purses. This was in contrast to the traditional Tibetan outfit—a *chuba* jumper dress donned over a wrap-style blouse in a contrasting pastel or bright color.

"You have to join us tonight at the party!" Pema invited Thupten. "It's my friend's birthday; you'll know most of the people!"

Thupten, being a fun-loving guy at heart, couldn't resist.

"I wouldn't go if I were you," Miguel recommended after we had settled into our room. "But if you do, stay out of trouble, and give us a report tomorrow."

"Yeah, yeah," Thupten laughed as he walked out the door.

Shortly after dawn the next day, Thupten charged back into our room.

"Well, what happened?" Miguel asked curiously.

Thupten shook his head and started talking faster than usual. "There were many people there last night, including Pema, and…" He hesitated.

"Dawa?"

"Yes, her. She was with her new boyfriend. Do you know who he is?"

Miguel frowned, "No. Who?"

"He's the son of the chief inspector in the Secret Police Department—you know, the one who arrested me this summer. The guy was stunned to see me there!" Thupten was noticeably disconcerted. I could almost hear his heart racing. Mine skipped a beat too.

"He probably couldn't believe that you came back to Tibet after what happened!" I blurted out. "Like, how could anyone be so crazy? So, what did you do?"

"I just glared at him." This was a deliberate act of irreverence on Thupten's part; as if to say, "I'm back, what are you going to do about it?"

"Everyone at the party knew about my apprehension and that this fellow was the guilty accomplice," he continued. "It was really unpleasant. The entire evening was spoiled."

We sat in silence, our minds muddled with thoughts of potential repercussions. It had been less than twenty-four hours since our arrival, and already, the first crisis had emerged.

"No more parties, no political activity, and no working the underground on this trip!" Miguel demanded. "It's imperative that we agree to focus on the task at hand. This is of utmost importance. We cannot afford to get distracted."

To emphasize the seriousness of the matter, he said, "We have to know what's going on with you and where you are 24/7. You need to call us three times a day or come by our room to communicate with us."

"Okay, okay, no problem," he agreed.

This wasn't realistic. Thupten, being a free thinker, would never contact us that often. By insisting on three times a day, perhaps we would hear from him at least once.

Perfect Circumstances

Since our senior monk's relatives were our key contacts in Lhasa, I told Thupten, "You should go see Khenrab's family and let them know that we're back."

"It'll be less conspicuous if you go alone," I continued. "They were really concerned about you, so they'll be relieved to see that you're fine. Please be mindful of why we're here and stay out of trouble!"

"That's exactly what I was intending to do," Thupten agreed. "I think that their son Tenzin Lodoe is here from Dharamsala."

Following the centuries-old Tibetan tradition of admitting one child into a monastic institution, the family had sent their Lhasa-born son to India for ordination. Lodoe was a tall, lanky monk, one of the many shy boys whom we had known for years, but apart from a polite nod and greeting, we had never spoken. He arrived from Tibet in 1983 during our year's stay in India. We often saw him sitting on the veranda outside his uncle's room, reciting scriptural verses aloud from the stipulated hundreds of folios that monks had to commit to memory.

I couldn't help wondering if Lodoe might play a role in our search.

Following the same rule that we had made for Thupten—to not dilute our energy and remain inconspicuous—we were content to remain within the confines of our hotel. Aside from completing our daily meditation practice, we passed hours watching television. It had limited channels, but it was enough to keep us entertained. We had a choice of BBC news, old reruns, or music videos. As for food, there were the choices of a café, a Chinese restaurant, and a buffet menu in the mezzanine.

Later that day, a knock on our door signaled the return of Thupten. He was invigorated—a complete turnaround from our earlier meeting. Upon taking a seat by the window, he quickly told us details of his visit with Khenrab's family.

"I took the bus downtown after leaving here this morning," he said. "It's really easy to get around Lhasa on public transportation these days. Besides, riding the bus removes the probability of being shadowed. If someone gets on and off the bus with you, that's a sure sign."

"I went right to Khenrab's apartment. He and his wife Yudron were having breakfast, so I joined them."

"She's a good cook, isn't she," I interrupted, trying to slow Thupten down.

"Yeah," he nodded, "and she makes some of the best Tibetan tea. Anyway, I told them that His Holiness has determined that one of the names on the list is Rinpoche's reincarnation."

"They knew about the list of boys?" I asked.

"Of course, it was through them that I met the person in the Office of Vital Statistics, but they never saw the list since I had to leave so unexpectedly."

Thupten continued. "I informed them that the chosen boy's name is Tenzin Losel. When I mentioned the parents' names—Kalden and Khandro—Yudron exclaimed, 'We know them!'"

"What?!" I exclaimed. It couldn't possibly be this easy!

"So, this couple does have a son, he's supposed to be quite young," Thupten kept talking. "They don't know exactly how old the boy is, but think that he's about the age that His Holiness indicated."

"Well, what do you think?" Thupten was wide-eyed.

"They know Rinpoche and his parents?" Miguel asked, somewhat in disbelief. "Do they know where they live?"

"Yes! They're supposed to be very nice people. Personally, they don't know them well, but their daughter Dekyi, and son-in-law Samten, are well acquainted with them. Previously, they were neighbors in the same housing complex."

Thupten took a deep breath before continuing, "The boy's father is said to be from rural Sakya, and the mother is a native of Central Tibet. They recently moved to a new home in Lhasa provided by the government agency the mother works for. I think that it's in the new subdivision on the east side of town."

Predictions given by the Oracle and several lamas back in 1987 came to mind: they had implied that when the timing was right, we would have pivotal support. The prophecy appeared to be coming true.

Miguel and I stared at each other, speechless, our jaws agape. We wouldn't have to find a needle in a haystack after all, in a society where it was forbidden to even inquire about the existence of the haystack itself.

I suddenly felt a surge of urgency. "What should we do?" I asked. "Can we have them contact Rinpoche's parents and arrange a meeting for us?"

Thupten was reflective, now calm and calculating, "Let me talk to Dekyi and Samten."

The Long Wait

In our hotel room, with its view of the distant hills, Miguel and I watched Grand Slam tennis matches on satellite television. While we waited, exerting nothing more than brain energy, seeing the athletes compete with such endurance was a good reminder of effort and perseverance.

We patiently sat out the weekend, taking advantage of the leisure time while we could. It was surprising that we didn't have TV at home in Hawai'i, but here in Lhasa, we could watch tennis and replays of "Faulty Towers," a British comedy.

We alternated our meals between the Western coffee shop and the Chinese restaurant, ordering from the à-la-carte menus. Meatless choices were limited, so my typical meal was quiche made with canned spinach and processed cheese. Miguel's standard was a well-done yak burger.

We loved to people watch. Whenever we got bored with TV, we moseyed downstairs and claimed a corner table in the dining rooms or chairs in the mezzanine overlooking the lobby. Foreigners and Tibetans alike congregated in the hotel foyer and its restaurants. For fun, we would try to discern who was American or European, identified the leaders of the tours and counted the number of people in the groups, and pointed out the lone trekkers. We could tell that most of the Tibetans lived abroad by the way they dressed, although a small percentage were locals.

Coming and going, we went down the back stairs, and slipped out the exit and side gate. On the rare occasion when we used the front entrance, we walked swiftly through the lobby, and kept our focus on the door. We avoided making eye contact with anyone. I was worried that we would run into people we knew. Such occurrences were inevitable, even in a place as distant as the Tibetan Plateau.

To get around Lhasa in 1987, we walked, rode two-speed bikes, or piled into trailers pulled by farm vehicles. Now, buses and bicycle rickshaws provided transportation in the city from east to west. More affluent people cruised the streets in private automobiles and jeeps.

On Sunday afternoon, after what seemed like a long retreat, we ventured beyond the walls of our safe haven for some fresh air and diversity. We braved the front entrance, passing staff members and guests in the lobby, then dashed across the boulevard to the bus stop on the corner.

The society circles of Lhasa had come out to attend a function at the Government Opera House located opposite our hotel. How beautiful the Tibetan dancers and singers looked in their vivid costumes and headdresses, a stark contrast to the army uniforms of the Chinese officers and their primped-up wives with pale, powdered mask-like faces.

Before long a crowded bus came by, jammed with passengers, a balance of Tibetans and Chinese. From behind the dusty windowpanes, we observed all the astounding changes in the west Lhasa landscape as we headed downtown.

At the convergence of several major avenues, a giant bronze yak—symbol of resilience and strength—marked the official entrance into the city. At the intersection, amidst honking vehicles, a uniformed police officer directed traffic with animated hand gestures and a loud whistle. Government and financial offices occupied this section of town. From here, the roads diverged, one looped around the backside of the Potala Palace, the other in front. Our bus continued along the road fronting the Potala. We had often walked these streets in 1987 and remembered some of the buildings. One was the bank where we changed our dollars for renminbi. Another was the Foreign Registration Office to extend visas, and also the police station (now rebuilt) which had been torched during the demonstrations shortly after we left Tibet.

Seats opened up as people disembarked, and we were able to find a bench together. A few people studied us, likely wondering what an Asian woman was doing with a Caucasian man. But most were uninterested; some had their eyes closed, using the time to catnap. We pulled the buzzer as the bus approached the Jokhang and Barkhor. It felt good to be outdoors away from the TV and to see what the marketplace had to offer.

Merchant stalls sold Chinese brocades, assorted fabrics for dresses and blouses, costume jewelry, offering scarves, and incense. Many of these items were imported from Nepal or China. The merchandise was of mediocre quality, probably because both the businesses and customers could not afford costly goods. In the larger, well-stocked Chinese stores, one could find anything from bolts of cotton velvet to canned goods, and lots of packaged candy.

Food and vegetable markets were located in the outer areas of the bazaar. Meat was not sold in the Barkhor around the Jokhang Temple, for good reason. We were nauseated by the sight of carcasses of recently slaughtered yaks alongside their heads. The flesh swarmed with flies under the midday sun. When a customer wanted to buy some meat, pieces were hacked off with a bloody cleaver or an axe. Mangy dogs laid close by, in hopes of being tossed a morsel. Life was raw and not sanitized; here, the cruel realities of survival and the food chain were plainly visible. It was a poignant reminder of the Buddha's teaching on the suffering of cyclic existence.

Nevertheless, it was a vibrant scene. Tibetans in coexistence with Chinese migrants who were conspicuously out-of-place. Ostensibly, religion was now a freedom of expression under communist rule. At makeshift stands, photos of various lamas, loose folio scriptures bound in bright cloth ornamented with patches of brocade were on prominent display. Meditation implements, such as vajras, bells, hand drums, and mala prayer beads were also available for purchase.

Meat Market on the outskirts of the Barkhor

Vegetable Market

Earnest displays of faith and spiritual practice were everywhere around the Barkhor area. Young and elderly aspirants prostrated their entire bodies at the temple's entrance. Monks garbed in maroon robes could occasionally be seen. Matted-hair yogis sat on the bare ground and chanted haunting melodies to release karmic debt as passersby dropped alms into well-placed begging bowls. Pious pilgrims with thick pads on their knees and wooden clappers strapped to each hand recited Refuge prayers and the names of the Buddhas. With each repetition they took a step, prostrated, stood up, took another step and so forth, thus circumambulating the Jokhang. Some of these devotees had journeyed that way from as far as Eastern Tibet, a vivid testament that the human quest for spiritual enlightenment cannot be quelled by oppression.

Despite their hardships, most Tibetans continued to exude positive attitudes and flashed toothy smiles. This often revealed gum disease due to poor dental hygiene accelerated by vigorous brushing, plus the introduction of sweets into the once alkaline diet. In our meander through the market, we were struck by how ubiquitous addictive substances had become. Besides sugar, an abundance of affordable nicotine and cheap alcohol had been introduced into this society. Given the high unemployment rate, increased alienation, and a sense of hopelessness, substance abuse had assimilated into certain segments of modern Tibet.

Effortlessly, without realizing it, we had roamed into a seedy section of town. Young men played pool in dark caverns, others gambled on tables outside taverns, all the while chain-smoking and drinking quart-size bottles of beer. They were dressed alike, in dingy white tanks and loose polyester trousers held up with stretched-out leather belts. It was midday, but instead of being at work, they squandered the prime of their lives and self-esteem. It was a pathetic sight and our expression must have reflected our feelings because they reciprocated with languid gazes and vacant stares.

"Let's go," I said, tugging on Miguel's hand. "That's enough exposure for today."

We stopped for some bread at a bakery run by a Chinese woman, likely an immigrant with a business subsidy from the Chinese government. Nearby, an open rickshaw was available, so we climbed in and headed "home." Keeping our heads down, we huddled under the soiled canopy for protection from the sun and evade the curiosity of the throngs of pedestrians on the street. We were just half a block from the hotel when another rickshaw pulled up to our right.

"Ma-ri-ya!" a voice yelled out.

"Oh, my god! Miguel," I murmured, bewildered. "Who is it?" Hoping that I was wrong, or that whoever it was would go away. I turned my head in the opposite direction from the voice, pretending to be busy talking to my husband.

"Ma-ri-ya!" The man was determined, calling louder from the rickshaw, which had slowed down and was now alongside us.

There was no choice but to acknowledge his presence. I leaned forward to spot a Tibetan with a clipped crew cut dressed in lay clothes. He was waving his hands enthusiastically.

I waved back with a broad smile, "Tashi Delek! How are you? It's so good seeing you!" I greeted cheerily, asking, "how are the Nechung monks?"

"Good! Very good! We're all fine. Please come by the monastery!"

"Of course!" I assured him. "We just got here, but will come to see you all soon!"

Satisfied, he bid us farewell and the rickshaw sped off up the road.

"Who was that? Do we know him? Is he a monk?" Miguel was eager to know.

"Wow, I can't believe that he saw us," I said. "That was Rabgyela from Nechung, we met him in 1987."

"That's amazing you remembered him," Miguel remarked, duly impressed.

In reality, we had no intention of going to Nechung Monastery. Khenrab had filled in some of the missing details as to what had happened a couple of months earlier. After Thupten had rushed back to India, a squad of officers had gone to the monastery seeking information. Luckily, the monks were unaware of Thupten's activities; all they knew was that he had been in Lhasa but had not visited them. We were reminded that as long as our friends remained uninformed, they could plead innocence with complete honesty if questioned—and hopefully stay out of danger's way.

By Monday, the city crawled with security again. Though the respite was temporary, we had savored the rare taste of freedom. This must be what life was like before the existence of the police state. Finished with their duties at the dedication ceremonies in Shigatse, they were back in full force. The secret police quickly discerned that Thupten had returned, and plainclothes agents were assigned to monitor his every move. They were hard to miss amid the casual Western tourists and Tibetans in the hotel lobby.

"The communist government should train and dress their operatives better," I commented, referring to their conspicuous ill-fitting suits, starched white shirts, and scuffed leather shoes.

Thupten was irritated at first; then, he found their pursuit rather amusing and decided to take an active role. He turned it into a game. Whenever possible, he created a diversion and sent the agents into a tizzy of confusion. Miguel and I avoided appearing with him in public so that we would not be linked as a team.

Although only a few days had passed, it felt like months. Being "hands-on" people, we wanted to see some progress. The clock was ticking and we were becoming increasingly impatient. Because the situation was precarious, we had intentionally stayed away from Khenrab's family. But it was time to consult with them again. The three of us needed to see them together.

Miguel directed Thupten to take the elevator downstairs. "Casually walk through the lobby, cross the street, and wait for us at the corner. Marya and I will go down the stairs and out the back. We'll be right behind you."

Thupten agreed, with an added suggestion, "Let's catch the bus downtown. It's cheap and convenient."

We carried out the plan and pretended to be strangers, merely three people waiting for the bus. Miguel and I chatted away in English. Thupten acted disinterested, seemingly oblivious of his two shadows who hovered nearby; yet, their presence didn't elude any of us. Would they be so blatant as to follow Thupten onto the bus?

The shuttle arrived shortly and the three of us boarded. Doors closed behind us. As we shifted our balance in the moving vehicle and headed toward the rear of the bus, we felt a sense of triumph when we caught sight of the agents' perplexed faces through the back window.

Thupten went ahead to the housing complex, while we lingered on the street. An old Tibetan woman had spread out some items for sale on the sidewalk outside its gates, so Miguel and I stopped to finger the goods until we were certain that no one was watching us. Inside the courtyard, people were everywhere—there were some folks doing laundry by the well and elderly women were cooking in a makeshift kitchen on the veranda outside their cramped quarters. I felt their penetrating eyes on us, as we hastily made our way across the grounds to a flight of stairs.

Tension increased palpably when we entered Khenrab's apartment. Our hosts were too gracious to verbalize what was on their minds, but their thoughts and body language said it all: "Being entangled with you could put our lives and future at risk. You will leave Tibet and go back to America, but this is our home."

Everyone was a potential spy with watchful eyes and attentive ears. Where human intelligence lapsed, surveillance cameras—on the corners of buildings, entryways, around the Barkhor—filmed every move.

"We cannot trust anyone. Every person is a potential informant," the family told us repeatedly. "Even if our neighbors mean no harm, they could tell others that we keep company with foreigners. Gossip is rampant, and people have nothing better to do than speculate and spread rumors. Our association with you will most certainly arouse suspicion, and the fact is, you are here to conduct a clandestine activity."

This was the sad reality. We knew all too well that if we visited too often, someone would connect the dots and trouble would erupt.

Anticipating our questions, Khenrab spoke. "Our daughter and son-in-law have been busy, but they did contact Rinpoche's family. There's a good chance that Rinpoche's father will be back in Lhasa today or tomorrow."

"What should we do?" Thupten asked with furrowed brows.

"Your first meeting will be critical," Khenrab's wife said. "Both parents should be present. They need to make your acquaintance, assess their options, and jointly decide what to do."

Then Yudron looked me firmly in the eye. "We'll ask Dekyi or Samten to pay another visit to Rinpoche's home. If his father is back, we'll tell them to set up a meeting for you right away. We'll let Thupten know as soon as we have any news."

We were grateful that, despite the tremendous risk, Khenrab's family was still willing to help us with our quest.

Caution and Terror

Although Thupten had restrained himself from overt political activity, he still made contact with various friends. After the initial few days of quiet, our hotel room became a hub of activity once again. We were glad to provide a safe place for people to speak frankly about their hopes and fears and to process their anguish. The space enabled them to have an open dialogue and reflect on the realities of an uncertain future.

People came because of Thupten. His enthusiasm reinforced their beliefs and fueled their desires for an autonomous Tibet. They discussed strategies for demonstrations. Some talked about their children in India. Others wept openly when they recounted the torture of loved ones. We heard accounts of bravery and selflessness—tales that had been told verbally and had now become oral history. These were the legends of heroism and resilience.

Many Tibetans had pent-up frustrations after living under the decades-long oppression imposed by the communist regime. Key components of Buddhist principles include training the mind to never lose one's humanity even in the face of brutality. In spite of this, anger can still erupt—often leading to desperate means.

There had been recurring protests and displays of civil disobedience where people shouted slogans such as "Long live the Dalai Lama!" and "Independence for Tibet!" Protests were peaceful. But inevitably, in the fervor of the moment, violence broke out when the crowds were confronted by heavily-armed paramilitary police. The demonstrators would have had nothing more than sticks and stones against their artillery and weapons.[24]

We heard the story of a teenage boy who had been involved in such marches and had thrown rocks at buildings and broken windows. Consequently, he became a wanted man and hunted as a symbol of dissent. The police promptly planted moles in the close-knit community in an attempt to infiltrate the political underground and procure the intelligence they desired. They located the home of the teenager's parents, stormed into their house, and ruthlessly beat the couple for information. The sister, a twelve-year-old girl, was standing by the stove making tea. Not getting answers from the parents, one of the agents pulled out his pistol and put it to the girl's head. "Tell us now, or we'll shoot her!"

"No, no, please! Believe us, we don't know where our son is!" Their pleas were of no avail. They shot the girl right in front of her parents. As they marched out, one of the Red Guards announced, "This will happen again to someone else until we get what we want! We will be back!"

The Chinese authorities were diligent in their hunt for active dissidents. Once discovered, the penalty was swift and decisive. This policy continues to this day.

---

24. *In recent years, pent-up frustration has led to self-immolations all over Tibet.*

Karmic Connections

Thupten had been on exceptionally good behavior, dropping by frequently at unpredictable times. His arms were usually laden with gifts for our monks in Dharamsala. I sighed each time he came, knowing that we were expected to take all these bundles back to India. Our "base camp" began spilling over with boxes of books and open duffels filled with miscellaneous foods, shoes, and clothes.

"We're supposed to go to Khenrab's again this afternoon," Thupten announced the day after our meeting with him and his wife. "I think they may have some good news. You guys should come at three o'clock."

This would be our final visit to the Khenrab family's Barkhor apartment. Their daughter Dekyi and her husband Samten belonged to a small cross section of younger Tibetans who were well educated and employed by the Chinese government, yet maintained traditional values. She worked in an office, he in a bank. Dekyi's looks resembled her mother's—tall and regal, with the distinct features and sophistication of Lhasa women. Soft-spoken and courteous, she had the well-honed manners of a central Tibetan native. Samten was an outspoken extrovert. Both were supportive of our mission and readily offered to help. They were inspired to be part of this journey and showed no hint of apprehension.

"Rinpoche's father teaches school in Sakya and is away for months at a time. He just returned to Lhasa last night!" Samten said, tacitly acknowledging that Tenzin Losel was indeed Nechung Rinpoche's reincarnation.

We were thrilled and expressed our delight.

"The family actually lived in Sakya for several years, after their children were born. Rinpoche has a younger sister," Dekyi told us. "The mother is from Lhasa and moved back to be close to her mother. She also wanted the kids to have a better education."

"You used to live next door to them, right? Why did they move away?" I asked, taking my chance to pose questions.

"The unit belonged to the grandmother. It was way too small for so many people," they explained. "Besides, Khandro found a job after moving back to Lhasa, and the firm provided them with housing."

"Hmm, so the father works full time outside the city. Does he come to Lhasa only for vacations? How long does he normally stay?"

"We don't know," Samten said. "Kalden wanted to be here with his family but the authorities wouldn't grant him papers for permanent residency in Lhasa. The government dictates where people live. Changing residential districts can be complicated."

"Okay, but the father is back in town now," Miguel said. "We would welcome meeting the entire family so that we can move forward with our plans."

Our friends quickly put the matter into perspective. "You've got to be sensitive," said Samten. "You're going to tell these folks that their son has been recognized by His Holiness the Dalai Lama to be the reincarnate lama of Nechung Monastery. And…you want to take him to India and ordain him as a monk. These are not small considerations for any parent. We personally wouldn't know how we would react if this happened to us. Would you?"

It was a candid appraisal, and it caused us to pause for reflection. What were we thinking? We had not even met these people, and already we imagined taking one of their two children to India. They might not be so eager to give their one and only son to complete strangers!

Now and then, at moments like this, a slight doubt gnawed at my resolve. So many factors could affect the outcome. I nodded my head, yet remained optimistic.

"But," Samten continued, "since Kalden is back in Lhasa with his family, there is an opportunity for a conversation. You meet them and let things unfold."

"It may take time for them to decide," he hinted.

"We know that you're anxious about this," Dekyi added. "So we're going to their house this evening and will try to arrange for a get-together tomorrow."

Later that night, Thupten gave us the news that we had been praying for. Khandro and Kalden had agreed to see us the next day, after Dekyi and Samten relayed to them that their son had been recognized as a high lama by His Holiness.

"What was their reaction?" I asked, wide-eyed, sitting on the edge of the hotel bed.

"Apparently, they seemed in awe and overwhelmed. But, they were noncommittal and didn't say very much."

I was slightly disappointed. More affirmative remarks would have been encouraging. Nevertheless, the next piece of the puzzle was in place. We had an appointment.

It was opportune that Dekyi's brother was in town. Being the sibling of trusted friends of Rinpoche's family and a monk from Nechung in India would give further credence to our proclamation. We devised a plan. Thupten and Lodoe would dress in their best monk's attire and go first to Rinpoche's house. Together they would deliver the official stamped and signed letter of recognition from His Holiness. That would be validation indeed.

However, before moving ahead, we had to deal with the plainclothes agents who were pursuing Thupten. We decided to renew our connection with an old acquaintance whom we had met in 1987. At that time, Miguel gave Ashangla a bottle of cognac hand-carried from America. He in turn, shared his prized tiger bone liquor, and the men bonded over stiff drinks.

Ashangla was well connected in political circles. He was acquainted with the heads of various branches of the government, and his position gave him clout and access to classified information.

"Of course, I will help!" Ashangla said. "I'll make some phone calls and find a way to stop the detectives from following Thupten. Don't worry! I'll take care of everything."

He reached out to the director at the Security Office and invited him over for drinks. Before long, it became clear that the agents following Thupten had been given orders from an ambitious bureaucrat who was vying to advance his career. Having presumed Thupten was engaged in subversive activities, he thought exposing potential wrongdoing would raise his profile and put him in line for a promotion. The security director exposed this unwarranted use of manpower and effectively put an end to the maneuvering of the contender. Ashangla's intervention gave us the latitude to move about without further interference. Nevertheless, we had to be vigilant.

Wednesday, September 8th

Thupten and Lodoe were to go to Rinpoche's home early the next day to deliver the recognition letter from His Holiness and offer silk scarves from Nechung Monastery. If everything went smoothly, Thupten would fetch us. He came by our hotel room at dawn, and together we stretched out the ten-foot-long *katas*. They were pure white embossed with auspicious symbols and prayers. We folded them into accordion pleats with their fringes neatly tucked inside.

"Okay, I'm going!" Thupten said at the door. He looked perfect with his cleanly shaven head and maroon robes offset by a saffron sleeveless shirt—the ideal picture of an ordained Buddhist monk.

Miguel patted him on the back and held his hands. "Regardless of what happens, come directly back here afterwards, okay? Be very careful!"

"Sure, sure! See you soon!" he assured us and was off.

We recited our prayers and kept busy by doing laundry and watching MTV. It was 1993, and the popular bands of the moment were Pearl Jam, Nirvana, and Soul Asylum. It was fun listening to music in Lhasa of all places—something that we never did in our Hawaiian hideaway.

Eventually we got dressed in the clothes that we had brought for this very occasion. Because they were quite wrinkled from the weeks of travel, Miguel used the time to iron—a chore I disliked. I fidgeted with my floor-length Tibetan *chuba* and tried to adjust the collar of the silk blouse that refused to lie flat under the formfitting garment. "Do I look all right? Remember all the gifts, okay? Where are the *katas*?" I was nervous. My mind was moving at a frenetic pace, but I made no attempt to restrain it and blabbered away. "I wonder how Thupten's doing? What time is it? Are our watches correct?"

Miguel was cool as usual, outwardly at least, but I knew that he was excited, too. He calmly made more coffee—not that we needed more caffeine. He looked so handsome with his dark hair slicked back, dressed in his signature button-fly Levi's and hand-spun long-sleeve cotton shirt from our favorite shop in Delhi.

Before long, we recognized Thupten's rhythmic knock. There he was, his winning smile lighting up the room.

"Well, what's the boy like? Is he special? Did he show signs of knowing you?" I couldn't ask my questions fast enough. "Can you tell that he's Rinpoche's reincarnation?"

"What are the parents like?" I pressed on. "What did they say?"

"He's about eight years old, sweet, tiny, and very quiet. His parents are humble and unassuming. Lodoe and I gave them the letter from His Holiness and told them that their son had been recognized as the reincarnation of the Nechung Lama. They must be in shock right now!"

I passed Thupten a cup of tea, and he took a quick sip.

"They didn't say very much. But they were receptive and seemed to have faith in His Holiness and the Dharma. They've been to Nechung Monastery and the Nechung shrine in the Barkhor."

"What was their house like?" Miguel asked.

"Modern and clean. They'll appreciate the gifts we brought from Nepal."

Thupten looked at his watch. "Now it's your turn to meet Rinpoche and his family. Are you ready? We've all been invited to lunch at noon." He sounded self-confident, clearly in his element. He reached for the presents. "I'll carry these," he said. "You two bring the *katas*."

"Are we going to Rinpoche's house?" I asked.

"Oh, no, that's too dangerous. Dekyi and Samten have offered the use of their home. So, I'll leave first and will wait for you there. Give me a head start, then go down and catch a rickshaw. Take it to Banak Shol and wait on the street outside the hotel. Lodoe will meet you there. He knows where to go. Just make sure you're not followed."

As if our ride had been prearranged, a lone rickshaw waited outside the Lhasa Hotel. We hopped into our chariot and instructed the driver to take us to Banak Shol.

The minutes ticked by as we lingered outside the hotel, watching for Lodoe, uncertain whether he would be walking or riding. We felt exposed waiting on the street in our fancy clothes, such a contrast from the average Tibetan, Chinese, or Westerner. Passersby pierced us with their eyes, prying for a hint of who we were.

Finally, we heard a voice from an approaching rickshaw. It was Lodoe. "Hey, come on, get in!"

We squeezed, all three of us onto a narrow vinyl seat designed for two. We had experience traveling this way in Delhi. We knew the best fit was for me to balance on Miguel's knees, since it was inappropriate to press up against a celibate monk. We were highly conspicuous—a Chinese woman in a Tibetan dress sitting on a Caucasian man's lap with her arms wrapped around him, while riding alongside a maroon-robed monk. Thank goodness we were on the edge of town where traffic was light, and the driver quickly turned onto a deserted back street.

The route will forever remain a mystery in my mind. The wheels of our carriage turned corner after corner, taking a course that could not possibly be tracked. Several malnourished, scraggy dogs barked and chased us down the gravelly streets as we passed numerous unmarked buildings with not a single human in sight.

Finally, Lodoe pointed his finger and leaned forward telling the driver, "Turn right into that alley. Stop there."

As I alighted from the rickshaw, my heart fluttered, causing me to take a few deep breaths. Ten years had gone by since our precious Rinpoche had passed away. Miguel and I had both matured, having carried the responsibility of managing the temple all on our own. For the past decade, we had been waiting for this very moment. Suddenly the magnitude of our role in this assignment became overwhelmingly tangible.

We walked through a walled entrance into a small courtyard filled with dahlias and nasturtiums in vibrant fuchsia and shades of citrus. Blooming roses in pastel pink grew alongside the pathway leading to the house. Dekyi and Samten greeted us with wide smiles. "Please come this way. Everyone is upstairs."

The couple escorted us indoors. It felt like we were honored guests invited to a propitious private event. We ascended the short flight of stairs to a landing from which we were led into a living room with wool-rug covered floors, carved-wooden armchairs, and low tables. Single platform beds doubled as couches. Floor-to-ceiling armoires lined the back wall and left side of the room; the upper portions of the armoires were cabinets with glass doors. Inside were Buddha statues swathed in brocades, religious texts, and assorted religious accoutrements adorned in metallic gold and silver.

It was only later that my mind registered these lustrous details. Upon entering the room, all we saw was the small boy. Rinpoche sat cross-legged on one of the beds, his silhouette softened by the diffused light of a nearby window. His slight frame was clothed in a silk-satin *chuba* that was chocolate brown with circular patterns and worn over corduroy pants. These must have been his best clothes—his New Year's outfit that was worn only on special occasions. His hair was closely cropped short like that of a monk. Composed, he sat with his hands placed one upon the other, as if in a meditative posture. He looked at us politely, poised beyond his years.

Nechung Choktrul Rinpoche at our first meeting on September 8, 1993

Our Rinpoche had passed away in his late sixties, and we were now in the presence of an eight-year-old boy believed to be his reincarnation. We did our five-pointed prostration thrice, barely able to contain our exhilaration. Miguel completed his prostrations and stepped forward to offer his *kata* to the boy. As if seeing an old friend, he said, "Rinpoche, how are you?"

I followed shyly.

The boy took the *katas* from our hands and presented them back to us. Miguel took a seat on the bed next to Rinpoche, as only a Westerner could do. This would be considered too forward a move according to Tibetan protocol. I positioned myself a polite distance away on the side platform, at a right angle from them. It seemed silly to feel bashful with such a young boy, but my timid side surfaces when I meet lamas—and this was no ordinary child.

Nechung Choktrul Rinpoche with Miguel

Miguel squeezed Rinpoche's hand tightly, as if to make sure that this unbelievable moment wasn't a dream. "Do you know us?" he asked in a central Tibetan dialect with his West Coast American accent.

Rinpoche responded with the slightest smile.

Our sense of intense familiarity in those first moments with Rinpoche were extraordinary—beyond what words can describe. We were witness to a consciousness that had transferred from one being to the rebirth of another—from the venerable lama whom we loved so dearly to this boy in Lhasa. And this recognition was made by none other than His Holiness the Dalai Lama himself.

What happens after death? Is there reincarnation, and if so, what mental or physical traits pass on? And is there a heaven and a hell? Such questions have continued throughout the ages by people of diverse cultures and religions. Yet, here we were, with genuine conviction that this child was the reincarnation of our teacher.

Miguel handed Rinpoche some small gifts—a ballpoint pen with a fine point, chocolates, and a round tin of Danish butter cookies—all things that his predecessor had enjoyed. The boy accepted them graciously.

Dekyi served us tea and biscuits, and some creamy "white rabbit" Chinese candies from a wooden bowl, then vanished into an adjoining room with Thupten, Lodoe, and the rest of the family, leaving Miguel and me alone with the young lama.

"Do you know what's going on?" Miguel asked. Rinpoche's nod was barely noticeable, but seemed to say, "Sure, I do." As we sat and drank tea, Miguel kept the conversation going—verbalizing how happy we were to finally meet him after waiting so many years, and of course, letting him know who we were.

After what seemed like half an hour, someone came in and asked if we were ready for lunch. We nodded courteously. Thupten, Lodoe, and the family started filing back into the room and stood alongside each other in front of the armoires. Everyone was beaming. After all, it is no small honor when His Holiness the Dalai Lama personally recognizes one of your own as being a high lama.

Khandro, the mother, was petite and pleasantly plump with a round, affable face. The father, Kalden, was taller, dignified, with a scholar's demeanor. Both were younger than either of us. The maternal grandmother was probably in her late fifties, a typical Lhasa lady dressed in a standard black *chuba* with a cotton blouse. Her son, Rinpoche's uncle, was there as well, a young man in his late teens with thick, bushy hair.

Two other women were present to whom we were not introduced. We had not intended to involve anyone but the immediate family; their presence made me a little nervous. Likely, they had come to help with lunch. If Dekyi and Samten had invited them, they must be dependable; so, we needed to trust them as well. We later heard that the women were neighbors and close friends.

Feeling uncomfortable being the only ones seated, we motioned for everyone to sit down. The father accepted, and we soon engaged in polite conversation. Miguel asked him about Sakya, the region where he was from, and his work. He wanted to know our story—how we came to be connected with Rinpoche's predecessor and the monastery. Thupten had already given them a rundown of our background, that we were from America and were close disciples of the former Nechung Rinpoche. They had been told that we were part of the delegation that came from India. Undoubtedly, this was the first time that these folks had met anyone from the West.

Our hosts had set out a simple meal of "sha-dreh," meat stewed with potatoes served over rice. Everyone ate heartily—except Miguel and me. Typically, we don't eat much at meals with company; it's hard to talk with one's mouth full. This situation was even more exceptional.

After lunch, Thupten and Miguel presented Rinpoche's parents with the gifts that we had brought from Nepal. These included an electric blender to make Tibetan tea, fragrant soaps, and a soft, woolen shawl for the mother. They accepted the packages politely, with both hands. As was Tibetan custom, the presents were not opened immediately but placed aside to be unwrapped later.

Based on our warm reception, we deduced that the parents were Buddhist minded and not influenced by communist rhetoric. We learned that they were acquainted with Nechung Monastery. Our own association with Nechung, a respected pillar of Tibetan culture, added to our credibility. These were all positive signs, and I assumed that it was unnecessary to give a lengthy explanation or justification for why we were there.

Even so, all eyes in the room were on us, observing and noting our every word and gesture. Silently, I thanked Rinpoche for encouraging us to learn Tibetan and speak it fluently. In our years living and working with Tibetans, we had developed a deep affinity with lamas and laypeople alike. Aided by our command of the language, we were able to bridge the boundaries of cultural differences.

"Did your son ever show signs that he was a lama?" I asked. "Do you remember anything he said or did that made you wonder if he was different from a regular child?"

"Nothing in particular," Khandro answered. "Though occasionally, when we would discipline him, my son would say: 'You better be nice to me. Otherwise, some people from a monastery in India will come and take me far away!'" She giggled as she recalled these prescient words.

The formalities were over; it was time to get down to business. Directing his attention to the boy's parents, Thupten said, "Now that Tenzin Losel has been identified as the Nechung Lama, what do you suggest we do? We all know how quickly gossip spreads in this community, so we must make plans and move fast." Ultimately, the decision was up to his parents; we could not move forward without their full participation.

Rinpoche was quietly attentive. He appeared to comprehend exactly what was going on, yet showed no signs of fear, attachment, or rejection. He calmly listened as we discussed his future and the course of events that would change his life.

"Time is of the essence. If it becomes known that your son is the Nechung Lama and the reason we are here is to take him out of Tibet, we all risk being in trouble."

Thupten continued, honest and deliberate in his message. "We can't afford to make any mistakes that will endanger anyone's life."

He paused, and then asked, "What do you think?"

"Once he got older," Rinpoche's mother, Khandro, murmured thoughtfully, "we had considered sending Tenzin Losel to a boarding school in India or to a government school in Beijing."

"He's a smart boy, and the Chinese government gives scholarships to children who excel in their grades," she paused…"But I didn't think he would leave for another few years. He's still so young." She lowered her eyes in reflection.

There was a hesitancy in her voice, perhaps she was not prepared to be separated from her child. My heart went out to her. "If you're not ready for your son to leave yet, we understand, but you need to make a decision."

Khandro nodded, followed by a hushed silence in the room. She may have already decided, I thought, since she didn't say: "No, he cannot go with you."

Kalden, the father hardly spoke, but in his quietness, I sensed tacit approval and support.

Miguel took the opportunity to make the bold move as if the parents had given us their consent. He cautiously but firmly asked, "Should we leave in a week?"

"That's best," Thupten concurred. "We should try to get it together within seven days."

"How will you travel?" Kalden asked.

"There are only two choices," Thupten replied. "We can go overland by jeep to Dram, cross the Tibetan-Nepalese border, and continue by road to Kathmandu. *Or* we can take a plane from Lhasa to Kathmandu."

To ease the angst of separation, I thought that the parents might conceivably want to see Rinpoche off and to travel with him as far as feasible. So, I dove straight into the logistics and asked, "What sort of identification papers does Rinpoche have? Whichever route we take, do you want to go with us?"

"The only papers my boy has are from school," Kalden said, "which is adequate for around here—but not for airport security."

He then suggested a possible option, "I've heard that you can buy identification papers suitable for travel by plane to Nepal and India, which would be useful for going overland as well. There's an office downtown that does this, but I'm not sure where it is."

"If that works, we can fly and avoid that exhausting road trip. That would be great!" Miguel exclaimed.

"I don't know if those documents are legal, although the rumor is that people have used them successfully," Kalden continued, furrowing his brows. "Supposedly, they can be processed quickly, provided you have a lot of money."

It was amazing, to think that we had just met these folks a few hours earlier (it was still uncertain if they would join us) and we were already discussing the details of leaving Tibet with their son. Incredible, really. Although Khandro and Kalden had not explicitly verbalized their consent for Rinpoche to go with us, they were engaged in the planning and offering suggestions. This display of willingness to work with us was all the affirmation we needed.

"I'll check into it," Kalden assured us.

"We'll cover all the costs," I said. "Just let us know what you find out about acquiring ID for Rinpoche. Meanwhile, we will check into flights and availability. In case we need to go overland, we'll also look into jeeps and potential drivers."

To my surprise, Khandro announced, "We probably won't go with you."

No one questioned the reason. Whatever their decision, we respected it.

Miguel turned to the young lama, who had remained silent. "You are aware that we're taking you to a monastery in India, and that ideally we'll leave within seven days, right?"

Rinpoche looked back at him, unblinking, so Miguel pressed on. "Is that okay with you? Are you ready to go with us?"

"Yes," he nodded. His answer was decisively clear.

His resoluteness made me tear up. "How brave," I thought, "for an eight-year-old to leave his family and go to a foreign land with three apparent strangers."

Then came the photo op that would capture and memorialize this auspicious occasion. In the courtyard, against a backdrop of blooming nasturtiums, we posed with Rinpoche, his family, and their friends. We thanked everyone, bowed, and took our leave.

The mission was acknowledged. The stakes were high. There was no time to linger.

At present, only a few people knew what was going on, but news *would* soon spread. The reincarnation of the Nechung Lama, recognized by His Holiness the Dalai Lama, now *that* was worthy gossip. Needless to say, suspicion, speculation, and intrigue would follow. Already, Dekyi and Samten's friends knew. Surely they could share the secret with others. Rabgyela—the monk from Nechung—knew that Miguel and I were back, as did Thupten's friends. Neighbors would soon question the unusual comings and goings. Word of our mission would inevitably get out and spread around Lhasa. This would naturally attract the attention of the Chinese authorities.

We had given ourselves one week—seven whole days to work out all the details: acquiring identification papers, determining the port of departure, and deciding on the best mode of transportation. Given the immensity of the task, could we map a successful strategy in such a short time?

We recognized the near impossibility of our undertaking, yet we had absolute confidence of success. We had been offered the role of a lifetime and given an open script with a generous plot, as well as the challenge to develop the story with precise details of cast, stage, and settings. There was the distinct consideration of scenario changes, but we never thought of any alternative endings. Triumph was our sole objective.

For us, having connected with the key characters so quickly was a promising sign. We knew that additional players would join us on the journey. Who were they? What combination of interdependent causes and conditions would lead us to achieve our goal? We had no choice but to listen to our inner voices and trust them. To do so, we dove into the pools of our mirror-like wisdom for answers.

Nechung Choktrul Rinpoche on September 8, 1993.

Thursday, September 9th

O n the same morning that we had our meeting with Rinpoche and his family, Kunzang Lama—the car salesman whom we had met in Kathmandu—checked into the Lhasa Hotel.

"Lama's here!" Thupten announced that evening, thrilled.

"So?" I responded, blasé.

"Lama had intended to drive in from Nepal and be here sooner, but the recent monsoons have badly damaged the roads again. So, he took a plane instead," Thupten reported. "When the roads reopen, which should be any day now, his employees will bring in a fleet of used cars."

"After Lama gets rested," he added excitedly, "we'll get together and make a plan for Rinpoche's escape."

"Now that you've met Rinpoche, you can fly back to Kathmandu," he told us. "Lama and I will drive overland with the boy."

Evidently, Thupten's "*we*" did not include Miguel and me. He reiterated what he had suggested back in Nepal. My defenses shot up like invisible horns. I looked at Miguel and made a face, certain that we both had the same thought: "Yeah, *sure*! We'll leave and let you and Lama take over. How absurd!"

Since arriving in Lhasa, Thupten had not spoken of this preposterous plan. I had hoped that he had given it up and come to his senses. Yet here we were. His proposition was simply not viable. Why would we entrust this mission to an individual we didn't know? We didn't have Thupten's same blind faith in Kunzang Lama. He had no directives from His Holiness; nor was he affiliated with Nechung Monastery. He had not met the young lama and his parents; nor had he been acquainted with his predecessor. Kunzang Lama was accountable neither to His Holiness nor to Rinpoche's family. If our operation failed, he would simply move on.

Thupten was well-trained in Buddhist philosophy, prayers, and rituals, but clearly, he lacked a common-sense approach. I had no doubt that he meant well; it simply had not occurred to him that his proposal was not practical. While his openness was refreshing, it frequently led him to trust the wrong people. Moreover, his youthful spontaneity meant he seldom pondered the potential ramifications of certain actions. Thupten's recent detainment and interrogation under precarious circumstances, plus the stolen vestments that he had entrusted to a complete stranger during our 1987 trip convinced us that we could not delegate the decision making to him. We would not leave and idly wait around in Kathmandu. To succeed, the mission would require the insight and skill of all of us working as a team. Our involvement was *not* negotiable.

I tossed and turned that night. It was vital that I use the techniques of mental self-examination to check for any signs of ego and self-importance. After all, this wasn't about us; it was about getting the job done. If that meant it was more efficient without the two of us, then we should accept that reality and put our bruised egos aside. On the other hand, if we were correct in our assessment—that our involvement may be useful—then we must persist. Nevertheless, we had to be tactful in how we handled the situation. We did not want there to be any internal conflict between us.

The night was long and dark. When I finally drifted off, I fell into a round of bizarre dreams that woke me.

"How should we proceed?" I mumbled to Miguel in my stupor. When he didn't answer, I gently nudged him to stay awake with me. "Hey, I can't sleep," trying to get his attention.

"What are we going to do? We can't just leave and trust Thupten and Lama to do the job."

"Don't worry," Miguel replied, half asleep. "We've come this far, it'll all work out. There's nothing you can do about it now anyway, so try to get some rest."

"We should explore our options," he rolled over, looking at me. "Let's see what travel documents Rinpoche's father comes up with. It would be great if we can all fly, but without proper IDs, going by plane will be out of the question."

Always the thoughtful one, he added, "We're going to have to play it by ear, honey. That's why we have to stay and help make the decisions as the situations arise."

"Yeah, we certainly can't do that sitting in a hotel room in Kathmandu," I said, heartened to know we were on the same page. "Besides, Rinpoche's parents *may* still want to go with us. They said that they won't, but I can't imagine why not."

Yes, our plans were far from certain and I was perturbed. Perhaps Thupten didn't reckon we were an indispensable part of the expedition, but he was not in charge. We were all equals. I could not allow his opinion to dampen my enthusiasm.

By now, Miguel was fully awake, listening to my musings. "One thing that Kunzang Lama *could* help with is hiring a jeep if we go overland," I said. "He supposedly knows some good drivers with vehicles."

"Don't forget, honey, according to reports, the border is still closed," Miguel reminded me. "They've been closed for almost three months because of the heavy monsoons, and there's been no traffic overland to Kathmandu from the border. They're still repairing the roads…" and with that uncertainty, we fell asleep.

Thupten dropped by our room in the morning. He was as insensitive as the previous evening. As if his plan had been finalized, he proclaimed, "Lama and I have talked. He knows someone who can take us to Dram."

"Before we leave Lhasa, Lama will call Nepal," he continued. "He knows a Nepalese general with good credentials, so he'll ask him to come with a vehicle to meet us at the border. That way, Lama, Rinpoche, and I can transfer into the general's car and ride to Kathmandu."

He looked at Miguel, then at me, "You two should buy airplane tickets and fly out."

Thupten's lack of sensitivity stung. There had been no dialogue, no request for our input, no concern about our opinion. How could he not know that we were sincerely invested not just in finding Rinpoche but also in accompanying him all the way to Nechung Monastery in Dharamsala?

I let out a deep sigh and bit my lip, and again questioned Thupten's judgment in tactics and choosing allies. I cast my eyes downwards, not able to look at him. Miguel was speechless. It was an awkward moment. Our silence expressed our feelings more than any words could.

We had not had breakfast, so we ventured downstairs for some cafeteria food. Winding our way through the crowded lobby, we heard a loud, somewhat familiar voice: "Marya! Miguel!"

"Oh, my god. Who is it now!" I looked wide-eyed at Miguel. It was too late to retreat; there was no place to hide.

We turned around to see a tall, bearded man grinning and waving to us from across the room. It was Terris, an old friend from Hawai'i who had trained as a traditional thangka painter in Nepal in the early 70s and had moved to the islands in 1976.

"Hey, I heard that you guys were in town!" Terris' voice boomed as though he spoke through a microphone. "Have you found Nechung Rinpoche yet? Is that why you're here?"

We wanted to disappear into thin air, but knew we had to react graciously. Everyone was staring at us. Were there agents in the crowd?

We gave Terris a big hug, "Great to see you! What are *you* doing here?"

He introduced us to the petite Eurasian woman with him. "This is Leslie. She's been studying thangka painting with me. We're working on a project for Tsurpu Monastery outside of Lhasa."

"Oh, what is it?" Miguel asked.

"It's an appliqué thangka," Terris replied. "The monastery used to have this huge, scrolled masterpiece that they rolled out for viewing once a year at Losar, but the communists burned it. We've been commissioned to remake it with no cost restraints; so, we're using the best silks and brocades."

Terris seemed to have forgotten about his earlier questions, so we happily kept the conversation going. "How large are you talking about?" I asked, somewhat curious.

"Large enough to cover the entire hillside across the river from Tsurpu," he answered. "You know the design of the thangkas, with the key Buddhas in the center, surrounded by images of the retinue seated in the background? Well, this is so spectacular that each corner figure—proportionately a small percentage of the main image—well, these are the size of a human!"

The thangka did sound impressive. We had only seen these in photographs. How fantastic that Terris was working on one, and for Tsurpu Monastery, the seat of the Karmapa.

What was more important to us was that the more he talked about his work, the less likely we needed to talk about ours.

"You aren't doing this alone, are you, just the two of you?" I wanted to know.

"No, no, we're working with the Lhasa Tent Company," Terris noted. "Leslie and I are pencil-drawing the figures to get everything to scale in the traditional way. Then the workers cut the silks and brocades and embroider them onto the images. They're really good because they have experience sewing and appliquéing on those fancy Tibetan tents. It's such an inspiring project. We're so stoked!"

After extolling the magnificence of Tsurpu, the Karmapa, and the appliqué project some more, Leslie finally said, "We've got to go or we'll be late for our meeting. You guys should come down to the Tent Company to see what we are doing."

"Sure, we'll try to stop by," Miguel said, knowing full well that we would not risk being compromised again. I glanced around the lobby. By now, almost everyone had cleared out, and I was thankful to see that no one was paying attention to us.

Friday, September 10th

Early the next day, Thupten stepped into our room. He was in an uncanny, pensive mood.

I broke the ice by asking, "How's it going with Kunzang Lama?"

"Fine," he quipped, "except, he's not sure if he can leave by Tuesday."

We were taken aback. This was a complete turnaround from the previous day.

"We still want to leave within the week, don't we?" Miguel asked, putting an emphasis on *we*. "It's down to five days now. We'd better figure out what we're doing."

"Lama has unfinished business so his departure may be delayed," Thupten said, visibly disappointed.

"It's alright. You guys should still go by plane and spare yourself the long road trip. Why tire yourselves out, when you can relax in Kathmandu? In any case, if Lama can't go, he'll get a jeep for me, and I'll go with Rinpoche to Dram by myself. His friend, the general, could still meet us at the border."

"This is our opening," I thought. "Try to use facts and logic to extract Thupten from his fantasy."

"Hmm, okay," I said. "We should revisit what we know about the border. Let's say you drive with Rinpoche and get past the first checkpoint at the Everest turnoff. Then there are two additional control stations at the Tibetan border, right?"

Thupten nodded.

"So, the second checkpoint will be at Dram, manned by Chinese soldiers. Then you go the eight kilometers downhill until you arrive at the Friendship Bridge, the third checkpoint, which is similarly guarded."

I paused to check Thupten's expression to see if he was following my reasoning.

"From there," I continued, "you proceed across the bridge to reach Kodari on the Nepalese border. That means you have to deal with four security inspections just to get that far. If the roads on the Nepal side are still in disrepair, there will be an impasse, with no vehicle thoroughfare. At which point will this general meet you?"

Thupten, as usual, came back with a quick response. "He'll come up to the immigration station at Dram. He's a five-star general and will do whatever it takes to get there. Lama will even have him bring his son's school ID."

"What for?" I asked, wrinkling my nose.

"Lama's son is about eight years old and looks kind of like our Rinpoche. The general will bring the boy's school clothes too, so Rinpoche can change into them and take on the boy's identity from the border to Kathmandu."

"Huh? None of this makes sense!" I snapped.

"It does! Lama is really together. He'll take care of *everything*," he said, "This plan will work! Don't worry!" Thupten was back to his cheerful self. He stood up and gave me a whack on the back.

It was irritating to hear Thupten gush about Kunzang Lama and his abilities. I didn't want to be biased, but we didn't know this man or his level of competence.

"Miguel and I are *not* going alone by plane!" I blurted out. "We are *all* sticking together! If Rinpoche's father can acquire ID papers that will pass scrutiny for air travel, then we'll *all* fly. Otherwise, we will go overland, *together*. There's absolutely no way we're leaving you to do this alone, with or without Lama!"

"Kunzang Lama can help though," Miguel added, trying to soften the intensity of the discussion. "The road trip is a definite possibility, and it would be great if he can find us a reliable jeep and a trustworthy driver. Since Marya and I don't know him, we should see him again and have a conversation."

"It's imperative to have a candid discussion," Miguel continued. "For example, I can't believe that this general you mention would really show up at the Dram border, because all the reports indicate that the roads on both sides of the border are still closed."

"What do the roads matter?" Thupten asked, frustrated with our analysis.

"Thupten! Think!" I shrieked, my voice an octave higher. "If the roads are washed out before the Nepalese border crossing, how can this guy drive up in a jeep to Dram on the Tibetan side of the border? How can he conceivably meet us there with a car?"

"And the roads are washed out on the Tibetan side too!" Miguel added. "Most likely, cars won't even be able to drive all the way to Dram. Even with a four-wheel drive, we may have to walk the last few kilometers."

Miguel peered into Thupten's face for a reaction, "Think about it. None of your plan makes any sense."

Thupten was lost for words. For once, he didn't defend his proposal or debate us. Looking rather glum, he said, "Okay, I'll talk to Lama," and shuffled out of the room.

Saturday, September 11th

We did our laundry again—a good therapy for our state of mind. We filled the bathtub with hot soapy suds and lathered up our clothes and undergarments. Miguel pulled out a rope from his travel kit and crisscrossed it from the windows to the bathroom door. Voilà, we had a clothesline, and soon, dripping clothes were hanging everywhere. The moisture felt good on my thirsty skin and legs which had broken out in dragon-like scales.

Thupten came by to see us, and we were happy that he was communicating. He ducked beneath damp jerseys and jeans, then sat down on our bed, the only dry spot in the room.

"Did Lama contact the general in Kathmandu?" I asked.

"Yeah, he called yesterday, but the general wasn't home, so Lama left a message with his wife asking him to meet us at the border in a few days," Thupten replied.

I winced. "You mean he never talked to this guy? How do we know for sure that he's coming?"

Thupten picked up on my annoyance. "No, Lama didn't speak with the general," he said with an exasperated sigh, "but he'll get the message. I'm sure Lama will call him again. There's no doubt that he'll be there."

A rebuttal was on the tip of my tongue, but I chose to keep quiet. It didn't matter anyway; everything was hypothetical at this point. We were three days away from our scheduled departure and numerous details had still not materialized. We weren't even certain we were going overland.

Later that afternoon, the phone rang. Thupten was on the line. "Come down to Lama's room. He has some time right now."

We dashed into the elevator and arrived within minutes. Who did we find in Kunzang Lama's room but Dawa—one of the slender, fair-skin girls that we had met on our first day in Lhasa. Lama was a good-looking man with silver-gray hair. He was suave with the demeanor of a high roller. With a lifestyle that many would envy, women were attracted to him and readily flirted with him. Dawa was there asking for help with a scholarship and student visa to Nepal. Lama made a joke about how girls showed up at his hotel room to ask for favors, especially to get out of Tibet. I mistrusted Dawa and thought her to be superficial and manipulative.

Knowing that we needed to speak with Lama in private, Thupten quickly ushered her out of the room.

Lama confirmed what Thupten had told us. The Chinese agencies that purchased his cars were balking on payments. He needed to stay in Lhasa until he received funds for an earlier shipment. Thus, leaving on Tuesday was impractical for him. Miguel and I were relieved.

Kunzang Lama assured us that the general was dependable. "He's a very good friend of mine. I've asked him to do favors for me before, and he has never failed me. With the numerous stars and badges on his uniform, he'll be able to pass through security with ease. The guards won't look at him twice." He waved his hand matter-of-factly. "Besides, Rinpoche will pose as my son, wearing his school attire and carrying his ID."

"Where do we meet the general?" I asked. "How will he recognize us?"

Lama couldn't provide definitive answers. "You'll meet in Dram. It's a small village, you'll find each other easily," he said. "I've told the general what Thupten looks like, and that he'll have a little boy with him."

"And what if we're delayed?" I asked.

"He'll wait for you," Lama dismissed my concern with a shrug. "If you feel better about it and aren't in a rush, you can wait for me."

"Realistically, when do you think you'll be leaving?" Miguel asked courteously, as if we would consider waiting.

"Probably in another week, two at the most," Lama replied.

"We can't wait that long," Miguel stated, looking over at Thupten, who seemed to concur with a nod.

"We're still waiting to hear from Rinpoche's father about travel documents," Thupten said. "If he can't get the papers, we'll have to go overland. So, we'd appreciate it, Lama, if you could look for a car and driver."

"In any case, we want to leave three days from now," I said firmly, "on Tuesday."

Sunday, September 12th

"Lama reserved a vehicle and a driver for us," Thupten announced on Sunday. "So, we're all set—if we go by road." Concurrent with Kunzang Lama's seemingly bowing out of the picture, Thupten gave the impression he would acquiesce to our demand that he not travel alone with Rinpoche. We had jumped through a major internal hurdle!

But by evening, things had changed again.

"Lama doesn't trust the driver," Thupten relayed. "He has questionable ties to the government. Lama will find someone else and check out his credentials beforehand. It's good that he's being so cautious, but we may have to delay our departure a day or two."

Interesting, I thought; there must be more to the story. "Who was this man, and how is he associated with the Chinese authorities?"

Thupten took a deep breath. "He works in the office that processes the expensive identification papers we discussed at Rinpoche's house," he said. "His second job is driving for the government travel agency."

Then in a sober voice, "The day Rinpoche's father went to inquire about the permits, this driver was there. It's a small office, so now he knows of Kalden's attempt to buy papers."

I shook my head with dismay. Everything was uncertain—Rinpoche's ID, the mode of transportation, our plan of action, whom to trust…

If Kalden could obtain travel documents for Rinpoche, we would be guaranteed safe passage. We could fly and avoid that road trip with its multiple checkpoints. And, we would face only two points of entry: the Kathmandu and Delhi airports. Though taking a plane was our best option, in reality, the prospect of acquiring legitimate ID in our window of opportunity was dismal.

Miguel and I had had no direct contact with Rinpoche's family since our initial meeting. Messages were conveyed through our contacts, Dekyi and Samten. I questioned Thupten again, pressing for more details.

"How did you find all this out? What else happened? Was Kalden successful in buying travel documents?"

"No," Thupten shook his head. "Those papers take up to a year to process and the price is exorbitant. I went by their house last evening and got the update."

I cast him an incredulous look. "What? Hey, we had agreed to not see them until we were leaving! Why didn't you tell us earlier today that you saw them?"

"It was after dark, so I felt that it was safe," Thupten explained, evading my other question. "Anyway, since Rinpoche doesn't have suitable ID, I told his parents that we'll have to go by car and that we're still intending to leave on schedule."

"I do have some other news," he added. "Kalden has decided to accompany Rinpoche and the three of us on the trip to the border."

"Oh, that's wonderful!" I said. We had secretly hoped that Kalden would go with us. It seemed too abrupt to tear Rinpoche from his parents at their house. Traveling with us, even partway, would ease the finality of the good-bye and give us time to get acquainted. A proper send-off by Rinpoche's father would also be a stamp of approval.

"So, Rinpoche just has his ID from school?" I inquired.

"I don't know," Thupten shrugged. "I think that's what Kalden told us."

"It doesn't matter," Miguel said. "We'll take our chances and see what happens."

"I believe that Kalden's identification card gives him the flexibility to travel to the border," Thupten added. "If we get stopped, our story will be that Rinpoche is traveling with his father to see relatives near Dram."

So, it was decided. We would go overland. It was our only choice.

Lama found another jeep and driver from an agency that rented cars to Tibetans. That meant we could bypass the tourist agencies monitored by the government who profiled visitors and tracked their movements.

We quickly put down a deposit. Jeeps weren't easy to come by in this town, and we were fortunate that one was available. We were set for Tuesday morning, aiming to leave Lhasa as early in the day as possible. Independent travelers heading for Tibet's border try to arrive at Shigatse or Sakya by nightfall where hotel rooms promise a good night's rest. On the second day, they complete the substantial part of the road trip. Our intention was to follow this schedule as well.

Departure was less than forty-eight hours away.

After Thupten had gone to Rinpoche's house once, he felt comfortable dropping in to see them again. We supported his initiative to spend time with the family and encouraged him to share his personal experience of entering the monastery at Rinpoche's same age. It was important to establish open communications with the boy and his parents. Given the condensed timetable, they needed to prepare psychologically and emotionally for the moment of parting. As foreigners, Miguel and I could not be seen in the vicinity of their home, due to obvious security issues.

"How's the family doing? Are they ready for this?" I asked Thupten.

"Okay, but they don't talk much. They're very reserved, but unquestionably committed," he said. "Their connection with Nechung here in Lhasa has made all the difference."

"What about Rinpoche?" Miguel asked. "Has he said anything?"

"No, he doesn't talk either," Thupten frowned. "He seems to understand what's going on but is very quiet, so it's hard to tell what he's feeling and thinking."

Miguel and I listened attentively, glad that Thupten was sharing some information with us.

"Anyway," he continued, "the plan is that I will come here to the hotel on Tuesday morning at dawn. The driver will arrive early too. Then together we'll go to their home. They'll be expecting us and know we want to leave by mid-morning."

"It'll just be the immediate family members, right?" I felt the necessity to ask, knowing how elusive Thupten was. "Will there be any more surprises?"

Thupten hesitated, then chose his words carefully, "Rinpoche's mother has asked that we take her brother, Rinpoche's uncle, with us to India."

"Why, what for?" I asked, considering the implications of adding an extra person to the journey. "We couldn't possibly take him. It would complicate everything."

"They say that the uncle wants to be a monk. If he were to accompany Rinpoche, he could be his personal assistant and friend. Rinpoche and the uncle are very close. So, the parents thought that this would also make the separation less traumatic."

"Are they just asking or is this a condition?" Miguel asked. "I mean, if we say no, is it a deal-breaker?"

Thupten shrugged. "Don't know, I didn't agree to anything. I told them that I'd discuss it with you. It's best to let it be for now. We'll deal with it on Tuesday morning."

The moment of seriousness quickly vanished, and a hint of a smile appeared on his face, as if intrigued by the thought of our imminent adventure.

Monday, September 13th

By now Thupten had filled our hotel room with gift packages to be hand-delivered to monks and folks in Dharamsala. The favored items were made-in-China sneakers and food products such as dried meat and nuggets of strong-smelling cheese. We packed and repacked, trying to consolidate our luggage until we were down to a manageable number of bags. It felt like a replay of our 1987 experience.

"This is ridiculous. We can't take all these things," Miguel griped. "The letters are plenty, they're light and have a purpose. This other stuff is just extra weight. Let's give it back to the owners or just leave it behind!"

"It's okay, Miguel," I quipped, "forget it!"

But Miguel wasn't giving up. "If people want to send a present, they should send money. The monks can buy shoes in India, and why should we take all this food? Why are we carrying hundreds of pounds of candy, meat, and stinky cheese?"

Thupten chortled, not giving in, and I giggled at Miguel's persistence.

"What if the roads are still washed out, and we have to walk and hire porters to haul all this stuff like we did in 1987! Remember?"

We kept packing. What else could we do? No one had the heart to return the gifts, and it would be preposterous to leave them behind for the hotel staff.

It was our last day in Lhasa. We wanted to visit the Jokhang before leaving, to absorb that profound spiritual energy that exists in holy places. It must have been a religious holiday because the promenade around the Barkhor was particularly active. The place was full of people circumambulating; some were mumbling mantras while simultaneously moving the beads on their malas. We saw elders spinning their copper prayer wheels in a circular motion—a practice that the younger generation rarely embraced. At the entrance of the Jokhang, numerous people—from the old and weathered to the youthful and energetic, even children—stood and knelt in every stage of performing prostrations. Some prostrated on wooden planks, others simply onto the bare ground. The air was heavy with the intensity of collective faith and devotion.

As on previous visits to the Jokhang, we noticed pilgrims who had traveled from afar. They wore thick pads on their hands and knees to protect against the rough ground in the countryside and mountain passes that they had traversed as they performed their prostrations. From an upright position, they clapped their hands above their heads, at their forehead, and at their hearts in praise of the enlightened ones. Then they lowered their entire bodies into a full prostration onto the ground. Upon rising to a standing position, they stepped forward to advance, then repeated the series of motions. In that way, they had journeyed the full distance to Lhasa.

Everyone moved around the temple in the customary clockwise direction, although some tourists unfamiliar with this cultural tradition, walked counterclockwise.

Whitewashed urns at key locales around the promenade served as receptacles for people's offerings. Juniper branches, *tsampa*, powdered incense, and tiny label-sized rice papers imprinted with prayers and emblems were placed into flames on the hearths. Billows of smoke wafted into the air through fluted chimneys of the round-bellied vessels, creating an aromatic, mystical atmosphere. We breathed deeply, inhaling the richness of the occasion. It infused every pore of our bodies and imprinted itself onto every atom of our consciousness.

We stopped by the market stall to see Yudron who, with her husband Khenrab, had been indispensable to our connecting with Rinpoche and his family. "We're leaving tomorrow morning and came to say good-bye," I whispered.

Two women shoppers at the booth cast curious glances at us. So, we pretended to be prospective customers interested in the rolls of fabric and assorted trinkets on display.

"How much is this? What is this used for?" I inquired until we were alone.

"Everything is set, we've hired a car," Miguel said. "Kalden will go with Rinpoche and us to Dram."

"Did you go by the house to say farewell to my husband?" she asked.

"Sorry, we didn't think that it was safe," I apologized. "Please give him our Tashi Delek and thank him for us."

"Yes, it's better this way," she agreed.

"Thank you so much! Please thank Dekyi and Samten, too. We'll never forget what you did for us!"

With these words of appreciation, we slipped back into the crowd.

Tuesday, September 14th

After breakfast at our corner perch, I surveyed the lobby and noticed two Western staffers on duty at the front desk. A few guests milled around, but no one looked out of character. It seemed a perfect time to discreetly check out. The Lhasa accepted credit cards, which was convenient. We needed to use plastic whenever possible; we had a limited amount of currency, and many of our expenditures and services required payments in cash.

Miguel put away the remaining toiletries. Our bags were packed, and we were ready. Thupten soon came to the door.

"The driver's here, I've put my luggage in the car already," he said. "Okay? Let's go!" He grabbed as many bags as he could, and Miguel took the rest. I smiled. This was one of the benefits of traveling with two men.

We headed down the stairs leading to the rear exit where the driver had parked—an area not monitored by hotel surveillance. Our driver had an honest face and was friendly but not overtly. He gave me the impression that he had an even disposition as I watched him load the luggage methodically into the tan Landcruiser. The SUV was not new, but it was clean with comfortable-looking seats.

"This will do," I thought, "this driver and vehicle will get us there!"

Lama came down to say good-bye and shook our hands warmly. "Good luck," he said. "My associate will be at the border to meet you. I told him what you all look like. You'll recognize him easily. He'll be in uniform."

"With his badges, no one will look at him twice," Lama reiterated. "He'll walk you past the border patrol without suspicion, but should there be questions, Rinpoche will pose as my son. I'll call the general again to tell him that you left Lhasa today," he assured us.

"How are the roads?" Miguel asked.

"As of this morning, the last few kilometers on the Tibetan side of the border were still washed out," he said. "I heard that crews are working, but the ongoing heavy rains are slowing their progress. You may have to walk."

He placed his hand on Miguel's shoulder, saying, "Your driver will take you as close to Dram as possible. I've given him your deposit. Just pay the balance when you get there."

"Do you know when you'll head back?" Thupten asked.

"I plan to be back in Kathmandu within a week. Call me. Let's get together for lunch." A few more pleasantries and we were off.

Lhasa was beginning to wake up as we drove through the familiar streets—shopkeepers in the bazaar opening their doors, people out on early errands, and morning traffic on the move. I knew that this might be our last time in Tibet for a long while—this country that we loved, the source of our spiritual inspiration. A sentimental wave surged through me, moistening my mind and eyes. My thoughts floated back to our first trip in 1987 and the excitement we felt coming to Lhasa; with few clues of Rinpoche's whereabouts, we only knew that he was somewhere in this vast, mountainous land.

Finding Nechung Rinpoche's reincarnation in Tibet was quite an achievement, and that it had been almost effortless on this third trip was even more remarkable. We could only attribute our success to powers loftier than our own human endeavors.

Soon, Rinpoche would leave his parents and everything familiar to him. He would be traveling with us to a place far away. He was but a child. Yet, evidently, he was mature enough to comprehend the immensity of the circumstances.

Reincarnation, in Buddhist tenets, is the thread of consciousness that traverses from one life to the next; in the process, it carries habitual patterns and seeded tendencies. This entire subject is part of the deep, complex human quest, and the desire to discover the meaning of life, death, and beyond. And here we were, Thupten, Miguel and I, mere novices in training, fortuitous enough to not only witness, but to play a role in the discovery of the rebirth of a Buddhist master whose list of sublime reincarnations included some of the greatest spiritual teachers dating back to the eighth century and the early days of the dissemination of Buddhism in Tibet.

I became lost in thought as we drove through the neighborhoods. We passed by guesthouses where we had once stayed and could observe people busily starting a new day—vendors spreading out fresh produce on tarps, men pushing carts filled with wares, and dogs sniffing piles of trash looking for something to eat. Thus, the transient lives of sentient beings—born into this world to live, to work, and then to die. What matters is not our beauty, for that fades; nor physical strength, for the body becomes old and decrepit; nor our accumulations of wealth, for we cannot take that with us. Truly the quintessential importance is what we make of our lives and how we affect those around us. That early dawn in Lhasa, I contemplated these truths: how to integrate altruistic aspirations into our thoughts and motivation, and how to pair that with actions to benefit others in the world. That is what truly matters.

As I looked out the window catching glimpses of the fast-changing scenery, it all appeared like a shifting illusion—a magical perennial dance reflecting the interdependence of karma, interconnections, and phenomena arising from the pure space of emptiness.

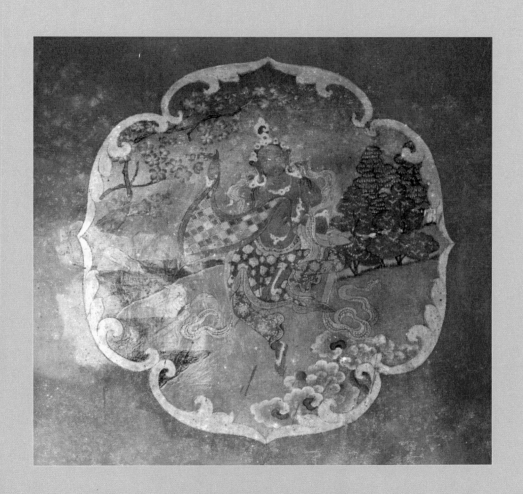

Offering goddess mural in Lhasa temple

THE ESCAPE:
September 14th–19th, 1993

Leaving Lhasa

Rinpoche's family lived in the east section of town near the Lhasa telephone exchange. The company where his mother worked as an accountant provided his family with housing, a common perk for middle management. Although we had checked out of the hotel early, it felt late when we finally arrived in their neighborhood.

Thupten, in the passenger's seat, gave directions to our driver, "Turn right at the next road, then right again into that first alley by those buildings."

As we approached the gravelly road, I noticed a man in his late fifties standing close to the junction by the alley. He was dressed in layman's clothes in shades of dark gray and a crumpled felt fedora shading his forehead and face. He seemed anxious, pacing back and forth, his head moving from side to side looking up and down the street as if waiting for someone. His restless eyes darted about until his glance fell upon our jeep.

I felt a sudden surge of adrenaline and then a tinge of fear. As our vehicle advanced and turned into the alley past the fellow, he squinted, trying to see through the tinted glass of our car.

"Oh, my god! It's Lobsang Zopa!" I exclaimed.

"No! It can't be!" Thupten cried. "Are you sure?"

Miguel couldn't believe it either. We all turned around in unison and stared through the back windows in disbelief. The man began to run after us and Thupten ordered the driver to stop. We opened our doors and stepped out.

"It *is* him," I whispered to the guys. "He's heading right for us!"

Lobsang Zopa was a former monk from Nechung Monastery in Lhasa. We had met him in the summer of 1987 when he invited us to his apartment in the Barkhor for tea. Tiapala had been friendly with Zopa and had apprised him that we had come in search of Rinpoche's reincarnation. "I heard that our Rinpoche was born in Tibet," Zopa had said, not hiding his arrogance, "so I'm already looking for him and may have some candidates."

Gossip had circulated about Lobsang Zopa and we had been warned to be cautious and not too forthright with him. Perhaps he was disliked due to his condescending manner or projection of self-importance, but we were given no specific reasons for the mistrust. "I'm a devoted disciple of the previous Nechung Rinpoche," he had told us. "I spent some hard-earned money to commission a 'look-alike' statue of Rinpoche. I'll show it to you." Zopa offered to look for boys with promising qualities born after 1984 and keep us informed. We never did see that statue, and in the six years that ensued, we never heard another word from him. Until now.

There was no way to avoid him, we were the only people in the lane. So, we turned to him, and with wide-eyed surprise, I exclaimed, "Tashi Delek, Kushog!" I used the respectful term "Venerable One," reserved for current and former monks. "What are you doing here?"

He glared at each of us through his bluish cataracts. With his right index finger, he tapped the tip of his nose, "I am Lobsang Zopa," he declared, his yellowed dentures clattering. "Don't you remember me?"

"Of course, we remember you!" Miguel declared, patting him on the back, "good to see you again, Kushog!"

Thupten stepped up, grinning, and held the man's hands; they gently touched foreheads in a Tibetan greeting.

I was very uncomfortable and my heart pounded. At least it was just Lobsang Zopa, I told myself, and not an officer of the Chinese regime. Yet, the obvious question was, why was he here?

"What are you doing here?" I asked, trying not to show my feelings.

He smiled mischievously. "I am Lobsang Zopa," he repeated, now pointing to his chest. "I know everything that goes on." With a smirk, he added, "I'm here to see friends."

We had no choice but to walk together, taking slow, calculated steps, hoping that this might make him go away. A few dozen yards later, shortly before reaching the gate of Rinpoche's home, we halted in an awkward silence. Clearly, Lobsang Zopa had no intentions to leave.

Out came Rinpoche's parents, Kalden, quiet and reserved, and Khandro, her warm bubbly self. "Tashi Delek, welcome, please come in!"

Within a minute, we *all* were within the safety of their home.

Rinpoche was seated on a low bed, dressed in a bright yellow collared shirt and matching fleece pants, so loud that they screamed, "Hey, look over here, folks. Here I come!"

"Perfect for a clandestine trip," I thought ironically.

I scanned the length of the modest, well-lived-in environment. Every item had a place, with not a spec of dirt in sight. Grandma, the teenage uncle and a couple of thirty-something women, probably family friends, were in the room.

The family evidently knew Lobsang Zopa, and were not at all surprised to see him, so I relaxed slightly. Was he a friend, a former neighbor of the family? Perhaps they were acquainted with him from their visits to Nechung Monastery. In any case, it was apparent that he had been invited for the occasion. We did not ask, no one explained, and there were no introductions.

Lobsang Zopa turned to the three of us and spoke, "You never contacted me! You never told me!" He pointed to his nose again, "but here I am anyway! I'm here to see my lama and to offer him a triple mandala."

He prostrated to Rinpoche with utmost respect. With his palms touching, he brushed his forehead, throat, and heart, then knelt, pressing his forehead, palms and knees to the ground. He did this five-pointed prostration thrice. Then from a nearby table, he picked up a Buddha statue, symbolic of the physical attributes of enlightenment, held it to his forehead, and offered it to the young lama. Rinpoche accepted the gift, and likewise, held the statue to his own forehead, then set it down on a side stand.

Then Zopa offered a text bound in saffron and red cloth, symbolic of the Buddha's verbal qualities. It was presented and received in the same manner. Lastly, he offered a small, bronze stupa, representing the wisdom mind of enlightenment. Thus, the presentation of the symbols of enlightened body, speech, and mind had been presented. He stepped forward, unwound a long white silk *kata* and passed it to Rinpoche, who blessed Zopa by draping it around his neck. The formality was completed by the light bumping of foreheads.

"I am so happy to see you today, Rinpoche," Lobsang Zopa said. "Now you will go to India. Be good and study hard. Your predecessor was a holy man and His Holiness the Dalai Lama has recognized you as his reincarnation. You must live up to Nechung Rinpoche's stainless reputation."

Rinpoche nodded, ever so gently, as to acknowledge that he had heard these words of advice.

The women served sweet rice, tea, and fruit. We took a few sips of our steaming tea, and instantly someone refilled our cups. Although eager to get going, we realized that memories of these parting moments with Rinpoche would be etched forever in the minds of the family. It was their call when we would leave, not ours.

Khandro handed us a care package for her son—a few toys, candies, some extra articles of clothing, photographs, and a thin book of prayers and writings. "These are some of my son's favorite things," said his mother to us. "It will remind him of home until he gets settled in the monastery."

Then Grandma spoke, directing her appeal to Thupten, then the two of us. "If you possibly can, we would be grateful if you take my son with you to India. He yearns to be a monk."

We had anticipated this. After Thupten had mentioned the family's wish for Rinpoche's uncle to go with us, we had not discussed the issue any further. We knew with certainty that taking the uncle was impossible. How could we say "no" in a skillful manner?

Rinpoche's mother chimed in. "My brother has taken care of Tenzin Losel since he was a child. They are very close. In India, he could continue to take care of my son. They could be monks together as well as best friends. It will make the transition so much easier. *Please* take him with you."

Thupten closed his eyes for a few seconds, thoughtfully choosing his words before articulating our perspective.

"It will complicate matters," he explained. "Uncle is rather tall. He's almost an adult. We don't know what will happen on this journey. It's crucial that we maintain a low profile and keep everything simple. Taking another person increases the risk. It could endanger Rinpoche and compromise our mission. We would like to just chaperone Rinpoche… for the time being. Once he's safe at the monastery, we'll find a way to send for Uncle."

As if the family had expected this answer, no one attempted to convince us otherwise. Nodding, Khandro softly said, "My husband will accompany Tenzin Losel to the border with you. I'm not going. We will say good-bye here." These words signaled that we could leave.

Thupten stood up. "Ready? Let's go."

I clasped Khandro's hands and looked deep into her eyes. Words could not express our feelings and gratitude. All that I could murmur was, "Thank you, thank you."

To give Rinpoche and his family privacy, we waited by the door with Lobsang Zopa. Miguel and I made small talk with him, while he and Thupten exchanged light-hearted banter.

Khandro knelt in front of Rinpoche so that she was about the same height as he. She hugged her son tightly, as if transferring all her love into him. Tears streamed down her cheeks as she choked with emotion while giving some last-minute motherly advice. Rinpoche remained calm throughout, demonstrating a maturity that exceeded an eight-year-old boy about to part from his mother and family.

At the car, we bowed and expressed our gratitude once more. Thupten, Miguel, and I sat in the back seat; Rinpoche and his father in the front. Through the windows, we waved good-bye, then, looking back, waved some more.

We were on the road at last.

Shigatse, where we had planned to spend the night, was hundreds of kilometers away. It was almost noon. The midday sun quickly penetrated the metal roof of our jeep, but a gentle wind blew through the open windows to invigorate us. I closed my eyes and felt the fresh air caress my cheeks, unraveling strands of my long, braided hair. I recalled a verse referencing a cool breeze that alleviates the scorching heat of day—that this, too, can be considered a blessing of the Buddha.

Within minutes we were on the main highway heading west out of Lhasa. Soon we saw the majestic silhouette of Drepung Monastery, with the seat of Nechung in the foreground. For just a second, the thought of racing up to our monastery crossed my mind, but I sensibly paid respects from afar, and hoped that our monks would forgive us once they learned of Nechung Rinpoche's discovery.

Picking up speed, we passed a dead dog and then another recent road kill. I looked at Miguel with raised brows and he nodded his head. "That's a good sign," we silently agreed.

Tibetans believe that seeing a corpse or passing a hearse when beginning an important undertaking is a sign that obstacles are carried away and pacified. Was it just wishful thinking, or was there reality to our conviction that everything would work in our favor, and that our guardian angels were with us? Our protectors had never failed us before, and we firmly believed that they would not abandon us now.

But then, only time would tell…

"You have proper identification for the boy, right?" our driver asked, snapping me back to the present moment.

Silence, until Thupten replied, "Uh, no…is that required?"

"Yes, definitely! Everyone, no matter what age, needs paperwork showing permission to travel in certain districts. There will be checkpoints where such proof will be mandatory."

"He's traveling with his father," Thupten said, "and being so young, we didn't think it was necessary, so we have no travel documents for the child. What do you recommend we do?" His feigned naiveté was convincing.

My initial impression of the driver was correct; he was a reasonable man. "Well, let's just see what happens," he said in an accommodating voice.

We were well on our way, and there was *no* turning back. Having Rinpoche's father with us made a huge difference, since the driver knew that Kalden would bear the responsibility if any problems were to occur.

Seated behind Kalden, I had a side view of his profile and discerned his apprehension on the absence of documents, though he didn't verbalize it. He and the driver began to chat, and soon established a rapport. As for Rinpoche, he had not uttered a single word since leaving Lhasa and showed no outward emotion.

The scenery was magnificent, the splendorous hills melded one into another, giving depth to the distant mountains. The heat made us drowsy and all three of us in the back seat dozed off to the drone of the voices.

Upon awakening from my slumber, I noticed that we were no longer on the paved highway, but on a one-lane gravel road. To our left, a hillside obscured visibility. On the right, steep precipices gave way to unparalleled panoramas of Tibet. Kilometers flew by, as did thick clouds of dust raised by our SUV's spinning wheels, coating my skin with fine powder.

We arrived in Shigatse before dusk and instructed the driver to take us straightaway to Tashi Lhunpo Monastery, which had been established by the First Dalai Lama. The town, originally built around the monastery, was now a sprawling city. Having heard much about the last Panchen Lama's stupa at Tashi Lhunpo, we wanted to see it. This would be the first pilgrimage site that we would visit with the young

Rinpoche. We parked outside the gates and walked into a compound of temples. Custodians were shutting down for the evening and some of the adjunct chapels were already locked. Then we spotted one building with a pair of hefty, twelve-foot doors slightly ajar, so we climbed its steep wooden staircase to peek inside. A striking image of Maitreya, the future Buddha, revealed itself.

Someone was inside, so we knocked lightly on the doors. An elderly monk appeared. "This temple is closed," he said. "Come back tomorrow."

Closed doors were nothing new to us, so Thupten insisted, "We are leaving for the border early tomorrow morning. This is our only chance to pay homage to the Buddha. It will only be a few minutes. Please!"

It worked. Soon we were circumambulating the statue of Maitreya, looking up into his eyes, prostrating, and making offerings. Upon leaving, we pressed some money into the palm of the temple keeper who seemed satisfied with his good deed.

"Hurry to the temple containing the stupa of the great Panchen Lama," he told us. "It may still be open since the monks have been conducting a Kalachakra ceremony there."

Minutes later we were gazing at the stupa—resplendently layered in gold, embedded with vintage coral, turquoise, amber, and *dzi* stones. It exuded opulence. More importantly, it induced a feeling of luminous tranquility. We could have spent all night in its marvelous splendor, enriched by the congregation of monks chanting and performing rituals.

The monks' rhythmic voices were melodic and soothing, accentuated by the occasional beat of drums, ringing of bells, and deep resonance of horns. While their harmonic chants for world peace filled the entire hall, the meritorious aspirations reached far beyond the limits of the temple walls.

We checked into a relatively new inn across from Tashi Lhunpo's main gates that served as a guesthouse for travelers and pilgrims. Miguel and I rented a room with single beds, while our friends stayed in a typical Tibetan dormitory with multiple cots.

Nearby was a mess hall that reminded us of the diners in China—cavernous rooms designed to seat hundreds. Such places become progressively louder as fried and salty foods consumed with alcoholic beverages hit digestive systems. Everyone was famished, so there was no choice but to patronize the establishment. A hush fell over the crowd when our team walked through its doors. We found seating at a round wooden table, a recycled cable reel for electric wire. The driver and Rinpoche's father ordered dumplings and vegetables for our party, plus beer for themselves and Miguel.

Shigatse was infamous as a hotspot for informants and moles. The stark room was full of men, mostly Tibetans and some Chinese. They made no effort to hide their conspicuous observation of us and eavesdropped on every word of our conversation. Miguel and I refrained from speaking much. We simply ate and listened while the noise reverberated around us. Despite the dubious circumstances, we finished our dinner without incident and retired to our rooms.

The First Checkpoint

The next day, long before dawn, the shrill ring of our alarm clock jolted us out of a deep sleep. We threw on our jeans, splashed cold water on our faces, and were wide awake. I went next door and knocked loudly until an indistinct murmur surfaced.

"Hey, it's time to go!" I called.

"Okay, okay," Thupten answered.

Soon we were in the SUV bouncing down the road. This time, Rinpoche and his father sat in the back on the passenger's side, with us behind the driver. Thupten was up front. We were crowded, but I was pleased with the new arrangement as it gave us the opportunity to be in close proximity to Rinpoche for an extended period of time.

The violet light of daybreak gradually illuminated the darkness of the still night. Each passing second revealed fresh silhouettes of our surroundings. Each turning of the wheels transported us closer to our destination.

Nestled next to his father, Rinpoche barely moved or fidgeted, his focus was straight ahead on a spot in the middle of the windshield. Occasionally we noticed subconscious gentle motions of his hands which were reminiscent of mudras—hand gestures symbolic of invocation, praise, and presentation of offerings.

Somewhere between Shigatse and the first checkpoint, our driver became notably nervous. He fidgeted with the wheel and his conversation with Thupten felt uneasy. I could sense his agitation and empathized with him. Understandably, the Chinese government was not lenient with those who deviated from protocol.

The checkpoint was located close to the Everest base camp turnoff along the desolate Friendship Highway leading to the border. We had knowledge of this checkpoint from 1987. Had anything changed in the six years since? What potential complications should we expect? About half an hour before we reached the site, the driver alerted us.

"We're almost there," he said, turning around, taking his eyes off the road momentarily.

"There'll be a building on the right as we approach, several guards will be inside. A heavy metal gatepost will block the road, so we cannot pass until our documents check out and the car gets inspected. So, the plan is…I will park the car…then we all need to go and present our passports or ID cards."

Pondering the seriousness of the situation, Thupten asked, "You've been through this before. What do you suggest we do with the boy? What's our story?"

"Well, Kalden has to take full responsibility for him," the driver responded. "He should say that he's taking his son to visit relatives near Dram. By coincidence, he met you and the American couple in Lhasa and caught a ride with you folks. This story will sound credible since Westerners are the only ones legally permitted to hire jeeps for tourism."

"What about the lack of papers for my son?" Kalden asked.

"That's a big problem. Even if the guards believe you, they will keep a record of your residential address, where you're going and your estimated return date, along with the boy's name and date of birth. A notation will be made in your travel permit to document that you and your son came through today. That means he has to be with you on the way back."

He grimaced, "So, if the boy is not with you…"

The checkpoint was exactly as described and how we remembered it. We pulled up behind two parked tourist vehicles whose passengers waited in line outside the building. The entire area crawled with police and soldiers. Some peered inside the visitors' cars; others stood erect with their weapons ready.

Our driver strode out and walked into the building. The rest of us stayed in the car, deliberating our next move in silence. The first group passed inspection, the gatepost rose, and they were off.

Without warning, a marked police vehicle drove up behind us, followed by another two jeeps filled with men in uniforms that parked alongside us. Suddenly we were encircled by officers.

What was going on? Were they onto us? How could that be possible? We had done nothing wrong…yet. This was not restricted territory and we had nothing "illegal" in our possession.

"Being stressed will only cause problems," I told myself. "Stay cool." If questioned, we had a convincing story.

One of the police drivers had positioned his jeep in such a way that it blocked the right side of our Landcruiser. He glared at us, honked sharply, motioning with his hands for us to move back, as if wanting to park between us and the remaining tourist vehicle. I looked back at him out of the partially open window, and reacted with nonchalance, even though my heart was racing. We continued to laugh and converse, all the while remaining vigilant.

A person of stature, noted by his air of importance, stepped out of the jeep. At once, the attention of the guards focused on him. A shock of recognition came next when we realized that this may be the Chief of Police from Shigatse, one of the most high-ranking figures in the district, with his aides. He paced around the gatepost exhibiting signs of impatience. I surmised that the chief was there to perform a routine inspection and wanted to get through the blockade swiftly.

We seized the opportunity. Within split seconds, we leapt outside, leaving Rinpoche in the back seat. The Landcruiser's doors closed behind us, concealing our little lama within. I'm not sure how that "decision" was made in that instant; certainly it was not verbalized. It was as if the choice had not been ours.

We queued up behind a Tibetan man in his thirties, dressed in jeans, hiking boots, and outdoor wear. He was part of the second group of mostly Westerners.

"Tashi Delek!" Thupten said to him. "How are you?"

"Oh, my goodness," I thought. "Now what? Another friend of Thupten's?" But they didn't appear to know each other, just a courteous acknowledgment.

Our driver stood with us, as did Rinpoche's father. I shared their trepidation. One by one, the tourists in front of us presented their passports, and then it was our turn. The driver and Rinpoche's father gave their responses as planned: they told the story that had been rehearsed, but omitted the fact that a boy was traveling with us. No questions were asked. Thupten, Miguel, and I made sure to look the two officers in the eye. They stamped our passports and handed them back. We could not have planned it better had we tried!

Rinpoche was still in the back seat, standing in the middle behind the rearview mirror, barely discernible through the tinted windows. His motionless shape blended perfectly with the shadow of our heaps of luggage behind him. It was as though he were invisible.

The officers finished rummaging through the tourist van ahead of us, then walked toward our Landcruiser. They were just a few feet away, glancing here and there distractedly. The rest of the force moved about busily catering to the demands of the chief.

I held my breath. Unexpectedly, everyone strode away. We were left unattended, as if they had forgotten we were there! In the car, Rinpoche slid down into the seat, hidden between his father and us. Our driver honked, gesturing for the guards to open the gate. The second tour group drove off. We cordially motioned to the drivers of the Shigatse police to go ahead of us, and they gladly zipped by. We were last in the convoy to pass through.

Whatever the explanation—whether it was the fortunately timed arrival of the Shigatse police, or the intervention of our guardian protectors—we had been shielded from a serious obstacle.

Shortly after leaving the checkpoint, we saw the police jeeps parked on the side of the road. Miguel and I frowned at each other. They had been in such a hurry. Why were they stopped? "Probably nothing to do with us," I told myself, "No need to worry, just relish this carefree moment." We smiled and waved to them as we sped down the road.

We were well into the highlands where there were few trees, only shrubby bushes dotted the hillsides, lone companions to the whistling of the wind.

Distant mountains extended far into the horizon, while tiers of foothills surrounded us in endless overlays of sage and burnished coppers. An occasional wispy cloud floated in the pure azure sky, appearing and disappearing into vast spaciousness.

High on the hill, we spotted open tents in the wilderness. The Tibetans recognized that this was an outdoor tea stand, and wanted to stop for a hot beverage and breakfast. Miguel and I looked at each other with the same thought: is this prudent? We preferred to keep moving and snack in the car, but the rest of our team was tired and needed a break. Since we had left Shigatse before sunrise, we had not eaten breakfast, and it was already lunchtime. Some food and caffeine would be welcome.

The driver drove the jeep off the road and made a beeline for the tents which were manned by a single person. One tent served as his kitchen with a fire ready to boil large pots of tea for thirsty travelers. The other had a few old chairs and makeshift benches, a place to picnic sheltered from sun and wind. At the insistence of

Rinpoche's mother, we had bags brimming with provisions. She had filled colorful hand-woven Bhutanese baskets with assorted sweets, cookies, and breads. We also found slabs of cooked meat, dried apricots, and fresh fruit. There was an abundance of food—way too much for six people to consume in two days. All we needed was some salty, butter Tibetan tea.

Famished, Thupten carved into the boiled meat and grabbed a large chunk, gnawing it with vigor. Kalden and the driver dug in with the same enthusiasm. Miguel and I had little appetite, perhaps it was the altitude or sheer nerves. I felt a strong urge to get out of there as soon as possible. Rinpoche sat quietly, almost fading into the background while the adults carried on loudly—laughing, telling stories, and enjoying themselves.

As if to validate Miguel and my concern, a jeep came racing up the hill, creating a small dust storm in its trail. It anchored itself roadside in plain sight. It was the Shigatse Police Chief.

"Thupten…don't look now," I said, "but the cops are parked across the road!"

There was an immediate silence. Everyone stopped talking and turned their heads to stare at the jeep. I sensed pairs of eyes peering at us through the lowered windows. Were we under suspicion? Had they allowed us to leave the checkpoint just to follow and observe us before pouncing?

The truth was, we were an odd bunch. It would be no surprise if we elicited curiosity. Or perhaps the policemen simply wanted to enjoy the scenery as we did.

Rinpoche stayed deep inside the tent, sitting on a low stool. How much of this intrigue did the child understand, I wondered?

What to do but carry on? Fired by adrenaline and caffeine, Thupten laughed loudly and grabbed another piece of meat. The driver and Kalden resumed their conversation. I sipped tea and nibbled on a stale biscuit, and Miguel bit into a piece of bruised fruit, all the while keeping the jeep and its passengers in our peripheral vision.

The jeep door on the passenger's side opened and out came one of the officers. He stretched, leaned on the jeep, and looked over at us. Soon they were all outside. The only thing to do was to remain calm.

The policemen paced around their car, lit cigarettes and had leisurely smokes. It seemed an eternity before the officers got back into their SUV and went on their way. We never saw the jeep again. It seemed to have vanished into the thin mountain air, and our worries evaporated with it.

Time, Space, and Elements

We consider the Toyota Landcruiser one of the best travel vehicles for the Tibetan highlands. As we luxuriated in its comfort, I mused on our previous road trip to the border in 1987. I was thankful that now we weren't on a tinny bus.

Drivers in Tibet must attend the same driving schools as those in India, we would joke. Their techniques are similar. Old buses grind up steep hills at a snail's pace, while sleeping passengers are smothered with dangerous levels of carbon monoxide. After peaking the mountain passes, these seemingly meek drivers turn into daredevils—turning off the ignition to save gas and speedily coasting the squeaky oversized tin cans down narrow, windy roads. Restroom breaks—as in stops to relieve oneself behind a boulder, next to a tree, or in the shade of plant foliage—are infrequent. Passengers are basically held captive for the duration of the ride.

Ah, yes, even though the Landcruiser wasn't new, this was a pleasant upgrade. We sank back into the leather seats and bathed in the warmth of the sun beating through the windows. It would be hours before we were to reach our destination. The lack of stimulation provided a temporary respite from our quandary—how would we get our little lama out of Tibet without incident. The only distraction was an occasional backpack or food basket toppling on us as we bumped along the Friendship Highway.

Rinpoche was wedged between Kalden and the door, sweet innocence snuggling under his father's protective embrace. He was impossible to read since he had not spoken a word or expressed any emotion since leaving Lhasa. The only thing he did recurrently, as on the previous day, was move his fingers in graceful gestures that resembled devotional mudras. We had to glance over frequently to be sure that he was there, that we weren't in the midst of a euphoric dream. On the road trip to Dram, we grew increasingly fond of this little boy.

We were traversing the Tibetan Plateau where it never rains. Humidity is nil, and the land arid, with the sporadic desert cactus or shrub accenting the terrain. Occasionally we encountered another SUV or a few adventuresome cyclists on mountain bikes. How did they do it, peddling uphill on these gravel roads at altitudes with rarefied oxygen? It exhausted me just to watch them. But then, we too, had no small challenge ahead of us.

Eventually, after intermittent stops and seemingly countless passes—each peak marked by flags blowing in the wind, faded and frayed from the countless prayers cast into the ten directions—we took a final break. We were about to descend into the valley leading to Zhangmu, the town on the Tibetan side of the Dram border and the entryway into Nepal. Thupten had brought new flags imprinted with mantras. These rectangles of cotton gauze were strung loosely together in primary colors of blue, white, red, green, and yellow, symbolic of the elements. We stretched them across the top of the world and watched them fly high in the sky, beckoning fortune and success. Mount Everest towered majestically in the distance as we chanted our prayers in harmony.

As our Landcruiser descended off the crown jewel of the Himalayas, we had ample time for contemplation. I reflected on the five elements—earth, water, fire, air, and space—and their significance in our lives. I thought of the border that we were to cross, a political division created by mankind. Caught in duality, our human minds erect artificial partitions to delineate where this grain of sand or that clump of soil is different from others. Whereas the nature of the earth itself, firm and nourishing, like a mother, openly supports the animate and inanimate without judgment.

A river rushing by our feet is superficially identical from one second to the next. Yet, the water that constitutes that river constantly flows and is continuously replaced; similarly, the ever-present stream of our consciousness is like that river, continually changing.

Through the smoke, hot flames reveal signs of a fire's existence. Does the flame that transfers from one torch to another still have the same identity, or is it different?

Air, although invisible, is the fundamental sustenance of life. Ungraspable, yet tangible and palpable to the senses, wind gently invigorates and dispels pollutants of the environment.

Space, pure empty sky, in which billowing clouds float to bring refreshing rain, is the abode for innumerable stars and planets, the sun and the moon.

The balance of the five elements in the inner physical body and the outer world is thus integral to the health of all living beings and the planet we share.

Certain aspects of life are gradual, like the process of aging. Change happens in such minute degrees that we ourselves are unaware of them. When did the innocence of youth turn to adulthood, to middle age, and the frailty of old age? What caused those lines of experience and maturity to appear in our faces? How does the passage of time defy our human reasoning?

Time sneaks up on us as one moment becomes the next, and days turn into weeks, months into years. The moment that was the future is instantly the elusive present, which immediately becomes part of the past. The three periods of time—past, present, and future—do not exist inherently. Interdependent upon one another, they exist conventionally as points of reference.

I think of time and space whenever we travel, possibly because modern modes of transportation take us rapidly from one reality to another. We soar vast distances, traversing through space in an "iron bird." Like time, natural space is limitless and without boundaries.

My attention eventually returned to our journey. The sun was low in the sky, and we still had a long distance to cover. So, our driver decided to take a shortcut cross-country rather than the switchbacks that wound around the mountain.

The jeep charged forward, its balding tires spinning so wildly down the hillside that it felt as if we would tip over. Our goal was to reach Dram before nightfall and find a secure place to stay for the night. We could clean up, get a hot meal, and some well-deserved rest. Specifically, we had to assess the situation at the border, ascertain the procedures, and devise the semblance of a plan for the next day.

It was questionable if we could even drive all the way to Dram. The last news that had circulated was that roads were still closed. Crews had been working around the clock to clean up the storm damage, and travelers had to walk a substantial distance to reach the border town. There was a good chance that our driver would drop us off, and we would hike the remaining kilometers with all of our belongings. Not a heartening possibility. We had way too much gear to trudge down muddy slopes in the impending darkness. More importantly, we did not want to draw attention to ourselves nor expose our party's unusual composition.

I winced and recited prayers under my breath. Our Landcruiser seemed to be losing its suspension; taxed, undoubtedly by the rigorous journey. We had left the city of Lhasa only two days earlier, but it felt as if ages had passed.

There was no sense in worrying. As His Holiness often advised, "If nothing can be done, why worry, and if something can be done, why worry." There was nothing we could do, so Miguel and I settled into the ride and drifted off as we plummeted down from the dust-blown highlands.

We woke up to an emerald rainforest. To our right, there was a river rushing through a gorge, below steep precipices. Plantains, ferns, and bright wildflowers were everywhere, dripping with moisture from the recent monsoon rains. It was warm and extremely humid. Miguel and I felt as if we were back in Hawaiʻi. The sudden drop in altitude was exhilarating. The changes in topography and temperature were dramatic.

Our jeep was now gliding on a narrow, winding road not much wider than a horse and mule trail. Multiple waterfalls cascaded down the face of the cliffs and grassy hillsides were transformed into muddy, slippery slopes. Dusk was fast approaching. Would the Landcruiser make it to the border without getting stuck?

As we turned a blind curve, another Landcruiser identical to ours appeared, as if looking into a mirror. This was the first car we had seen in hours. As is typical of macho motorists in this part of the world, our driver headed straight for the other vehicle on the one-lane road, towering cliffs on one side, steep canyons on the other. Moments before the seemingly inevitable head-on collision, he swiftly pulled over to allow the other SUV to pass. As it pulled alongside, we all strained to catch a glimpse of its passengers.

"Hey!" our driver yelled out to the other driver. "What are you doing?"

The other man stuck his head out the window and replied in a blaring, incomprehensible Chinese dialect.

The two drivers faced off from their seats behind the wheels. My gut response was, "Oh, no! There's going to be a confrontation over who's the King of the Road!"

A dialogue ensued, and soon, their obnoxious voices turned amiable. Before long, our driver seemed satisfied with the conversation, thanked the fellow, and bid him farewell.

"Good news!" he exclaimed. "My friend just informed me that the road is open all the way to Dram. The work had been completed only a couple of hours earlier, and his was the first car to leave in many weeks. We'll be able to drive all the way to Dram and get there by dark."

"That's a wish come true!" Miguel said, and we congratulated one another for our latest stroke of good luck.

The last stretch to Dram was a quick and easy drop through lush, verdant shrubbery. Towering trees with drizzling rain accompanied us all the way.

Dram—the Tibetan Border

Our Landcruiser wound its way through crowded alleys that were lined on both sides with rundown shanties, some two stories high with dimly lit storefronts and hole-in-the-wall eateries on the street level. Zhangmu at the Dram border was not much different from other shabby border towns, just smaller. We certainly didn't make the discreet entrance appropriate for our mission. Instead, our driver honked relentlessly, navigating through the throngs of men, women, children, and dogs that packed the streets. It was the time of day when hungry folks were out looking for something to eat. Finally, we arrived at the lower edge of town.

The driver knew exactly where to take us—to the only tourist hotel in town—a drab, cement Chinese fortress that was several stories high, built on the mountainside. Its only redeeming charm was a grand entrance and clear glass windows that stretched upward, giving an unobstructed view of the road. Jeeps and trucks were lined up on both sides of the narrow road in front while dozens of people milled around.

We parked in the first available spot near the hotel, happy to be there at last, yet also anxious about the critical next steps. We carefully surveyed our surroundings in preparation for our border crossing attempt in the morning. The lighting at dusk combined with our exhaustion made every detail almost surreal.

Straight ahead was a metal guardrail, and beyond that, signs marked the restricted territory where no unauthorized vehicles or people were permitted. A small building with counter windows stood alone just beyond the barrier. This, we noted, must be immigration control.

Across the street from the hotel was a Chinese guard post, two stories high with shaded windows on the second floor. Armed soldiers outside kept constant watch over the movements of visitors at the border. Everyone was under surveillance day and night.

Although late, it was still light. The communist government had never established a separate time zone for Tibet; it was on the same Central Standard Time as Beijing and the rest of China.

To get to the hotel's reception area, we had to cross a short walkway that led from the street to the hotel's inner sanctum. We grabbed our backpacks that contained essential items and left the driver with the rest of our luggage. A big puff of air exhaled involuntarily from my mouth, "Let's go!" I said to Miguel. What could we do but drag our weary bodies into the building that would be our home for the night?

The lobby was full of Westerners standing around—trekker types with guides, porters, and heaps of baggage. Hollow and sparsely furnished, the lobby resonated with loud noise and voices all talking at once in half a dozen languages—German, Nepali, Chinese, Tibetan, Hindi, and, of course, English.

Our team had not discussed how to behave in the hotel, but we understood that Miguel and I would check in on our own and act like we didn't know the Tibetans. No one was in line at the front desk, so we casually strode up and ask for a room from one of the few available receptionists. Rinpoche and his father found an empty chair in the corner and waited patiently. Thupten stood by himself to rent a dormitory for four.

"Yes, we have a room for two," the clerk told us. "We need your passports, which we'll keep for the duration of your stay. They'll be returned to you upon checkout."

Our passports? No way. Too much was at stake. "What do you mean?" I protested. "Why can't you just look at them? You can't keep passports all night!"

"These are the rules. Give me your passports, or I can't rent you a room," the clerk said impatiently eyeing the next set of guests clamoring for attention. By now, more people had arrived and stood behind us, pressing into our backs, waving money and passports trying to get assistance. Among them was a man in a dark blue tracksuit with white stripes down the legs. He stood uncomfortably close and seemed to study us.

A little white lie seemed the only recourse in dealing with this clerk. "Listen, we left our passports in the car, along with our luggage," I said, trying to sound reasonable. "We'll go get them and bring them to you, but why not assign a room to us now and give us a key? That way, we won't need to start all over again."

The clerk could see that the line behind us stretched toward the front door. He jotted a note in his logbook and selected a room key. "Your room is on level two down those winding stairs," he said. "Bring back your passports right away. I'll be waiting for you."

He clamped his thin lips together, as if pondering his next words. "Someone will be here early tomorrow morning, so you can retrieve your documents then. Be ready to checkout after breakfast. Immigration control opens early, but its agents are on duty only briefly. All visitors will get their papers processed at the same time and everyone leaves together."

We nodded politely, acknowledging that we had heard his instructions. Miguel held out his hand, trying to not act too eager. The clerk handed him the key with hesitancy.

The hotel was built on the side of the gorge. Its guest rooms and restaurant were located downstairs from the lobby which was at the street level. Our room was close to the end of a long, unlit hallway in a nondescript gray. It was dark and dank. We opened the window shutters to let in fresh air and the last rays of daylight before nightfall. It was quiet with no one in sight. We needed a refuge, not only a place to rest, but also the privacy to strategize. This was the perfect hideaway.

Miguel threw our backpacks on the dresser and turned on a dim table lamp between two single beds. As much as I wanted to relax, there was still work to do, and the passport issue lingered over us. We tucked them into our jean jackets and trotted back upstairs. The crowd around the reception desk had swelled into such a chaotic mass that no one but Thupten noticed us slipping by. He sauntered toward us. In the instant it took to brush shoulders, he said, "I have a dormitory for Rinpoche and the three of us in the Tibetan section. Where are you guys?"

"221," Miguel breathed.

We headed outdoors and took the bags needed for that evening from the car. "Please wait here for a few more minutes," I said to the driver, who looked exhausted and was chain-smoking, probably his third or fourth cigarette since our arrival. "Thupten has booked a dorm for you all, he'll be coming out soon."

Both sides of the guard post were now lined with vehicles, including trucks filled with cargo for deliveries to Tibet. Empty jeeps and eager drivers waited in anticipation for the next wave of customers going to Lhasa.

We reentered the hotel. Our clerk, buried deep in paperwork behind the counter, was too busy to notice us. We dashed through the lobby and down the stairs to our room, mindful to lock the door behind us. Though springy and well-used, the bed was our compensation for enduring the arduous trip overland. How many other weary travelers had slept on it? What did it matter? We were more than content to lie down, stretch our cramped legs, and ease our sore backs. For a few minutes, we closed our eyes and consciously tried to keep our minds free from thought.

A familiar tap on the door; it was Thupten. I leapt off the bed and opened the door.

"Rinpoche, Kalden, and the driver are in the dorm," he said in a serious voice that reflected our mood. "I'm going out to find the five-star general that Kunzang Lama sent. He has to be in town looking for us. I'll be back."

Miguel and I never believed that the scheme involving the five-star general was a reality, but Thupten was optimistic. He was convinced the general would be our saving grace and was obsessed with finding him. We had no bright alternatives to offer and were just too tired to object.

"Go ahead. We're going to stay here and get some rest," Miguel said. "It's probably best that Rinpoche stays out of sight until we've made some progress with our escape plans. This place is crawling with undercover agents. You saw the surveillance post across the street, right?"

"Be careful, and come back soon," I added. "We haven't eaten since the first checkpoint, so we need to feed everyone. Since this is a Chinese-operated hotel, the restaurant will probably be opened for a limited time."

Thupten agreed with a nod.

Reclining in the dimming light, my body was still, but my mind raced on. I couldn't fully relax. With the seconds ticking away, it would soon be midnight, then dawn, and the inevitable moment when we would have to leave.

Thupten returned after some time. He had failed to find Mr. Five Star. "I walked up and down the streets and scoured the town," he reported with downcast eyes, "but I found no one that came close to resembling him."

"He must be here," he continued, with a glimmer of hope in his voice. "Lama promised he would get a message through and that someone would be here to help us. He'll definitely come, either tomorrow morning or the following day." But there was a hint of quandary.

As we sat silently in rumination, raindrops began to fall, pitter-pattering on our windowsill. The view from our room was awesome. We were on the edge of the cliff, surrounded by dense vegetation. Clouds rolled in, enveloping the valley and gorge below us, seeming to reveal ethereal goddesses dancing in the grottos and mist. The rain steadily intensified. Before long, the heavens opened up, releasing a seemingly infinite reservoir of pure water. Flashes of lightning and the occasional roar of thunder charged toward us from the distance. Perhaps the titans or local deities were in battle or doing aggressive sparring. We took the impending storm to be a positive omen of purification and cleansing in preparation for the new day.

On the eve of potentially the most perilous mission of our lives, for some inexplicable reason, we had no fear. On the contrary, we felt assured of our success.

Dinner in Darkness

"I'm starving!" Miguel exclaimed, looking at his watch. "Let's go eat before the restaurant closes."

It was a feeding frenzy in the overcrowded dining hall. Some people sat on chairs encircling round tables, while others squeezed together on benches at oblong tables. Ravenous travelers and their guides were consuming quarts of beer and eating family style from large platters of vegetable and meat dishes placed in the center of the tables. They had individual bowls of rice and their chopsticks moved constantly from platter to bowl to mouth. The cacophony inside outmatched the pounding of the intensifying storm outdoors.

After a short wait, Thupten spotted an open table in the middle of the room. So, we rushed over to take it. Faces turned, and for an instant, the loud echo of hundreds of voices seemed to subside. Surreptitiously, Miguel and I scanned the entirety of the room. We tried to keep our energy neutral and project the persona of ordinary tourists wanting supper after a hard day of traveling. Even though the restaurant felt safe, there was no telling who was who in this crowd.

Thupten ran upstairs to invite the driver to join us. He told Rinpoche and his father to stay put and that he'd bring them dinner.

Miguel and I wanted to ensure that we got a hot meal, knowing too well that supplies were scarce and quickly consumed. Instead of waiting for the frantic servers trying to keep up with their customers, we headed for the kitchen. It was uncluttered, with large counters holding basic root and leafy vegetables, slabs of meat, trays, and utensils. I was pleased that the place was relatively clean with no flies or signs of rodents.

For simplicity, we ordered the standard fare: flat steamed breads, rice, fried meat, and a choice of vegetable. The dishes arrived one at a time. Miguel and the driver drank a couple of room-temperature Tsingtaos, the export-quality Chinese beer. Thupten and I had plain tepid tea to help wash down the salt and oil in the food. Our mood was light. We might as well enjoy the moment!

When the entire meal was on the table, Thupten heaped two plates full of food, saying, "I'll take this to Rinpoche and Kalden…will be right back."

The Dram night sky offered spectacular dinner entertainment. The storm had positioned itself directly above us, and lightning flashed at swift intervals. Thunder roared, and rain pounded down heavier by the minute. Gusts of wind whipped through the capacious dining hall, creating an even more theatrical effect. The clashing sounds of nature outside merging with the human commotion in the restaurant nearly deafened our senses.

Suddenly, without warning, the room went black.

For a mere second, the chatter ceased, absolute silence reigned. Then a symphony of voices and nervous laughter erupted. We heard shuffling in the darkness, people anxiously searching for flashlights, candles, any type of illumination. It wasn't long before votive candles flickered throughout the room, providing enough light for us to finish our dinner and retreat to our rooms.

Before long, Rinpoche, his father, and Thupten appeared at our door. We conversed in the darkness. Kalden took the opportunity to get to know us better. He wanted to hear more about our relationship with the previous Nechung Rinpoche. It was understandable—he needed to be convinced that we would be equally caring for his only son whom we were taking far away. After we crossed the border, father and son might not see each other again for some time.

We gladly obliged, happy to bring to memory details of our unique experience living and studying with a Tibetan lama of rare caliber. Young Rinpoche listened attentively as we relayed the story of how we met his previous incarnation in 1975 and overcame the challenges of language, diet, culture, and other obstacles. We conveyed to them the kindness, patience, and generosity of our teacher and described how he had spent the last years of his precious life with us in Hawai'i.

When we mentioned His Holiness the Dalai Lama's name, their ears perked up. We discussed His Holiness' impact on the world and how we had hosted him at our Hawai'i temple during his second trip to North America. We told them that another visit was scheduled for April of the following year; and conveyed that after accompanying Rinpoche to Dharamsala, we would go home to begin preparations for the spring event.

Throughout, our voices remained a bare whisper. There was no telling if we had eavesdroppers with their ears pinned to the door or next to the thin walls of the room. The mood was serious. Reminded by the flashes of lightning in the night sky, we knew that these priceless moments were fleeting. Morning would come soon, and we would part ways. What happened next would alter the course of Rinpoche and Kalden's lives.

As the evening wore on, the ramification of the imminent separation hit Rinpoche as he realized the radical change he was about to face. It was the first adult experience for an eight-year-old boy who had lived a very sheltered life. He buried his head in his father's lap and began to sob uncontrollably.

There was nothing that any of us could do. No words of comfort could we offer, no outpouring of love could we generate to console this child. Only the warmth of being in his father's arms could soothe the pain. The situation must have been equally difficult for Kalden, but he showed little outward sentiment. It was a process they each had to suffer.

Cool breezes floated in through the open windows soothing us with a gentle embrace. The downpour of rain was relentless. Sheets of water penetrated every atom of earth and space. It filtered through trees and dripped from branches. The moisture soaked into our thirsty skin, still parched from the Tibetan Plateau. We tasted the freshness of renewal around us. We were completely encompassed by the roar of the river rushing through the gorge, enhanced by the rumble and thundering clap of the sky dragon overhead, matched in intensity by the downpours.

We sat in stillness and waited for a break in the turbulent storm as the outer noise merged with the swift current of thoughts in my mind. In time, the boy's tears ceased. Rinpoche had cried himself to sleep.

After bidding us good night, Kalden carried his son to their quarters. We had bonded. A deeper trust and friendship now existed between us. We would not have any face-to-face or verbal contact with Kalden again.

Guides of the Night

Alone in the room with us, Thupten said, "You two should leave in the morning with the other foreigners. I'll stay behind with Rinpoche. We'll leave this hotel after you depart and move up the hill. We'll rent a small room and I'll make a call to Kunzang Lama in Lhasa or to his wife in Kathmandu to make sure that the five-star general comes to help us. We'll wait for him."

He emphasized his words as if to lend them validity. "Five Star *will* come with the ID papers and clothes for Rinpoche, and we will get in his car and drive to Kathmandu."

"This is therapy," I thought. "He's just saying this to make himself feel better."

"No! Absolutely not!" Miguel said emphatically. "We have a one-hour window tomorrow morning to leave, and all four of us are going together. We are *not* going anywhere without you and Rinpoche."

"Thupten, you are more at risk than we are," I said, glaring at him. "We have American and Canadian passports. You entered Tibet as an overseas Chinese and you're already on a police blacklist. If anything goes wrong, we can back each other up. If we're caught, certainly we can be charged with kidnapping, espionage, plotting against the motherland, and thrown in jail. *But*, being foreigners, we have some leverage; we can cause a commotion, raise the issue of racial discrimination, and bring up human rights abuses."

Thupten sat quietly furrowing his brows but offered no rebuttal. So, with a sigh, I continued my reasoning, "You, on the other hand, have a Chinese government-issued visa and therefore have submitted to being a citizen. They can cast you into prison indefinitely without bail or counsel, torture you, and your whereabouts may be unknown for years."

"Besides, *how* will Mr. Five Star get here? You do know the roads on the Nepalese side of the border are still closed, right? Huge stretches of road are still not functional. *Even* if some sections are intact, no one can drive through the washouts—five-star general or not. Can't you comprehend that?"

The tone of my voice must have revealed my frustration. Thupten retorted, "Well, in the next few days, the weather *will* clear up, and the road *will* be repaired, and the five-star general *will* come for us." He was clearly becoming just as obstinate as we were. His jaw was set and arms were crossed—body language that strongly implied he was not budging!

But to remain in Dram longer than an overnight transit was risky. No doubt, one of the numerous operatives would catch on. Travelers never stayed more than a night at these border towns. We had to leave the next morning with the other tourists!

"Anyway, it doesn't matter," Thupten huffed. "I'll wait here with Rinpoche, and if the general doesn't show up, we can go the way that most Tibetans do—over the mountains."

"What are you talking about!" Miguel countered, clearly irritated. "You cannot be serious! How will you know where to go?"

"I'll find a guide to take us, that's what people do. Just give money and someone will do the job," Thupten claimed. "They know the trails and will take us to a place where we can hike into Nepal by ourselves. It'll be easy!"

"No way are you going over the mountains with Rinpoche!" Miguel declared, shaking his head incredulously. "The kid's not strong enough for the trek; he doesn't even have adequate clothing or shoes. There may be soldiers monitoring the trail, it'll take days if not weeks, and the longer you're out there, the more vulnerable you will be! And what about food and the weather?" Miguel questioned, "I have a list of reasons why you cannot do this!"

"This is going nowhere," I thought. Somehow, we had to reach a consensus and get on the same page.

"Listen," I said calmly, "it's just not prudent to stay. You've already been detained, blindfolded, and interrogated. We're lucky that you weren't harmed. You're on record admitting that you are in Tibet looking for a reincarnate lama. How long do you think it'll take before one of these agents gets suspicious seeing you and Rinpoche day after day?"

Thupten was quiet, so I continued. "True, the Chinese government currently is disinterested in reincarnate lamas and knows nothing about reincarnation. True, their intelligence gathering is not sophisticated. So what? Dram is a small place, and people can differentiate the locals from outsiders. You'll be really conspicuous. All it takes is a phone call to Central Intelligence to put two and two together. We would never consider leaving you and Rinpoche here alone without backup. I don't know how, but we have to leave tomorrow together."

We were out of words, on edge, and had no game plan. For three people who were always in control with something clever to say, this brick wall was disconcerting indeed.

Not the one to sit still, Thupten soon announced, "I'm going out."

"In the dark? In this storm?" Miguel asked, raising his eyebrows in disbelief. "Where are you going?"

"Remember the group of Europeans at the first checkpoint by the Everest turnoff? When I saw the Tibetan guide, I thought that I knew him. But couldn't figure out who he was. Since I'm not in monk's robes, he didn't recognize me either. I've been trying to place him ever since. We ran into each other upstairs, and I remembered…" Thupten paused, then resumed talking in the darkness.

"A few years ago, he came to India to see His Holiness, but he didn't know anyone in Dharamsala. Our monastery assisted him and offered him food and shelter. You know how we're always doing that."

We nodded…

"I didn't have a chance to talk to him earlier, because everyone was checking in and he was busy. I think I know where he's staying. I'll try to find him to see if he can help us." Thupten stood up, grabbed one of the flashlights, and headed out into the night.

Now it was just Miguel and me, sitting in the dark with a single flashlight beam aimed at the ceiling, watching the intermittent bursts of lightning bolts in the distance.

It was disturbing to have such a disparity in our approaches. I felt sad at the notion that we might be instrumental in causing Rinpoche any trauma. Tinges of guilt arose thinking about his painful feelings. How would he feel in the morning? Would he still come with us? Would it be possible for his individual karma and our collective one to create the right conditions for a safe passage in the face of an impossible mission? What about Kalden? Was he still willing to send his son with us after witnessing the boy's emotional outburst? So many questions and no answers.

Depending on the circumstances, Kalden may or may not be a sole passenger returning to Lhasa with our driver. Only karma and skillful maneuvering could determine the outcome. Miguel and I knew that the five-star general was not in town. The likelihood of him showing up in the morning to save the day was zero. Meanwhile, Thupten was roaming around in the dark, searching for someone to petition help in a clandestine mission that was operated on a "need-to-know" basis. Here, alone in the shadows, I allowed myself some private moments of insecurity.

Before midnight, Thupten returned with no significant results. He had gone to the section of the hotel where tour groups stayed. With his torch in hand, he knocked on doors and made inquiries. Eventually, he found the room where the Tibetan guide was staying, only to discover that he wasn't there, but out on the town partying with friends.

"It's okay," Thupten assured us. "I'll go see him before dawn." He sat in a chair by the open window and gradually dozed off.

I couldn't sleep. Sitting in bed leaning against the headboard, I wanted Miguel to stay up with me and share my restlessness. I tried my best to keep him awake, but after listening to several rewinds of obsessive jabber, he mumbled, "Go to sleep. We need to be alert and ready for tomorrow."

Time passed slowly. Each minute felt like an hour. I wanted it to be morning, but the night lingered on—as did my thoughts that enacted a multitude of scenarios. It continued to rain. The torrents raged down the gorge, its reverberation echoed the cascade of my deliberations. In my head I played the lists of what-to-dos, what-to-say, and what-ifs of the next morning. Despite the outer noise and inner chatter, mists rendered the air around us magical. The sky dragon kept me company, speaking to me, hinting cryptic messages in his expressive thunderous roar, as if saying, "Decipher this, and you will have your answer."

In the dark moonless night, I could spot twinkling lights in the small villages far up the hill. As the night wore on and the storm let up, stars shone through the dissipated layers of clouds, revealing constellations and galaxies light-years away. It was an enchanting evening after all…a night of mountain vigil.

To Leave or Not to Leave

The next morning before sunrise, Thupten tiptoed out of our room so as to not disturb Miguel, who was still sound asleep. "I have to go, will be back soon," he whispered.

It was critical that we make our move that morning. I was convinced that the only chance for a safe passage out of Tibet was to join the other tourists in the one-hour opening available to us. The chaos produced by groups of people should create the distraction we needed for that opportunity. Somehow, we had to slip Rinpoche past the heavily guarded immigration station and down a long stretch of dirt road thickly shaded with trees and patrolled by armed soldiers. We needed to reach the Friendship Bridge and then pass through the next checkpoint and beyond. How we would achieve that was yet a mystery.

Lost in thought, I didn't notice that the storm had completely stopped and the black of night had transitioned into heather gray. Another day was dawning, and Miguel was beginning to stir.

Thupten tapped lightly on our door and pushed it open. He had found the Tibetan guide, the man he had recognized the day before, asleep in his room, still happily drunk, if not a little hung over. His name was Kalsang, which translates as Fortunate One. Tibetans gave inspirational names such as wisdom, love, accomplishment—good qualities to aspire toward, aiming at higher motivation and purpose.

"Can he assist us?" I wanted to know.

"He knows some porters who are trustworthy and may be able to help, but has no way to contact them. He said that they usually show up outside the hotel looking for work. So, we'll have to wait till sunrise."

"Why porters?" I asked. "To carry our bags?"

There had been a hint in Thupten's voice that the workers might perform more than their routine services to serve a more significant objective. Could Kalsang's savvy knowledge of the interplay of individuals at the border help facilitate our needs? It was imperative to identify all the players who might be involved, even if we didn't know faces or personalities yet. We had to discern how to integrate our mission with the other elements of the production on the Dram stage.

"Kalsang suggested we hire porters to escort Rinpoche past the immigration station," Thupten said. "Generally, these guys only transport loads for tourists. But once in a while, a courageous one will consider doing something riskier—*if* he's paid enough."

From our prior experience, porters had arrangements with the Chinese guards to service the area between Dram and the Friendship Bridge. Only a select few had permits to cross the bridge and go as far as the Kodari immigration station on the Nepalese side. In all probability, they had an informal porters' union. These men—denizens who trolled the border region day and night—were familiar with every-one that worked the circuit, and newcomers were subjected to a tough integration process. There was plenty of work during the season. Compensation and tips from most foreigners were lucrative; so, most of them would not chance losing this by getting involved with covert affairs.

"We understand," I answered.

By now it was light, with sun rays glistening off the moisture-laden vegetation. The air was alive with ozone, fresh and rejuvenating. Despite my lack of sleep, I felt invigorated. It was going to be a beautiful, sunny day. If everything went well, we would be in Kathmandu by dusk. If not…well, I didn't want to go there.

"I'm going upstairs to check things out," Thupten said. "I need to find Kalsang and see if he's located anyone to help us. We agreed to meet in the lobby around now. I'll be back." Thupten vanished again. Only one of us needed to be out there running around. We were the stationary members of the team for now, conserving our energy, prepared to move at the precise instant.

After Thupten left, I remembered Rinpoche. "Oh, we should have had him check on Rinpoche and see how he is. I hope that he's feeling better and still willing to go with us."

"Knowing Thupten, he'll make his rounds, don't worry." Miguel said, then added, "we have to stay calm and let things come together. It's 6:30 now, and the whole place must be buzzing. The tourists are up, eating breakfast and getting ready to hit the road. They're going to get everybody out of here in the next couple of hours."

Bang. Bang. Bang. Out of nowhere, someone pounded on our door, and it was not Thupten. A loud voice shouted something in Chinese; we surmised, "Hey! Open up! Open up now!"

I quickly crawled under the covers of the bed that had not been touched all night, faced the direction of the door, and pulled the light, thread-bared blanket over my shoulders and up to my eyes. This way, I wouldn't miss any of the action.

"Okay! Okay! I'm coming!" Miguel ambled toward the door.

Just then, the man on the other side barged in. I had neglected to lock it in my usual cautious way, since Thupten had been coming and going so often. The intruder was a thirty-something man dressed in fatigues. He was angry and belligerent. It didn't matter that we couldn't understand his words; his message was loud and clear.

He was the same fellow in the tracksuit who had scrutinized us the previous day when we were getting our room key at the front desk. Today, Camouflage Man, the nickname I aptly assigned him, was on duty in his role as a Chinese lackey.

"Listen, I don't understand a word you're saying," Miguel said in Tibetan. "Are you Chinese or Tibetan? If you're Tibetan, speak to me in your own language!"

Miguel's American-accented Lhasa dialect surprised the man. Hearing Tibetan come out of a foreigner's mouth stunned him into unexpected silence. Blinking, he blasted back in Tibetan, "You must leave here! It's time to check out now!"

This was my cue. Unrehearsed, I spontaneously pulled the covers over my head and moaned loudly, pretending to be ill. Surely, this man had seen many a Westerner come through Dram with dysentery, exhaustion, or altitude sickness.

"Can't you see that my wife is sick?" Miguel exclaimed. "She had a very hard night and can't move. I don't know if we will be able to leave this morning." Of course, we couldn't leave yet, we still didn't know what to do. We needed to stall and buy some time.

"Go away! Leave us alone!" Miguel made rapid motions with his hands to shoo the guy away.

Camouflage Man stomped off, cursing to himself. Miguel speedily bolted the door, but within fifteen minutes, he was back with a vengeance, rattling the doorknob. "Open this door! Pack your bags now! Everybody leaves this morning! No one stays in this hotel past nine!"

Miguel opened the door. I tossed and turned, groaning under the covers.

"We'll try to check out, but she's extremely nauseous," Miguel said, shrugging his shoulders. "If I can't get her to move, we'll have to spend another night."

Camouflage Man glared at Miguel. Aside from dragging me out of bed and personally hauling all of our stuff upstairs, there was nothing more that he could do but harass us.

Thupten came through the door next. Our room had become the stage for a sitcom, with one person after another entering to deliver his lines. It would have been comical, but the situation was neither amusing nor optimistic.

"Kalsang hasn't found the porters," Thupten said. "He went looking for them, but no one has shown up. And *no* five-star general either!" He sounded discouraged, as if needing to reassure himself that everything would be fine, he fell back on his old proposal. "Well, if nothing else, you can leave this morning, and I'll stay here with Rinpoche. In a couple of days, Lama will arrive, and we'll figure out what to do. Don't worry, we'll meet in Kathmandu."

I stared at him, took a deep breath, and shook my head in disbelief. It was pointless to respond. Instead, we packed the few things that were tossed on the dresser and crammed our extra clothes into the duffel. Thupten left again.

"Let's leave our things here and go upstairs," I said to Miguel. "At least we can see what's happening, and if there's any chance for us to leave today. It's time to take some initiative."

Miguel agreed.

The corridor was clear. Upstairs, the commotion in the lobby was as expected. Luggage was scattered everywhere. People were running in and out of the hotel, and some were starting to gather in clusters. It was the perfect time for us to emerge. In this whirlwind, we were just two more bodies in the crowd.

Outside the entrance by the roadside, we noticed two army trucks with cabs in front and large flatbeds with shallow sides, roofed over with olive canvass. These had not been there yesterday. Several young Nepalese men lingered nearby. They looked like independents, unattached to any group. "Were they for hire?" I wondered. It was worth finding out. We needed a couple of helpers, and neither Kalsang nor his phantom porters were anywhere in sight. I casually approached one of them and made a motion with my head towards the direction of the immigration station to illustrate my question: "You going?"

The youth appeared disinterested and replied with a flat, "No."

So much for that. I walked back indoors, shook my head ever so gently. Miguel caught on and in turn strolled outside. I positioned myself close to the stairwell, surveying the lobby. The previous Rinpoche had taught us to develop an awareness and perception of people. Their physical movements and facial expressions all reveal much about their inner character.

After being alone for just a few minutes, a tall, lean young man approached me. "What you need, madam?" he said in rudimentary English with a heavily laced Nepali accent.

I looked up at him. He was in his mid-twenties, seemingly streetwise, and looking for the job that would make his day. He wore a faded denim shirt and scrubby jeans, probably hand-me-downs from a Westerner leaving Tibet.

"Is that your truck?" I asked, pointing my finger.

"Yes, my truck. You need help? I help you go Friendship Bridge. How many people? How many bags? We help."

Another shorter kid in his late teens, possibly a newcomer to the trade, joined the young man. His sidekick perhaps?

Miguel noticed that I was talking with them and rushed over. I explained the conversation.

"So, you want to work, huh?" Miguel asked, patting the older boy on the back.

"Yes, sir!" flew back a fast, honest answer.

"Okay, you wait," Miguel said, putting his hand on the boy's arm to emphasize that they should stay right there. I had a good feeling about them. Miguel seemed to as well; we signaled our agreement by way of raised eyebrows.

We glanced around and spotted Thupten with Kalsang, so we headed for them. The tour guide had a group of people with him, including two Tibetans; they had congregated to the side of the lobby with their luggage—very proper and well organized. Thupten saw us and sauntered over to meet us halfway.

"See that guy over there in the blue shirt?" Miguel said, glancing discreetly in the opposite direction from where the Nepalese boys stood. "Says he's got a truck out front and that he can help us. Can you go talk to him?"

Thupten enjoyed the "let's make a deal" game and gladly obliged. From our vantage point, the negotiations appeared positive. No one threw their hands up in the air or walked off. Before long, Thupten flashed us a promising grin as he and Kalsang took our potential helpers by their arms and led them downstairs. We surmised that he was heading toward his dorm to finish the transaction in private. We nicknamed the taller boy Chambray, for his shirt, and his partner Junior.

Suddenly Camouflage Man resurfaced. He scowled at us—ready to pounce. Once again, we benefited from the commotion of the other travelers. The minute he turned his head away, we raced down to our room and prepared for checkout.

New Friends

Kalsang wasn't just a normal tour guide, he was the head of the guild for Tibetan guides, an organization for tour leaders, and was certified to work in all regions of Tibet. He was delighted to use his skills to repay the kindness that Nechung Monastery had shown him in the past.

Chambray was authorized to work the territory between Dram and the Nepalese immigration station—a permit very few porters had. How miraculous that he had materialized at the right moment! He knew the risks, yet had the confidence that he could fulfill the task. His services were not cheap; he demanded 5,000 Chinese yuan to do the job from start to finish. This was much more money than we had collectively. During our travels, most transactions were in cash, and it had been challenging to keep adequate amounts of currency in our possession. Thupten had to drive a hard bargain, we learned later.

"Hey, I'm a monk. I don't have that kind of money!" Thupten had protested. "The little boy you're taking across the border will go to India to also become a monk. It's impossible for us to give you 5,000 yuan. We don't have it!"

"No money, no deal," Chambray had answered, turning his back and pretending to walk away. Of course, Thupten knew this was all part of the negotiation. The morning was wearing on and most travelers had already hired their porters. We were his only hope for employment.

"Okay, I'll give you all the yuan I have, *and* I will give you this Swatch," Thupten said.

Chambray looked confused. "Swatch...What?"

On his wrist, Thupten sported a trendy Swatch watch in wild patterns of purple, electric blue, and magenta. It had been well used but still was in good condition. "This Swatch is worth 2,000 to 3,000 yuan. It's Swiss-made, almost new, one-of-a-kind! No one else in Tibet or Nepal has anything like it. Guaranteed!"

Thupten pulled the Swatch off and slapped it on Chambray's gaunt wrist. He reached into his pockets and his knapsack for bills, then shoved a handful of yuan into Chambray's outreached hands.

"Here! Take these Nepalese rupees too. Now you have all my money! Okay? Happy? Very good!" He laughed robustly and gave Chambray a friendly pat on the back.

It was a one-sided deal. Chambray was speechless, but what could he do? He was the proud owner of a Swatch and held a heap of yuan and rupees. Perhaps it was Thupten's persuasive powers, or the scarcity of jobs that morning, or the mesmerizing swirls on the face of the Swatch. *Something* induced Chambray to agree.

Subsequently, we learned that the going price for such an engagement was indeed 5000 yuan per person. How much did he actually give Chambray and Junior? We don't know for sure, since the bills were never counted.

Having made this verbal contract, the next component fell into place. During the height of tourist frenzy, Chambray would accompany Rinpoche past the immigration post and down the road where we would meet them. He seemed comfortable with this scenario and had previously executed a similar assignment. The truck was not factored into the arrangement. Chambray had told Thupten "no truck," citing that it would draw unnecessary attention.

"Two foreigners and a Tibetan hiring an entire truck would seem extravagant," he had told Thupten. "Besides, there's no place to hide the boy."

Thupten was thrilled to have found suitable helpers and initiate a plan of action. A major obstacle had been eliminated; along with it, the five-star general became a nonissue.

In the lobby with our luggage, Miguel and I waited eagerly for Thupten and Kalsang. People were checking out, rushing around, talking fast, ordering porters to take bags and other paraphernalia outside. Immigration control was about to open. I went up to the front desk hoping to discretely drop off our room key at the counter. There were receptionists there, but not the one who had checked us in. I swiftly turned to walk away before any questions were asked, but not soon enough. One of them pulled out a cardboard box and called out to me, "Madam, your passport. What country are you from?"

"Oh, no, don't worry, we have our passports already. Thank you, we had a great stay. Good-bye!" I hurried into the crowd, leaving behind a puzzled clerk scratching her head.

The lobby had begun to empty, the crowd was thinning; only Miguel and I, and a few stragglers remained. We felt increasingly vulnerable. Where were Thupten and Kalsang? Where were Rinpoche and Kalden?

In answer to our angst, Rinpoche and his father came up the winding stairway. Without as much as a glance in our direction, they walked past us, out the front entrance, and up the street.

Kalsang and Thupten resurfaced as well, with Chambray and Junior in tow.

"Marya and Miguel, join my group outside and go through passport control with them," Kalsang advised.

Outdoors, he said, "Grab your things and throw everything into the truck over there." He pointed to an old army truck, exactly like Chambray's, parked outside the immigration station. "That's the one we've contracted for my Swiss group. You and Thupten can ride with them as far as the Friendship Bridge."

We watched Rinpoche tightly holding his father's hand walk up the hill until they were out of sight. Junior helped take the rest of our belongings out of the jeep where our driver was waiting. We paid the balance owed him, plus a tip—a small token of our gratitude for someone so instrumental for our safe passage from Lhasa to the border.

We followed Kalsang's orders and went to the army truck. A driver and two others were seated in the cab looking bored. The back was heaped with luggage, to which we added our bags. At the lone immigration building, dozens of people were in queue. Once its passport window opened, one by one, the visitors handed over their documents and waited for the official stamp.

We started mingling with Kalsang's group to establish a rapport since they would play a significant role in the next phase. Miguel gravitated toward two Swiss Tibetans who were friendly and struck up a quiet conversation with them. It started with generalities—their background, Switzerland, the Tibetan situation in and out of Tibet—then inched toward the subjects of politics and His Holiness the Dalai Lama.

Kalsang's group was the last to go through passport control. He formally introduced us. "These people need a ride down the mountain. They will be riding with you to the Friendship Bridge."

"Welcome. The more the merrier!" someone said.

The Crossing

Chambray and Junior had met Rinpoche and Kalden briefly in the dorm during the bargaining process. The plan was Rinpoche and his father would walk up the road and have breakfast at one of the eateries. Chambray was assigned to find them and walk the young lama down the hill at the height of border congestion. They were to casually stroll past immigration control and down the dirt road, acting natural, like a couple of local boys. Not that Rinpoche blended in. Dressed in his yellow shirt and pants, you could see him coming a mile away!

Chambray walked rapidly up the hill, slowing down outside each food stall to peek through soiled windows. He finally spotted them having *momos*—meat and vegetable dumplings—a Tibetan favorite. They were surrounded by Chinese soldiers enjoying the same. The duo had walked out of peril's way smack into a tiger's den! We later learned that Rinpoche had been aware of their predicament, but once they entered, it was too late to turn around. Kalden had relished their last meal together so much that he didn't notice Chambray. It was Rinpoche who caught his helper's eye, cognizant that the moment of parting had arrived. He stood up bravely, said good-bye, leaving his father in the restaurant with the soldiers.

In line at passport control with our new friends, we watched our little-big man walk alongside Chambray with a similar stride as the previous Rinpoche—that of a very self-assured person. They approached the restricted area where we were standing.

A few arm lengths away, Camouflage Man was hankering for a reason to apprehend us. He had shown up during our interchange with the Swiss Tibetans. Now he was leaning on the passport counter listening to every word. He was fixated on us—obviously he sensed something was amiss—and was perplexed that he couldn't deduce what it was. To our advantage, the agent was so preoccupied with us that he failed to see the real prize.

Totally cool, Rinpoche strolled past us without a trace of hesitation. He and Chambray meandered around the bend. It was unclear as to how far they would walk; we just knew that we'd meet them somewhere down the road. Although we couldn't say with certitude, our helper appeared to be honest. We had trusted him with our priceless gem.

Miguel and I were the last to climb into the army truck's covered flatbed, which was about five feet off the ground. Riders had to hoist themselves into it. Being petite, I needed a helpful boost from my husband. Most of the tour group had propped themselves against piles of luggage. Thupten and Junior were onboard. There was sufficient head room under the canvas tarp for the men and porters to stand. They were to be the ones to off-load bags at the bridge.

I breathed a sigh of relief—nothing consequential took place at the Dram border. We had found ourselves some helpers and travel companions, if temporarily, to get us to the next checkpoint. Camouflage Man had been deserted. We merrily waved good-bye to his solitary figure standing by the immigration station through the tailgate.

A happy bunch, the Swiss folks were. They talked and giggled as the truck bounced down the rocky road. Between the driver's seat in the cab and where we were, a glass partition allowed glimpses of the course ahead through the windshield.

Where were Rinpoche and Chambray? Anxious to find them, we peered around the blind curves and scanned the area we had covered.

There! A brightly clad little boy and a tall young man were a few hundred feet ahead. They beckoned for the truck to stop. Thupten and Miguel banged on the cab window and called out to the driver, "Hey! Hey, stop! Stop now!"

The driver and his assistants turned their heads, frowning, with confusion written across their faces, like, "what's going on?" Nevertheless, the driver brought the vehicle to a screeching halt. Chambray grasped Rinpoche's hand and ran toward the truck.

Thupten unlatched the safety gate, and Chambray lifted Rinpoche into Miguel's arms, who positioned the little lama securely next to me. Chambray hoisted himself inside.

Thupten and Miguel pounded on the window and waved their hands briskly, both shouting, "Go! Go! Go!" The driver stared at them, shook his head, then pressed the gas pedal to the floor, and the truck lurched forward.

Our European companions were in awe, their eyes were wide with disbelief. They glanced at each other, looked at Rinpoche, and then at us. In a matter of seconds, they realized that another Tibetan was escaping his occupied homeland. This time, it was a child *without* his parents. The Swiss Tibetans, who we later learned had been adopted at about the same age, were visibly moved.

Rinpoche sank into the mound of luggage, tents, and backpacks. He was adorable with his cherubic face and quiet demeanor. Maternal impulses arose in the women, a natural response to want to protect him. One of them wrapped her arm around his shoulder when we hit a huge bump that tossed him into the air, then continued to hold him close.

We did it! We had successfully negotiated surveillance at the heavily guarded Dram border and were on the road out of Tibet with Rinpoche!

The Friendship Bridge

The truck charged full speed ahead hitting all the bumps. Most of the men were balancing themselves with a hand pressed on the canvas top and their feet braced. The women sat amidst the gear—tossing, rolling, and squealing loudly with each bounce. Every jolt sent a small shock up my spine. Still, compared to the treacherous hillside with loose boulders and sludge that we had to slide down in 1987, this was a breeze.

Abruptly, the truck came to a halt. We all raised our heads to see what was happening. A police vehicle was barricading the road in front of us.

Now what? Another roadblock? There wasn't supposed to be another checkpoint until the Friendship Bridge. Frantic, we looked around, anticipating armed officers stepping out of the jeep to encircle our truck. My initial thoughts were: Where could we conceal Rinpoche? Should one of us jump out with him and hide in the bushes? What story could we fabricate?

We felt trapped, our bodies were motionless. My agitated mind unleashed a myriad of thoughts covering a spectrum of wild speculation. Perhaps some people wanted to hitch a ride? Was this a random spot check? Were the cops onto us? Would everybody be forced out of the truck? Would they inspect it to see who and what was inside?

To our astonishment and relief, nothing happened. Nothing at all. The doors of the police jeep remained closed. No feet stomped out. No one approached us. There was no inspection. Just silence. After what felt like an eternity, but probably lasted only five to ten minutes, the motor started running and the police vehicle moved forward and continued toward the bridge. Our truck followed closely in its tracks.

Through the cab opening, one of the driver's assistants relayed a message explaining the reason for the unexpected stop. The jeep was transporting the Lhasa police chief and his subordinates to the border for a routine security inspection. Miguel and I looked at each other with bulging eyes, shaking our heads in utter disbelief.

I closed my eyes to envision the next episode of the unfolding drama. I saw another checkpoint—the third one—where the truck would stop. A multitude of armed men would be on duty outside a building that had additional backup staff. After clearing this staging area, we'd proceed to the Friendship Bridge, the connection between Tibet and Nepal. There, more guards would await at its entry. The bridge was narrow and stretched approximately two hundred feet in length over a swift river.

The truck came to a screeching stop at the anticipated checkpoint. Guards swarmed the area. Some stood their ground clutching weapons; others darted between the guardhouse and the bridge. Several of them moved toward our truck, prepared to conduct a thorough search.

My heart skipped a beat. We were sitting ducks in the confines of the flatbed.

But suddenly, the guards scattered. Most of them scampered into the station, leaving behind only a fraction of the force. The police chief's visit to the border had taken top priority. Inspection of the last tourist truck of the day was no longer important. I was astounded!

Seizing the opportunity, everyone grabbed random bags and tossed them out. The Swiss and their porters jumped off first, took their belongings, and headed toward the bridge. This created the perfect diversion. There were enough people—and attractive women—in the group to draw interest from the remaining guards. We were but an insignificant minority.

Whispers from Miguel and Thupten of "Go! Go! Go!" filled my ears. In fire-drill style, Thupten jumped out first, followed by Miguel, who reached up as Rinpoche leapt into his outstretched arms and alighted firmly on the ground in a single motion. I was the last out of the empty truck, landing next to the luggage, which had been reduced to our personal bags.

Rinpoche spontaneously picked up a sizable piece of furry marmot pelt and threw it over his right shoulder. It was light and draped down his back. He marched in the direction of the bridge with surprising confidence behind Thupten, Chambray, and Junior. The pelt had been a hurried purchase from a nomad sitting by the roadside on our way out of Shigatse. The call of the vendor had caught Thupten's attention, and upon query, he had discovered that the hide was the skin of a chipee, a furry

Tibetan marmot. One of the senior Nechung monks had requested this rare item to be used for ritual ceremonies.

Miguel and I retrieved the rest of our gear and followed behind them. We lingered long enough to allow Rinpoche and Thupten to get a head start for a logistical reason—if anything happened, we could spot it from our rear vantage point.

Several guards fronted the bridge access to scrutinize everyone who walked past, causing me concern. Spot-checking was common here, a final place to review documents, rummage through travelers' possessions, and badger them before they left Tibet. Their eyes followed Rinpoche curiously as each step took him closer to Nepal. What were they thinking? Perhaps: "Who is the kid? Is he one of the hired help? The younger brother of the two older boys? He's so young, but then, child labor is not uncommon in this part of the world."

Rinpoche would not be safe until he crossed the finish line at the other end. It was our move. We stepped within arm's reach of the guards and boldly stared each man squarely in the face as we passed. This distracted their attention away from Rinpoche who had by then reached the Nepalese boundary.

Halfway down the bridge, Miguel and I stopped and looked back to check on the Chinese soldiers, to be sure that they were not in pursuit. To our relief, no one, absolutely no one, cared about us. The guards were smoking and talking, ready to finish their shift for the day.

A rush of sentiment flooded me. I felt emotion rise to my throat and could see it in Miguel's eyes. When would we return to this country that was so dear to our hearts? We took one last glimpse of our beloved Tibet and silently bid her farewell.

The Nepalese Border

Kodari, on the Nepalese end of the bridge, was just as I remembered from 1987. A long horizontal metal pole blocked the road much like a cattle guard. This was the boundary of Nepal. As we had hoped, beautifully choreographed chaos reigned at the border outpost. The small building had not been renovated in the six years since our last trip. Outside were travelers, porters, rental taxis, drivers, and even a few buses. We were thankful to be in the midst of this confusion.

Thupten knelt down and held Rinpoche's hand, "Wait here!" he whispered. "Keep an eye on our luggage, okay? We need to get our passports stamped and will be right back!" With these words, we left Rinpoche, Chambray, and Junior standing to one side of the building.

It felt like a case of déjà-vu—everything was 1987 again. Inside the building were two men bent over the old wooden table busily stamping a stack of passports. To prove rightful access into Nepal, they had to use multiple stamps in various shapes and colors. Were these the same guys from 1987? Doing the same tedious job day after day?

A crowd of people encircled the table, trying to get their papers processed ahead of others. Thupten decided to be equally aggressive to show we were ordinary travelers. "Hey! Hey, you. Stamp our passports!" he called out, shoving our booklets at the men. "We've been waiting a long time!"

The noise outside was almost intolerable. A cacophony of loud voices competed with buses and cars that were revving up, honking, and spinning their tires.

Eventually, we were cleared and back on the street breathing car exhaust. The Swiss tourists were still hanging around trying to hire the last bus to Kathmandu. The remaining vehicles were all taxis. Upon catching sight of our team, the drivers accosted us with proposals and prices for their services. Our plan had been to hire a taxi, so Thupten began the negotiations. After a short time, he settled on a deal with one of the drivers, and we started to put our luggage into the trunk.

It was about then that the Swiss Tibetans approached Miguel and me. "Do you want to ride with us?" one of them asked. "We've hired the bus, and there's plenty of room for all of you."

"The boy and the monk can come for free," said the other, "if you two are willing to share the expenses with us."

Another unexpected twist! I recalled all the upcoming checkpoints, at least six before reaching Kathmandu. Being with the Swiss had already proven advantageous; their presence drew attention away from us at Dram and at the Friendship Bridge.

"Safety in numbers," Miguel smiled.

"For sure," I agreed.

"Thupten, come here a second!" I signaled. "This group has offered to share their bus with us. Maybe it's a good idea. If we're on our own in a car, there's no place to hide if we're stopped. It'd be really hard to explain why Rinpoche has no papers. There are a lot of checkpoints between here and Kathmandu. Remember?"

Without a second thought, Thupten agreed. He stepped away from the small mob of locals that had gathered around us. "Walk the boy down the road," he instructed Chambray, then pointed to the bus. "We're going in that. Once we have the child safely on that bus, I'll give you baksheesh, okay? You deserve a tip for your good work!"

We pulled the bags out of the taxi and threw them onto the bus.

"Looks like we're coming with you!" Miguel announced to the Swiss group. They applauded and welcomed us.

We had successfully crossed four major checkpoints—the Everest crossroads, the border town of Zhangmu at Dram, the Friendship Bridge station, and Kodari, the Nepalese border crossing. We were in Nepal at last, ready to face the challenges ahead.

Our spontaneous decision to travel with the Swiss group was opportune. As we tossed our gear into the bus, Thupten murmured, "How fantastic that they offered to let us join them. We have to stay together until Kathmandu. The company of these foreigners will be very useful."

The bus crew comprised of five young men in their mid-twenties and teens—a driver, a conductor, an assistant conductor, a mechanic, and a porter. Way too many, but this was typical in Nepal and India where the driver brings companions along for the ride, whether it's a short distance or a longer trip. Even in a small taxi, there would often be two extra people in the front seat, leaving the paying passengers in the back! It was impossible to dismiss any of the driver's helpers who earned little or no money without a major argument. Helpers do have a purpose though: they carry on a lively banter to entertain the driver and keep him from dozing off.

Our ride was basic transportation—a well-traveled bus with unpadded, metal seats. Windows by each seat opened sideways and were shaded with light cotton curtains that had been faded by many a bright, sunny day. Passenger gear and larger duffels were heaped high to the ceiling behind the driver on the right side of the bus. Everyone kept their smaller backpacks and personal items with them.

Miguel and I headed straight for the back, which had a long bench that stretched across the width of the bus. The rows of seats ahead of us were designed to seat two people, with a narrow aisle through the center. Thupten chose a seat directly in front of us on the left, put his pack down, then darted outside.

It would be dusk before we would reach Kathmandu. Our Swiss friends settled into their seats, trying to get comfortable. They spoke in rapid bursts of English and German as they wrestled with their belongings, trying to fit them on the seat, under it, and on the narrow overhead racks. Miguel and I were anxious to get moving, but we sat, and waited patiently while everyone settled in.

A middle-aged Nepalese man—I guessed in his fifties—boarded our bus. He hesitated at the entrance, scanning the interior with observant eyes, as if making a mental note of the passengers or possibly looking for a seat. He had an air of authority and resembled an Indian train conductor ready to hole-punch tickets. He carried no luggage, only a vinyl briefcase with worn-down handles. He wasn't part of the crew. Maybe he was just a local trying to hitch a ride to the next town.

He caught my eye and strutted between the rows of seats, heading straight for the back of the bus. He squeezed into the space between Miguel and me—smack in the center of the aisle.

"Hi!" I greeted him in a cheerful voice. "How are you? Are you the conductor?"

"No, I am an immigration inspector," He said in fluent English with a thick Nepali inflection. "I'm the head accountant of immigration for this border region. I'm going to the bank to do some business. It's in the next town, about twenty-five kilometers from here."

Miguel and I nearly choked. This couldn't be happening! How on earth could we be expected to disguise or hide Rinpoche from him?

I tried to act relaxed, while thinking: "come on, Thupten, get in here!" He was outside having a great time trading stories with the Swiss Tibetans. Finally, we could wait no longer.

"Excuse me," I said to the inspector, "we need to go outside for a minute." Miguel and I stepped over his legs and hurried outdoors.

We explained the situation to Thupten.

"No!" he exclaimed. "You must be joking!"

True, I didn't know whether to laugh or panic at the irony of it all, so I started to giggle nervously. "What are we going to do?!"

Thupten confidently said, "It's okay. We'll handle it. We can give him some money. Nepalese are easy. There's no turning back now!"

"Okay. But how exactly are we going to do this?"

We deliberated for a bit, but Thupten laughed, slapped me on the back, and repeated, in broken English, "It's okay! Easy! We pay him!"

We piled into the bus, the driver, his cronies, and the last of the Swiss. Nyima, the older Tibetan who was also the group's tour leader, sat in front of Thupten. Across from Nyima was Migmar, the other Tibetan, and his Swiss girlfriend. Everyone else was scattered throughout the bus. We were all there, except for Rinpoche.

The bus cranked up and started to roll down the gravel road. It managed to avoid cows, porters, and taxi drivers leaning on their vehicles, still hoping to get a customer. I held open the dingy curtain and peaked out the window.

And there he was, Rinpoche in his flashy yellow attire with Chambray and Junior!

"Okay! Stop!" Thupten was on his feet. He yelled at the driver so he could be heard above the motor noise. "Stop! Now!"

The bus came to a halt. Rinpoche and his two helpers jumped on board.

Thupten dashed up to greet them before anyone could react. He took Rinpoche in one hand, and with the other, put additional money into Chambray's palm, then patted the youth's back. "Okay, finish! Thank you!"

Chambray started to count the rupees and opened his mouth as if to object. But Thupten was done. He pushed Chambray and Junior out of the bus with a "Good-bye!"

A Small Bribe

Seated in the middle looking up the aisle, the inspector had caught sight of Rinpoche when he got in the bus. The kid was not exactly disguised. The young lama glanced shyly at the inspector and flashed a charming smile. The inspector smiled back, saying nothing. This was a good sign.

Nyima motioned kindly to Rinpoche, "Come here, sit with me."

His seat, two rows ahead of us, was already full—he and a bulky pack took up most of the room. Without hesitation, Rinpoche accepted his offer and slipped his tiny frame into the narrow space next to the window.

Miguel and I had intended to put Rinpoche in the back with us, thinking that we could conceal him with ease. Now the entire situation had changed.

Additionally, the bus driver and his crew were bewildered and not happy with the latest little passenger, so Thupten had to do some fast-talking to calm them down.

Meanwhile, we needed to befriend the inspector and turn him into a sympathetic ally. To break the ice, we began to engage him in conversation. It started with the usual questions. What's your name? Do you live nearby? How long have you worked at the border? What do you do every day? Most Indians and Nepalese enjoy talking with Westerners, and this fellow was no different.

"I have to deposit the money from today's visas. It's quite a journey, since the roads are in poor condition after the monsoons. I've had this job a long time."

Excellent. "Do you enjoy your job?"

"Yes, yes. I very much like meeting people from many countries."

"Do you go to Kathmandu often? Have you ever been to India?"

"No, oh-no. I never go that far. I just go between here and the next village. That's where I live alone. I rarely see my family. They live in Kathmandu. I come up here and work seven days a week. Every month, I work at least three weeks; sometimes I get a short holiday."

The amicable conversation eased my stress, at least for the time being. Our voices were loud enough so Thupten and our companions could hear. It was now the inspector's turn to ask questions.

"And you, madam, where are you from? Are you Tibetan?" he asked me. Still no mention of the boy.

"No, I'm Chinese," I replied. "We're from America. Have you been there? We live in Hawai'i. Do you know where Hawai'i is?"

"No, I don't go anywhere, madam," he said with a sigh. "I have no money. I have no chance to see my family but once a year."

This was our cue. We sensed where the conversation was going. I edged forward on the seat and lightheartedly tapped Thupten on the back.

"Hey, Thupten…"

"Thupten!" Miguel chimed in, laughing, "This guy says he doesn't have any money. He needs money to travel."

Thupten turned around and looked at the inspector with a grin. "Oh really? You don't have any money? Here, let me give you some!" He pulled the leftover change out of his pockets.

There wasn't much left—he had given most of his remaining cash to Chambray—just an odd mixture of Chinese, Indian, and Nepalese bills. Thupten shoved everything he had into the inspector's hand.

It was so little. I feared it would seem like an insult. We should give him more. So, I started emptying my pockets and found some crumbled American bills in small denominations.

"Oh, yeah, I have dollars, too!" Miguel said, reaching into his Levis and jean jacket to contribute.

We were starting to have fun with the inspector, whose hands were now completely filled with various kinds of currency overflowing into his lap. Although the pile was sizable, its sum was not substantial.

The inspector opened his briefcase and turned to Miguel, "*This* is the kind of money that I carry, sir," he said, as if it was the Caucasian who had deep pockets. He fanned a thick stack of bills—American dollars, European notes, Japanese Yen—all in large denominations. "This is real money," he declared.

Actually, we had less than a hundred dollars left on us. We had ventured on this mission with a modest sum of cash in our pockets, a credit card, faith, and a prayer. Clearly, we were over budget just with the basic necessities and transportation.

Here we were trying to broker a deal with a man who wanted more than we could afford. Fortunately, the interchange was playful and non-threatening—and still not a single word about our little Rinpoche.

"Oh, we don't have that kind of money!" Miguel winced, making one of his "what-to-do?" faces. "This is it. We've given you everything we have. Look! All my pockets are empty." He turned his pockets inside out and shook the dust.

We shrugged our shoulders and gestured with open palms. It was clear that there was nothing more to give.

"I see. That's too bad. No more?" The inspector's voice was acquiescent.

"You know," Miguel said, "it really doesn't matter what kind of money we give you—Chinese, Indian, Nepalese, American—or how much. This is a gift for you to spend as you wish."

"Very true, sir. Thank you. Thank you, madam." He carefully deposited the wad of cash into a personal muslin pouch.

Exchanges of baksheesh were not typically conducted in such an open manner. Customarily, people slipped it under the table, passed a bill while shaking hands, or tucked it politely into a newspaper while having a cup of tea. Although there were watchful eyes—the driver sneaked peeks of us through the rearview mirror, and his crew stared unabashedly—there was no fear of repercussions.

As the bus jostled down the road, our continued exchanges with the inspector revealed that he was sympathetic to the plight of the Tibetans. "Very unfortunate," he said. "Very many problems in Tibet now. The people are not happy there and try to leave all the time. I have seen too many of them caught and sent back. They go to prison for years and are tortured badly."

He pointed to the steep Nepalese hillsides with thick growth and tall trees that seemed impenetrable. "The refugees walk there," he explained, "to avoid the road, the check stations, and the police searching for documents."

We knew exactly what he meant. I grimaced, remembering the multiple checkpoints that were ahead of us. No sense worrying about them yet. We would just respond to each situation individually, as we had done thus far. Better to sit back and enjoy the beautiful Nepalese countryside with its fertile fields on terraced slopes. Now and then, we saw a villager along the road with his herd of goats, shooing them aside when the bus honked.

Barely had we de-stressed when the inspector said, "The next checkpoint is coming very soon."

To our left, just before the curve, was a small shack with several armed guards milling about the entrance. A sizable wooden pole barricaded the width of the road.

After a thorough search of a vehicle's cargo and passengers, if the guards were satisfied, they would give a holler to helpers who tugged the ropes to lift the pole and allow the vehicle through. Locals, as well as shepherds and their animals, merely walked around this setup.

We braced ourselves for the worst. Rinpoche was alert; he peaked through the window shades, then stood up to peer over the bars of the seat ahead of him. He had not made a sound since embarking the bus. I couldn't help but wonder what he was thinking and how he was feeling.

Our bus stopped by the building. The front doors opened and in marched an officer. He stood by the door next to the driver, severe, with sharp, penetrating eyes. Instantly he spotted the inspector.

"Good to see you!" The officer said. "Where are you going?"

"To town for business," the inspector replied. "We had a busy morning at the border. More visitors, now that the weather is better." He added: "These foreigners came from Tibet and are on their way to Kathmandu. No problems here."

He then politely asked. "How is your day?"

"Good, good." From where he stood, the officer made a cursory scan of the bus. "Well, see you later then!" He turned around and went down the stairs. A minute later, the guardrail swung upward for us.

Another blessing! What good fortune! Miguel and I each grabbed one of the inspector's hands and clasped them in appreciation.

He nodded with a sincere smile. The driver turned on the music. It blared Indian music from worn out amplifiers, likely a soundtrack from a Bollywood movie. I imagined the heroine singing in a meadow, her voluptuous figure wrapped in an embroidered silk sari that revealed a taut midriff. She would be dripping with jewels, ornate necklaces, earrings, and bangles. With a chiseled face full of emotion, kohl-lined eyes and glossy Bordeaux lips, she was seducing the audience. Her lover, roguishly handsome, would croon in a baritone voice while tossing her amorous glances. Ah, how the mind can wander…

Miguel rubbed my arm gently, snapping me out of my daydream. "Hey, Marya! We're back on duty."

It was another checkpoint and a similar guardrail. Nyima quickly threw his jacket over Rinpoche's head. The garment was large enough to cover the upper half of the boy's body.

The police officer came on board and walked down the aisle with slow, deliberate authority. With a hardened gaze, he focused on one person at a time and tapped his baton under the seats.

"He's searching for liquor," our inspector told us in a low voice. "There is big business in black-market moonshine here."

"Namaste-ji!" he called out to the man, who was about half way down the aisle, and had not yet noticed him. Instantaneously, the officer's demeanor softened, and he greeted the inspector back with "Namaste-ji!"

"There is nothing in here, nothing at all," the inspector volunteered, with a shake of his hands and gesture of his head, as is common in India and Nepal.

"I have been on this bus since the border, and I can assure you that everything is fine," he added. "No need to worry!"

"Thank you, Babu-ji. In that case, I will return to my station. Have a good day!" With that, he was gone, and we were through another station.

The inspector was forthcoming: He explained to us the different types of officials along this stretch of road and described how their uniforms and hats—in green or variegated shades of drab olive—distinguished the various categories of paramilitary police officers. That's how we could tell whether their job was to confiscate illegal alcohol or search for immigration documents; or, if they were just ordinary cops doing a routine check for vehicle registration papers. Their pay was meager and the "real" money came from bounties and bribes. This information was intriguing as well as practical, and it gave us great insight.

Our fellow passengers were chatty and relaxed. Although we didn't know one another, and besides for the Tibetans, didn't even learn each other's names, we had bonded on this exceptional journey. Only the bus crew seemed edgy—for good reason. I sensed that they would demand additional compensation for their services. Rinpoche was riding with them without the necessary papers. If the boy were discovered, they could be in serious trouble.

"Starboard side!" one of the Swiss members called out. Everyone sat up straight, the jacket was again tossed over Rinpoche, and we were ready. This time, however, the guards didn't care about us. Two were inside the shack drinking tea and playing cards. Leaning against the shack's open door, another was basking in the midday sun and taking puffs from a cigarette. He waved us by. We, in turn, leaned out of the windows to wave our greetings. If only it was always that easy.

"We will stop again soon," the inspector informed us. "They are still working to repair the washout in the road."

"Will there be a roadblock with police?" I asked.

"No," he shook his head. "It is not near a checkpoint."

Before long, we saw the heavy equipment and men working in the hot Nepalese countryside. The bus stopped by a makeshift tea stand where a man in light cotton pajamas boiled tea on a single gasoline burner for the workers and passersby. Glass jars half-filled with cookies were available to complement the sugary milk tea.

Several cars waited to get through on the opposite side of the construction site. I surmised that they were on their way to Dram. Little kids ran around barefoot and snotty-nosed, laughing merrily and having fun.

We went out to stretch our legs and sip some tea, but Rinpoche remained in his seat. He stared out the window, quietly observing all that was new around him. There were small streams of running water on the side of the road where the children tossed stones and got their feet wet. We bought tea for everyone on our bus. This seemed to take forever, but it didn't matter since we had to stay until the road was fixed anyway.

It was there that I realized that my trusted black carry-on was missing.

While everyone stood waiting for the tea, I ran back onto the bus. The heap of baggage was immense, and each bag heavier than the last. I moved one backpack after another aside until I reached the bottom of the pile, but I still could not find my leather duffel bag.

Meanwhile, chatting away, my dear husband and the inspector were fast becoming friends, the latter acknowledging again. "I know that the Tibetans are having a very difficult time. They live in an oppressive society and under deplorable conditions." He was a kindhearted man and had witnessed many fleeing refugees robbed of their possessions and dignity on this road. Many were deported back to Tibet and forced to work on road gangs as punishment.

The inspector didn't appear to have serious problems in his life, perhaps just a lack of money. He led a simple existence, going back and forth between the border, the bank, and his home. "I have a very wonderful family," he said. "I love my children and want them to have a good education. I will go visit them soon." He was intelligent and articulate; we deduced that he was well educated and came from a high-caste family.

"Miguel!" I whispered into my husband's ear. "My bag's gone! I can't find it anywhere!"

In the bag was my day planner with contacts and addresses. More importantly, it included Rinpoche's extra clothes, snacks, family photos, and the sentimental things that his mother had packed. The thought of him not having these deeply saddened me.

"Should I hitch a ride back to the border to find it?" I asked.

"Wait a minute," Miguel said. "Let's think about this rationally before we do anything. First things first, the inspector is leaving, so we need to say good-bye to him."

"Very happy to meet you," the inspector said. "Have a safe trip, *and* good luck!"

"How will you get to the bank?" I asked with concern.

"It is not far from here, and I'll enjoy the stroll. They will soon finish the road repairs. Perhaps I will see you in town later." He bid us farewell and shook our hands. We watched as he ambled through a trench and climbed over rocks and debris. On the other side, he quickly caught another ride and was gone.

A Matter of Courtship

What were we to do about my missing bag? Retracing our footsteps back to the border was probably not the wisest choice, since the chance of finding it was next to zero. A thief would have already lugged it off and rummaged through its contents, only to find it had no monetary value. Moreover, the same logic at the border had to be applied here—we needed to stay together as a team. Our journey was indeterminate enough; there was no reason to add more variables to the equation. The best thing to do was to view the loss as having removed a potential obstacle and keep moving.

I retreated back to the bus to sit out the delay with Rinpoche who sat alone with his head leaning against the window frame. He tossed bread crumbs into the moving stream outside and watched the children float makeshift paper boats in the water. Other than sharing the time and space, we didn't communicate in words.

"Chielo! Chielo!" the conductor yelled. "Let's go! Go!" The construction on the washout was complete, just wide enough for the bus wheels to drive on. Our companions filed in and took their places. The driver revved up the engine and the assistant conductor counted the bodies on board with his fingers. Satisfied that we were all there, he struck the patchy, metal ceiling, calling again, "Chielo, Chielo, Chielo!"

We bounced on the newly formed strip of gravel and down the one-lane road. Everyone was delighted to be moving again and engaged in lively chitchat. As I gazed out at the passing countryside and intermittent farmhouses, the attachment to my recent loss rapidly faded. Gradually, the population became denser and the next town appeared. Stores were open for business, selling everything from rustic wooden furniture and hardware to edibles. People milled about in the streets enjoying the sunny weather after the storms. Our driver parked in front of one of the larger cafés. As soon as we disembarked, we ran into the inspector.

"We meet again!" Miguel said with open arms. I greeted him too, but with a slight apprehension. Had he changed his mind after he'd left us at the washout and decided to collect on a bounty?

But there was no hint of betrayal. He gripped our hands solidly and bid us farewell once more. "Come back to Nepal again, and best of luck to you all!"

Our group had seated themselves in the restaurant so we joined the party. The place had four tables to accommodate up to about twenty people. Two large plate-glass windows gave us a clear view of the street. This was advantageous. Since we were not that far from the border, it was still necessary to be vigilant. We ordered sweet fresh-lime sodas—our standard drink when traveling in South Asia and a perfect refreshment for the hot, dusty trip. The Swiss congratulated us, toasted our joint success, and treated us to the meal. They were courteous. Although they must have speculated as to who the boy was, no questions were asked. We opted to not divulge that he was a reincarnate lama.

The distance between Kodari and Kathmandu was about 116 kilometers, and we had not reached the midway point. This meant another four to five hours on the road. Everyone was tired, but we had to keep moving. There were still checkpoints to cross before reaching the city, and we hoped to arrive before dark with our precious package. It was better not to tempt fate.

Shortly after our lunch break, back on the road, someone shouted out, "Here comes another one!" Sure enough, another station was on the horizon. "Let it be trouble-free," I thought, "simply raise the guardrail and let us through." My prayers were not heard.

Two police officers came on board. One guarded the entrance. The other headed straight for us with a harsh expression. The four Asians—Nyima, Migmar, Thupten, and I—were his target.

"Show me your passports!" he commanded.

Nyima pulled his out of a shirt pocket and promptly handed it over. The policeman took great pains in studying the Swiss Tibetan's ID, as he hovered over him and Rinpoche.

In haste, Nyima had thrown his backpack into Rinpoche's lap and the jacket over him. So hurried was the action that he had failed to conceal the back of the lama's head and shoulders. It was too late to readjust the cover. Nyima pressed his left forearm on the pack in attempts to disguise the child's body as part of his luggage. The configuration was odd and conspicuous. Worse, I feared that Rinpoche's legs and feet dangled from the edge of the seat and could easily be seen.

The boy remained motionless. We all tried to act cool, but my heart was pounding. I silently called for help from the Nechung Protector. "*Please!* We need some supernatural intervention!"

Instinctively, Migmar's girlfriend, whose name we later learned was Tilda, stood up and waved her ID at the officer.

"Hey, here's my passport. Look at mine!" She was almost in his face. "We're traveling together in one tourist group," she continued. "We're from Europe and live in the same town in Switzerland. We all have proper visas and documentation. Don't worry. Want to see mine?"

Her effort to direct the man's attention to herself on the opposite side of the aisle was timely. Tilda was an attractive German woman in her early thirties with blondish hair and a lovely figure—a perfect distraction. This chap was no different from other men, unable to resist the flirtations of women.

Tilda, seeing that she had caught his interest, continued to entice him. "Hey, are you hungry? Would you like to eat a banana? Here, have some of our fruit!" She started to peel a banana for him. "Here, have this. It's very good." She stretched her arm past Migmar and seductively held the ripe fruit in front of the poor fellow's face.

Tilda's trick worked perfectly. While the policeman shifted his stance toward the woman, Thupten pulled the fold on the crumpled jacket completely over Rinpoche's head.

The scene was comical, and we laughed aloud in amusement.

A smile broke out on the officer's face, and he, too, started to chuckle.

The deputy officer, our driver, and the conductors had turned around to watch. Everyone was bursting with laughter, dissipating the tension. Nyima was out of the picture, and so was the fear of Rinpoche being detected.

The officer glanced perfunctorily at Tilda and Migmar's Swiss passports. "No problem," he said. Then he turned to Tilda. "No, thank you," he said, shaking his head, rejecting the banana with an upheld hand.

We held our breaths, anticipating that he would step toward Thupten and me. Instead, he nodded at us as if to say "okay, whatever," then gestured to his partner that it was time to leave. "You can go, everything is fine," he told our group.

"Yay! Namaste!" we cheered. "Thank you! Good-bye!"

They looked satisfied and swaggered off. Our bus trundled on.

There was an outpouring of relief, followed by a release of nervous laughter and an exchange of self-congratulations. We had made it through the eighth checkpoint.

How many more rough bumps laid ahead? It didn't matter, we had to ride this roller coaster till the end.

Unfortunately, the driver and his crew had become increasingly nervous. Our last close call had confirmed how we were at the razor's edge of discovery. If caught with a refugee, they could lose their jobs. Although their wages were meager, it still meant freedom from toiling at menial labor or begging on city streets. Moreover, there would also be steep fines in excess of what could be earned in a lifetime as well as the probability of incarceration. So, they demanded extra money for their troubles. We had intended to give them a tip upon arrival at our destination, but not the sizable amount that they wanted. The driver pulled over in a convenient spot under a shady tree. He gave Thupten, Miguel, and me an ultimatum: either we produced more rupees or this was the end of the road for us and the boy.

"What are we supposed to do?" Miguel argued, "Take our stuff out and hitch rides to Kathmandu? You'll have to refund us for what we paid you!"

"We rented this bus!" one of the Swiss cried out, accompanied by the whole-hearted support of the others, each adding their remarks. "We made an agreement. They paid their share! They're our guests and travel partners. This is *our* bus, and the monk, the boy, and the couple are coming with us!"

At heart, the bus boys had no intention of giving up their fare or giving us a refund. The money they collected at the border was only a deposit, and they counted on the balance at the end of the trip. The gratuity alone would likely be more than their total earnings. In all fairness, a bonus was not unreasonable, given the weighty assignment.

"So, what are we going to do?" Miguel asked, weary of the interchange. "Are we just going to sit here for the rest of day?" His challenge was directed at the conductor and the driver; they were the apparent bosses and the ones with English comprehension.

"Sir, this *very* dangerous," the conductor said, defending his crew's position. "We cannot continue. Big trouble if we get caught!"

"Well, we can't stay here!" I interjected, crossing my arms. "There are too many of us to hitchhike, and Kathmandu is too far away to walk. Besides, you took our money and we made a deal."

"Madam, we want more money for extra difficulty. You never tell us about boy in beginning!" one of them said.

He then turned his plea to rouse Thupten's sympathy: "We work very hard, Guruji! My friends and I have nothing!" he said, raising his voice. "Nothing. This no good, no good at all!"

It was up to Thupten to utilize his skills. "Okay!" he piped up in his broken English. "Now you drive, we go Kathmandu. We give you more money. No problem. Okay?" He slapped the driver on the back twice, then grabbed the conductor's hand, "In Kathmandu, we give you big baksheesh!"

They were still reluctant. Perhaps, they assumed that the two Westerners were bankrolling the whole expedition, and that the monk was not holding the purse strings, nor the one to gift them with additional rupees.

So, Miguel reassured them. "When we get to Kathmandu, you come to our hotel, okay?" he said in his straightforward manner. "You will know where we stay, so you come tonight. We'll give a present for you and your friends to share."

Miguel's tone was sincere. "We'll be as generous as we can with you guys. We know what you're going through for us, and we appreciate it. This is very important. If we succeed, you will have done a great thing!"

They lit up. A sign of acquiescence crossed the faces of the two main guys, along with a tinge of smugness. They assumed they would be well compensated. But Miguel and Thupten had been vague about the payoff, spoke only of baksheesh, a tip; so, the amount of the gift was ours to determine.

"Chielo! Chielo! Let's go!" Thupten exclaimed.

Simple Human Smile

"How fortunate that we joined the Swiss group," I whispered to Miguel. "What would have happened if we had just hired a taxi? Where could we have hidden Rinpoche? Surely we wouldn't have gotten far." I shuddered at the thought.

The bus boys seemed to have worked through their negativity, and turned the music back on full blast. We reached into our bags for some snacks and passed around nuts and dried fruit, and the Swiss shared their chocolate and biscuits. The sugar gave us a much-needed boost. The mood became light and jovial.

This was rudely interrupted when seemingly out of nowhere, two uniformed officers appeared in view. They stood in the middle of the narrow road with machine guns slung over their shoulders. Their hands instructed the driver to halt the bus. A rush of fear surged through my body; I saw the same in Miguel's face. We braced ourselves...

A guardhouse was concealed at the edge of the forest, tucked away from the road so as not to be spotted. Three additional men, heavily-armed, were standing by this station; one of them, holding a rifle and baton, quickly joined the other two officers on the road. This was the most weaponry we had encountered since the Tibetan-Nepalese border. Between the Friendship Bridge to Kathmandu, the Nepalese Central Intelligence Division (CID) had established its tightest security until about the halfway point, thus the requisite checkpoints. The main purpose was to apprehend refugees fleeing Tibet lacking legitimate papers; once discovered and captured, punishment would be dealt accordingly. And as the border inspector told us, there were consequential arrests made for transporting bootleg alcohol, smuggling, and other illicit activities.

We were grateful that there was time for Nyima and Thupten to carefully adjust the jacket over Rinpoche. Having learned from our previous experience, we ensured that not an inch of the boy was perceptible, at least not from the waist up. In addition to the trusted backpack wedged between Nyima and Rinpoche, the Swiss Tibetan had shoved another medium-sized duffel onto Rinpoche's lap. It was full and heavy. The contents organically shifted and reshaped itself to fill the empty space between Rinpoche and the bench in front. Perhaps it was my wishful thinking that we could fool the commandos; the entire heap indeed resembled a pile of luggage.

The Captain marched up the bus stairs with an assistant in tow, while the third man guarded the entry. Tall and burly, they projected a somber, no-nonsense attitude; undoubtedly trained in the art of combat, they had the demeanor of hardened killers. Their dark eyes were sharp and incisive, noting each of our concerned faces and taking inventory of the objects on board. Their lips were pursed tightly as their muscular hands clenched their weapons. I had no doubt that they would shoot a person in the back if he tried to run away. We would not want to be in a confrontation with any of these men. It was clear that neither Tilda nor I would be able to use our feminine charm on these guys.

How were we going to get out of *this* grim situation? I closed my eyes and once again, invoked the help of the Nechung Protector to eliminate danger and obstacles.

"Whose bags?" The Captain roared, poking at some random bags in the luggage compartment behind the driver. "Let me see what's inside."

Miguel and I touched each other's hands. I leaned forward and discreetly tapped Thupten gently on the back of his neck.

"Yeah, yeah," Thupten mumbled.

Thankfully, the bags selected for inspection were not Nyima's or ours. If so, we would have had to leave our seats and move away from Rinpoche, the focal point of our concern, leaving the boy vulnerable.

Two members of the tour group stepped forward to identify their bags.

"Open them," the Captain barked, pointing his finger.

They nervously complied.

The Captain looked, but quickly lost interest. He moved down the aisle and gave his aide the pleasure of tearing apart another tourist's knapsack.

"Under these seats—why so many bags here?" He had bent over and discovered a number of smaller carry-ons. "Who's the owner? What are they? You speak English?" He kicked the bags with his boot and glared at someone in the row in front of the Tibetans.

The Swiss man in question, who was not fluent said, "Yes, sir. No, sir, I speak no English." He said something to his partner, who translated, "He said that there's nothing of importance; just some personal items and film that he took on this trip, but you are welcome to look for yourself."

Were Rinpoche's little feet dangling below the edge of the seat? "Make those feet vanish, Rinpoche!" I pleaded silently. A virtually undetectable movement took place in the load next to Nyima. Had he intuited my panic?

All three commandos were now digging through several bags simultaneously. There was nothing of interest—no evidence of terrorist activity, no gold or other valuables to confiscate. They were plainly rummaging through people's dirty clothes, underwear, smelly socks, shoes, and toiletries. When not looking fierce, they maintained solemn dispassionate expressions.

The Captain now stood over us. He looked up at the shallow metal overhead rack and saw leftovers of food and drink. He bent forward to look under Migmar and Tilda's seat and found nothing. Then he peered under Nyima's seat, and at once straightened up—emotionless, as though he had seen…Nothing!

My heart skipped a beat. Rinpoche had managed to become invisible again!

"Wait, don't be too confident," an inner voice advised. "The Captain hasn't gone yet; he's still hovering over you. What if he poked at that pile of 'luggage' next to Nyima and demanded to search it?" The consequences would be bleak.

Knowing that these men were trained to watch people's reactions, we acted indifferently, gazing blankly at the Captain as if we had nothing to hide. Then, unconsciously, without any premeditated thought, I flashed a smile. The Captain stared back at me with a mildly perplexed look; he blinked, and a faint twitch appeared on his lips.

Did anyone ever treat these guys as human beings? Or were people so afraid of them—as we were, waiting for them to go away—that they invariably reacted with gritted teeth?

Miguel followed up with a wide grin. "You see," we telegraphed with our empathetic smiles, "we recognize your human nature and understand the need to inflate your ego, but it is a fabricated illusion. It is as fragile as a bubble and can be shattered in an instant. Just like us, you want to be happy and free of life's problems. In that way, we are the same."

For a mere second, the Captain's tough stance relaxed, his locked jaw softened, and a shadow of a smile emerged on his thin lips. We had cracked the walls of his impenetrable shell and touched a strand of humanity. But as quickly as the emotion materialized, it vanished. He bellowed out a command to his subordinates, clipped his heels as he spun around, and marched off the bus.

Whether the turnaround was the Captain being caught off-guard by the simple human interaction, or the recognition that his harassment was a fake display of power, we will never know.

One thing was for sure, our protectors were taking care of us.

We had maneuvered through nine checkpoints safely and were exhausted. Battle fatigue had set in. I honestly didn't know how much more stress we could take.

It was a relief to have survived the challenges of the journey thus far, and I was grateful for the team spirit that had been generated. It didn't take long for everyone to relax. The loud, scratchy music was back on, and some people started to hum and sing along with the Indian songs, making up their own verses to the tunes.

The tenth checkpoint soon came into sight. "On the left!" Tilda called out. There wasn't much time to react. The lone guard looked as if he had been napping in his plastic chair all afternoon; he couldn't care less about our rickety old bus. The rail guard went up, and he allowed us to pass with a motion of his head.

This was a complete reversal from the last ordeal. Considering the lax attitude, we deduced that security along the road may have finally eased up. Our Swiss friends suggested that they take turns being on duty. Each stop became easier. The checkpoint monitor would call out a warning upon seeing a station, but at these latter posts, the guards did not care who was coming or going. At a couple of places, they didn't even look up.

Now that the danger was past, the crew was having a good time. When passing a station, the driver would bravely honk the horn, as a gesture of appreciation. Some of our group would lift their curtains to wave to the guards. Even Rinpoche had surfaced from beneath his disguise as a pile of luggage. Folding back a corner of the curtain, he viewed rural Nepal as the kilometers flew by.

"Please, no more incidents," I sighed, as we raced toward Kathmandu.

"We'll be there before sunset!" Miguel said with excitement in his voice. "In time for a long shower, a cold beer, and a good hot dinner." It was humid and the thought of washing off the dust and perspiration was marvelous indeed.

Miguel's prediction was almost correct. We would have arrived in Kathmandu by dusk if our bus had not broken down. We had just passed another station, where there was not a soul in sight. Rolling down the hill, it felt as if the tires had run over something jagged. Within a minute, the bus chugged to a complete stop. We were banked on the left side of the road against the face of a cliff on a blind curve. "Perfect spot to park," came Miguel's dry comment. Yes, why hadn't the driver pulled over where we could see around the corner and down the road?

The crew got to work with some basic tools aged with grease and dirt. Surprisingly, there was a threadbare spare in need of air. Other than a patch, there were no noticeable holes.

Everyone got out to stretch and breathe some of the fresh country air. Our parking spot was hazardous. Two of the boys were stretched under the vehicle with their legs extended into the road. Although there was no obvious threat, we felt exposed. Random officers may well drive by on security patrol.

Rinpoche stood in a patch of weeds observing all the newness around him. It was disconcerting to see him in that bright yellow outfit looking rather awkward amidst the group of Western tourists.

Our worries were unwarranted. The crew finished their repairs, and soon we were headed for Kathmandu. The sun was setting as we approached its urban sprawl. People and cars were everywhere, everyone was trying to get home for the evening. Our bus was just another vehicle that added to the congestion. There was one final checkpoint before we entered the city limits. The policemen were drinking tea, smoking, and conversing in and outside the station. They couldn't be bothered to stop anyone and waved us through.

Everybody beamed with joy. We leapt to our feet, clapping, cheering, and hugging each other. We had all bonded in an extraordinary way through all the risks— unshakable support, conviction, and perseverance. If Rinpoche had not been on the bus, the journey would have been just a trip on a bad road from the border, but *this* was an unforgettable adventure for every one of us.

It had been an extremely long day. Dram, that morning's point of departure, seemed in the remote past. As I recalled our successes of the day, Tibet seemed light-years away, yet remained ever-present.

I recounted all the stops, the frighteningly close calls, the kind cooperation from strangers, and the spontaneity of each situation. From Lhasa to Dram, at the Friendship Bridge, and from the Nepalese border to Kathmandu, we had skillfully maneuvered through no fewer than sixteen checkpoints. Each successful passage was unique and in its own mysterious way demonstrated that people in the world can thrive because they've learned to work together with reliance and trust.

A Brief Respite

W e were dropped off at the edge of Thamel, the tourist section of town. "Buses are not allowed into Thamel," the conductor told us. "The streets are too narrow."

And there we were, Thupten, Miguel, and I, standing on a street corner with a heap of luggage and a child. Cars, trucks, and scooters whizzed by in all directions, along with the occasional meandering cow. A traffic cop at the intersection paid no attention to us.

"We made it!" Miguel exclaimed. "We're in the clear! No one will notice us here."

"Besides," I said sarcastically, "the heavy smog in this city could easily cloak us."

Nyima settled the balance with the driver and conductor. They looked at us as if to say, "Well folks, you're in Kathmandu and we're ready for that bonus that you promised."

"Can you come by our hotel tonight?" Miguel asked. "I don't want to pull out money in public."

The conductor understood and gave a slight nod.

"How will you know where we are?" I asked. We ourselves didn't know yet.

"No worry, madam," he said wryly. "We will know."

"Okay," I thought, "if you're not worried, neither am I."

We picked up our gear and skirted around the traffic. The task of finding lodging proved effortless, since there was an abundance of guesthouses in the area. Later that evening, we joined our Swiss friends for dinner.

"We're here for a few more days," Nyima said. "Then we'll fly to Delhi to spend a couple of weeks in India before we return to Switzerland."

"We're going up to northern India," Thupten said. "My monastery is there, and that's where the boy will be ordained as a monk. Please come and visit Nechung, if you're in Dharamsala."

Before we finished our meal, who should turn up in the café but the bus driver and conductor. They *had* found us—apparently quite easily. Thupten and Miguel took them aside to give them their bonus. It was well deserved, and we had no hesitation in giving them most of our remaining cash. Luckily for all of us, Miguel had discovered some extra bills in another pair of jeans. The men were thankful and expressed how gratified they were to have helped us.

Kathmandu was not the last leg of our journey. We still had complications and challenges ahead, but none of that mattered that evening; we just wanted to revel in the triumphs of the day. Everything else could wait until the next morning.

First on our to-do-list was to get Rinpoche a change of clothes. He needed to blend in with the crowd and possibly pass for our son. It was a natural family—a forty-something couple with a child together with Thupten, who could easily pass for an uncle or older brother.

In a two-story mall in the center of the city, shopkeepers had ingeniously converted tiny spaces into packed displays for their merchandise. Almost every square inch from floor to ceiling had items for sale. Amidst the shops selling electronics were an equal number of purveyors selling household goods. There were "boutiques" that appealed to the fashionable with knockoff sneakers and Western attire, and fabric stores carried bolts of cloth with multiple patterns and colors in brocades, cottons, and silk for made-to-order outfits. We purchased a golf shirt, jeans, and a baseball cap for Rinpoche. This made us feel like proud parents of a very adorable boy.

Nechung Choktrul Rinpoche with Marya and Miguel in Kathmandu, Nepal

As aromas of spicy curry wafted in our direction, we realized that it was time for lunch. Around us lay a spectrum of stalls and tiny cafés with different fare. Local foods included deep-fried pakoras stuffed with cauliflower and potato, dahl, rice biryani, chicken tandoori, and whole wheat chapatis fresh from brick ovens. Pizzas, lamb burgers, sandwiches, and spongy cakes spilled out of fast-food outlets. Health-conscious folks could choose fresh watermelon, orange, pomegranate, and apple nectars from juice bars.

Our decision on where to eat was usually determined by cleanliness. If the dining area looked hygienic, we assumed that the food was equally decent. That day we chose a mom-and-pop joint and ordered a lunch heavy on protein and vegetables, plus a tray of saffron basmati rice. Sweet lime sodas complimented our meal, cooling our palates of chilis and rich flavors.

Afterwards, we wandered at leisure through the bazaar, with Rinpoche alternately holding either Thupten's or Miguel's hand, absorbing the new experience with wonderment.

Our respite was over too soon. We had to get back to work and figure out how to get Rinpoche safely to India. If we were to fly, that meant clearing immigration at *two* international airports—Kathmandu and Delhi. This would be no easy task, when legitimate identification papers were a requirement.

We did have a plan. It pivoted on Venerable Tenzin Choephel, one of the most dependable monks at Nechung in Dharamsala. We first met Tenzin in 1981 when he was a novice. During our year sabbatical in 1983, he was in my English class when I taught a phonetic system of reading and writing to five monks. Tenzin learned to speak fluently with scarcely an accent. He also spoke several other languages and had the competence to communicate smoothly in diverse cultures.

Before we left Lhasa, Thupten had telephoned Tenzin Choephel to say that everything was on track and that we would be in Nepal with Rinpoche in a few days. Tenzin quickly acquired a note from the Liaison Office of the Home Affairs Ministry in Dharamsala. It stated that Tenzin Losel was a bona fide monk at Nechung Monastery; he had visited relatives in Kathmandu and was returning to India after his trip to Nepal. There was no mention of a birthdate nor was a photograph included. The note had an official stamp from the office authenticating its validity. He also prepared an Identity Card from the monastery to certify that Rinpoche was one of its monks. It showed Rinpoche's name and year of birth, as well as date of issue. All the necessary information was typed in, leaving blank the places for a photograph and signature. Tenzin Choephel gave this letter and ID card to a colleague who hand-delivered them to the Tibetan Bureau in Kathmandu.

In an old-fashioned studio lit by bright lights with artificial backdrops of wallpaper landscapes and vases of pastel silk flowers, Rinpoche sat on a wooden chair to have black-and-white passport-sized photos taken for his ID. The setting reminded me of a vintage sepia photo the previous Nechung Rinpoche had taken in a Lhasa studio from the mid-forties.

The Tibetan representative was expecting us when we dropped by the bureau to pick up the documents. Thupten glued Rinpoche's photo on the monastery card, and the young lama signed his name in cursive script. It was the signature of a child still learning to write. We stapled the other photo to the top corner of the letter. These were Rinpoche's official travel papers!

It was time to move on. Although we had planned to fly, we revisited the option of going overland. That route was notorious for being troublesome in regards to distance, bad roads, and tight security. Checkpoints similar to those we had encountered from the Tibetan border would continue all the way to the Nepalese-Indian border. We had heard that upon arrival at the crossing, everything would be removed from vehicles and passengers were strip-searched. Stories abound of Tibetans being turned back in both directions. So, we decided it was best to take our chances with an airplane.

We were resolute about the success of our mission. To have found Nechung Rinpoche's reincarnation so effortlessly, to have secured the blessing of his parents, and to have escaped detection at those multiple checkpoints was a sheer miracle. As a team, we would be able to work our magic; trusting our instincts and combined abilities, we would successfully escort our precious lama through the last stages of the journey. Besides, our experience told us that inimitable opportunities cropped up to bend the rules.

"Hey, we're on a roll, right?" Miguel said, ready to finish the job. "We can't lose, and will not be stopped! We're going to keep on going…all the way to the monastery!"

"Hmm," came my quiet response, trying to not be overly confident.

The four of us had moved up the hill to the Hotel Vajra, a guesthouse removed from the honking cars and hustle bustle of the tourist town. It had intricately carved doors, antique furnishings in the lobby, and art by local artists. We had a breathtaking vista of the cityscape below us. It was also close to Swayambhu, the stupa that housed relics of the Buddha. It was an ideal refuge where we could get to know Rinpoche better.

"Kunzang Lama is back from Lhasa," Thupten announced. "He invited us to his house for lunch tomorrow."

"Wonderful," I said wryly, "I'm curious to know if the five-star general ever showed up at Dram."

We took a taxi to Kunzang Lama's house. His wife was there. She was a witty modern woman, and they seemed to be a well-matched couple. Over a home-cooked meal, we discussed the Dram border.

"Did the five-star general ever show up?" Miguel asked.

"Oh, yes," Lama answered. "He just returned yesterday. He arrived at Dram a few days late, due to the road closures and other problems. But he stayed two nights and looked all over town for you. You had already left. He brought my son's clothes from school, provisions, and a car. You could have easily left Tibet with him."

On the mantle were photos of his family, including the boy who was supposed to look like Rinpoche. We saw no resemblance whatsoever. His son was older, taller, and heavier. There was no way that Rinpoche could have passed for this boy. Nor did we have any proof, other than Kunzang Lama's word, that the general had indeed come for us at Dram. That was all irrelevant, so we graciously thanked him for his efforts.

Before leaving, Thupten suggested that we visit Swayambhu, home to a high lama named Druptop Rinpoche, a friend of the previous Nechung Rinpoche. We climbed the steps leading to the ancient temple and its adjoining quarters as chattering wide-eyed monkeys curiously watched us stride by.

As we approached, we could hear the rhythmic chants—invocations to Guru Padmasambhava, the patron saint of Tibet, and to the Nechung Protector. It was a special lunar day. The prayers were auspicious, as though the ceremonies were held for us, a thanksgiving for the safe escape of our Rinpoche.

We prostrated at the entrance and an assistant monk immediately beckoned us to join the assembly. Druptop Rinpoche was warm and welcoming. He felt privileged to be the first lama to greet the Nechung Choktrul (supreme reincarnation) Rinpoche outside of Tibet. He'd had a close affiliation with Rinpoche's predecessor, and had played a notable role in Rinpoche's 1962 escape. Kathmandu was a divine respite indeed and upon taking leave from Swayambhu, we felt uplifted, ready for the next phase of our journey.

The Kathmandu Airport

Flight reservations were easy to make. Our flight to Delhi was scheduled for Saturday, September 19th. Before long, it was time to pack, envision our goal, and face whatever challenges were ahead.

Kunzang Lama drove Rinpoche and Thupten to the airport. Miguel and I met them there and checked in with no glitches, we merely needed to name the persons on the reservation and give the flight number. I wondered why there was no request to look at our passports. Since it was an international airport, surely proof of identification for travelers was required. "That must be at immigration control," I thought.

We had plenty of time to have tea and snacks in the air-conditioned restaurant and "talk story." Unlike arrivals with the excitement of guests coming and the anticipation of what may be forthcoming, there's often not much to say at airports when bidding farewell. Departures reveal the transient nature of meeting and parting. Travelers' minds are focused toward their next destination, while those staying behind think about getting back to work and the realities of life after the visitors leave.

We had over three hours to kill. I watched the minute hand of my Swatch move in slow motion and wished that we had not come to the airport so early. Yes, I too had a Swatch; it was a limited edition that I had bought at the old Hong Kong airport with a hot pink "auspicious knot" on a bright purple face. The knot symbolizes the interdependence of everything in life—how everything is interconnected and that ultimately nothing exists on its own.

I think it's rude to tap your feet or hands. But I was becoming increasingly impatient and did exactly that. "We should walk to the gate now," I suggested, eager to get through Immigration Control and Security sooner than later.

"Oh, no," Kunzang Lama said, "there's no hurry. Let's have some more tea."

"My goodness," I thought, "how much more small talk could we conjure up?" We'd already talked about food and the weather and the political problems of Tibet, Nepal, and India, and had come up with opinions for everything. There was nothing more to say, but we continued to sit.

Finally, Miguel and I stood up, "Really, we need to go," Miguel said.

Rinpoche had been munching on some finger food and drinking sweet tea. I imagined that he was anxious about his first airplane ride. Was he wondering what the planet looked like from the sky? Surely, he was speculating about the place that he was moving to.

We queued up at the rear of a long passport control line; there were only two immigration inspectors at the counters. Since it was midday, there were several planes leaving around the same time. The process was tediously slow, and the line barely moved. I started to panic.

"This is why I wanted to be early!" I said to Miguel. "Our plane will be boarding soon."

"It's okay," he reassured me, squeezing my hand. "We'll make it."

"It's all right, don't worry," I told myself.

"C'mon! C'mon!" Thupten called out, as if that might speed up the process. Stretching his neck out and looking at the passengers ahead of us, he said, "Hurry up! Hurry up!"

We watched as the other travelers got their passports stamped; they went through the metal detector and disappeared down the concourse. Everyone was through, except one old Tibetan man and us. He was traveling alone and couldn't communicate with the immigration officials who tried to speak to him in English, Hindi, and Nepali. He spoke an obscure Tibetan dialect, and even in the heat of late summer, was dressed in a heavy black-wool *chuba*. He presented a greasy, tea-stained booklet for his identification. It was unlike anything we had seen before—a passbook from some village in Tibet. It was bogus, yet just as credible as the ID that we had for Rinpoche.

"This is unacceptable!" the exasperated officials exclaimed. "Where's your passport? Where's your visa?"

Surely they wanted a break before being swarmed by the next wave of passengers. Thupten, Miguel, and I knew that this was our opening, the signal for us to intercede. Thupten translated the Tibetan's words and included his own persuasions. He pretended not to know Hindi, so Miguel and I interpreted for him. "Look at this grandpa, he walked all the way from his nomad tent in Tibet!" Thupten quipped in Tibetan, "What hardship! He's hardly eaten for days and hasn't taken a bath for months. Look at him! Poor thing! Let him go!"

Like characters in an impromptu play, we delivered our unscripted lines. The situation was most entertaining and soon everyone—including the officials—were laughing. The officers felt compelled to stamp the old Tibetan's booklet and waved him on.

By then, we had developed a rapport with the officers. They started with Miguel's passport, followed by mine, then Thupten's IC. An American, a Canadian, and a Tibetan refugee—everything was in order—so far.

"Japan?" one of the officials asked me with a grin.

"No, Chinese," I replied pleasantly, thinking to myself, "if you had read my passport, you'd have known my birthplace."

This was good, the more conversation, the better. Befriend them. Gain their trust.

"Where are you from? America?" the other inquired.

"Hawai'i," I replied with a broad smile. This was always a winning answer everywhere in the world. People's faces light up when they hear of these islands in paradise.

"Hawai'i, beautiful place!" the officer smiled back.

"Yes, yes, it's beautiful and very far away," Miguel piped in.

"It's beautiful here too, we love coming to Nepal and India," I said, beaming. "This is like our second home.

"Okay, okay! Go, go!" Thupten urged, grabbing my wrist, looking anxiously at my watch.

"Oh, we've got to go," I said. "We're going to miss our plane!"

This was true. We were way past boarding, and the plane was about to take off. Miguel had his arm around Rinpoche. His head was counter height, and the officers' attention now focused on the boy. Enough small talk, it was time to pass the stamped letter from the Liaison Office to them. We would only use the laminated monastery card as a backup.

The letter was an unconventional piece of identification, and both the officers squinted at the single piece of paper with its stapled-on black and white photograph. One of them picked it up and turned it over, thinking that perhaps there was more on the back. Their brows furrowed. They were confused and speechless. In the silence, one could hear a pin drop.

I became very nervous but still managed a mental chuckle imagining what these guys were thinking.

"What is this? Do you have anything else?" holding up the piece of paper, directing their questions at Miguel.

Rinpoche stood on his tiptoes, propped his head on the counter, and gave the men a disarming smile.

"No," Miguel answered matter-of-factly. "This is the boy's ID. He's a monk at Nechung Monastery in Himachal. He was here for a short visit and is returning to

Dharamsala to continue his studies." Pointing to Thupten, Miguel said, "he's a monk at the monastery too."

"Yeah! No problem." Thupten said, gesturing at the official letter. "This very good! Dharamsala office stamp here. I have same. Young monk, good, good, very good!" He patted Rinpoche affectionately on the head.

Our team looked genuine—a cute innocent child, an ebullient monk in his twenties, and an interracial couple. Clearly, we were not terrorists or smugglers.

"C'mon, it's okay. We've got to go right now!" I implored with a trace of desperation in my voice. "We're going to miss our plane! Can we please go, sir?"

Duly noting our sincere pleas and not knowing how to object, I detected the faintest hint of a nod. One of the officials stamped our letter with the exit stamp. Then, with a wave of his hands in the direction of security, a mere few yards away, he indicated that we could go.

"Thank you! Thank you!" We voiced our gratitude and gave both men solid handshakes.

Yes, we had passed the seventeenth checkpoint! But we had yet another predicament. The security metal detector wasn't functioning. Everything had been shut down since the rest of the travelers were long gone, and no one was manning it!

"Oh, no!" I cried. "You've got to be kidding! This must be a joke!" I threw up my hands, and turned around to catch the Immigration officials' attention with shock in my eyes. "What should we do?" I asked. The situation was so ludicrous.

"Can you guys come over and turn the machine on so that we can go through?" Miguel had become animated. Expressing disbelief that no one was there to man the station, he demanded immediate action.

Even Rinpoche looked inquisitively at the Nepalese guys, as if asking, "What's up?"

"That's not our job," they shrugged. "We don't have any authority to be at that security post."

What could those underpaid guards do? It wasn't as if the positions were interchangeable. There was no one to call and no place to go. We were caught in a tiny area between Immigration Control and Security, with no one in sight who could assist us! We were already late; for all we knew, the plane had already taken off. The thought of having to rebook our flights and repeat this entire scenario with different players was daunting.

Suddenly a voice shouted out, "Just go!" It was one of the two inspectors, waving his arms with authority. "Okay, okay, you can go! Go!" he repeated.

We charged through the dysfunctional metal detector with gratitude for their change of heart. Turning around, we waved. "Thank you! Thank you very much!"

We raced down the concourse toward our gate. We were over an hour late, but the plane was still there—with its doors wide open, it was boarding a few last passengers. Indian and Nepalese time had worked in our favor. The local deities and the wind horse of good fortune were flying by our side.

On to Delhi

Normally I sleep on planes, dozing off before they're even airborne, but this day was different. Relaxation was difficult since we still had one last hurdle before freedom.

Thupten sat next to Rinpoche who had a window seat and was staring into the clouds. Being exposed to a whole new world, what must he be thinking, I thought for the hundredth time.

Miguel held my hand discreetly and looked over at me, "We're almost there, just one more stop."

"Yeah," I said, "the good thing about the Delhi airport is that everything is familiar, and we know exactly where we're going."

We had passed through the terminal over a dozen times on our trips to India, often during the wee hours of the night. I pictured the layout of the airport and the escalator that delivered passengers down to the ground level where immigration officers would wait for the rich mix of international travelers and Indian nationals.

Indians were a colorful bunch and fascinating to observe—many still dressed up for travel in the day. Women often dressed up in embellished saris and other traditional attire with armloads of bangles and ornate jewelry. Sikh men donned colorful turbans that concealed their long hair and rolled-up beards. Those returning from abroad proudly sported new jeans and sneakers.

Most foreigners came from various Western countries and spoke English or a variety of European languages. These adventurers would be decked out in hiking boots, fleece pullovers and twill cargo pants, sporting camera bags and backpacks. With each passing year, we'd see more visitors and tour groups from Asia in the immigration lines.

We landed without incident. Several planes had arrived at the same time, from both east and west. Arriving passengers picked up their paces on the concourse, trying to get a few steps ahead of others so that they could be first in queue. We watched the little old ladies, the alpha males, even those with physical handicaps; all were hurrying as fast as they could.

"We're going into the fast line today, Miguel," I told my husband, as we scurried alongside the other passengers. "We will not get behind anyone slow with problems. Okay?"

It was an ongoing joke. Sometimes, one of us would wait in one line, while the other would stand in the next. That way, we could move laterally when one proved faster than another. I would make a terrible gambler since I consistently pick the wrong one.

"Sure, whatever you say," Miguel snickered. "Lady's choice."

At the top of the escalator, with a full view of the entire immigration area, we scoped out the scene. Seven counters were open with several hundred people in overflowing lines.

"Wow! After racing down here, I thought that we'd be here first," I said, disappointed. "But here we are close to the end again."

Next came the game of chance—choosing the quickest moving line. We had to use our analytical skills: Do those people have the necessary documents and visas? Will that officer be lenient on the individuals because they are visitors? Will he be tough for the same reason? Is one line shorter and being processed faster?

Dozens of tourists waited in the central aisle, mostly middle aged, clean-cut, and fairly well dressed. It was the shortest line. "We can't go wrong in that one," I thought; so, I suggested we join it.

"Looks good," Thupten agreed.

Miguel offered no opinion.

Well, guess what? I had picked the slowest line, the one that didn't move! We surmised they were Russian refugees with no proper travel documents. By the animated gestures and raised voices, we gathered that the group spoke little or no English. How they had gotten on a plane and arrived in Delhi, we will never know; they must have not checked for IDs and visas at the port of origination.

Several officials had gathered around this booth, curious onlookers amused at the entire incident. Meanwhile, people to the left and right of us cleared immigration one by one and disappeared into the next foyer to collect their luggage off the carousels. Steadily, the hundreds of passengers began to diminish while we remained motionless.

"I cannot believe this!" Miguel grumbled. "This is ridiculous. We're getting nowhere!"

Miguel is usually a patient man, but the one thing that frustrates him most is waiting in long lines. His tolerance had reached its limit, and he voiced his frustration loud and clear. Even Rinpoche, in his quiet nonchalance, began showing signs of fatigue.

We had been in line for nearly two hours, which is unusual even in this country. By then, our team had separated into three rows—Rinpoche accompanied by Thupten, Miguel in a second, and me in the third. But no matter where we stood, we always appeared to be at the end of the line. For some odd reason, we could not advance to a counter where we could hand our passports to someone. We were last *again*!

By then, everyone was gone except for the Russians and us. One official, surrounded by multiple sidekicks, was mulling over their plight. "Who are all those guys?" Miguel said snidely. "How many men does it take to stamp a passport?"

Most of the immigration officers had retired into back rooms, and the ones remaining were packing up their briefcases and rubber stamps. Several of them stood by the wall staring at us, laughing and joking as if they found our predicament extremely amusing. Looking over at them, I, too started to giggle. It *was* comical, and the best way to endure it was to not be the brunt of the joke, but to join the laughter.

Finally, Miguel and I walked up to a counter, hoping for some sympathetic assistance.

"Hey, can you help us?" Miguel asked, somewhat belligerently. "We've been here for over two hours! Everyone else that came in has gone except for us."

The fellow would not even look up. He had no desire to tackle four more cases. Instead, he said, "Sir, I cannot help you. This line is closed. Go over there." He pointed his finger to another booth at the opposite end.

We hastened over, but once again, received no service.

"You go there," said that officer, shooing us away, referring to no one in particular. "He can help you. My work is finished." Then with that distinct Indian gesture of swaying the head from side to side, he turned his back and walked away.

Besides the men dealing with the Russians, there was one last person at his station, a younger man in his early-thirties with a pleasant face who didn't look too burned out. He had met my glance for a second and then quickly turned his face away. "What the heck," I thought, "let's ask him." *Someone* had to come to our aid.

I started off with a big smile, then tried to hand him our passports and Thupten's IC. "Hey, how are you?" I said cordially, then kept talking to get his attention. "You're not leaving, are you? You've got to help us. Everyone is gone. We've been waiting and waiting. It's been over two hours. We've got to go. Our friends are waiting outside for us…"

I held out our documents at arm's length, shaking them every now and then, while extending my hand onto his counter. "C'mon, you've got to help us! You can't leave us standing here. You're the only one left."

After several minutes of this cajoling, his face cracked into a big grin, and he started to chortle. "Madam, I cannot help you. My work is finished for the day," he said. "Look!" He gestured to his cleared-off desktop, as if to say, "Even if I wanted to, I can't."

"No, no, you've got to help us. You know you can!" Then I added: "You're the boss here. You can do whatever you want!"

This caught his attention and his demeanor changed. He really wasn't the boss, but that didn't matter. He was proud that someone thought that he was important.

Miguel noticed this and stroked the man's ego even more. "Yeah, c'mon, you're in charge, you can do it! We come to Delhi every year because we love this place. We recognize you from our previous trips. You're a good man!"

"Babuji," Thupten called out, addressing him with a polite term for "sir." "Very good, Babuji! Very good job!"

By then, the young man was beaming from ear to ear. He opened Miguel and my passports and checked our visas. Then he pulled out a well-used logbook. In it, he wrote our names, passport numbers, visa numbers, and date of arrival. "How long are you staying in India?" he inquired.

"Just one week," I answered, "this is a short trip. We must return to Hawai'i."

"Hawai'i! You live in Hawai'i?" he said, starting to enjoy the interchange. "Is it beautiful there?"

We were enjoying it too, especially since he was stamping our passports. "Yeah, it's very beautiful—it's warm all year around. Hawai'i is a wonderful place, there are friendly people everywhere." Just keep talking, I thought, keep him interested and entertained.

He finished processing our entry and handed back our passports.

Thupten had no problems. Delhi was a principal port of entry and Indian government-issued ICs were familiar here. There are no complications if the ICs are current and an entry visa accompanies a valid "No Objection to Return to India" (NORI) stamp. He noted Thupten's information in his logbook and promptly handed the IC back.

"What about the boy?" the immigration officer asked. Miguel handed him the letter with the attached photo of Rinpoche.

"You have another passport?" He looked confused.

"No, this is it," Miguel said. "This is all we have."

"I cannot accept this," he said, furrowing his brow. "This is no good!" He shoved the letter firmly back at us like he meant business.

"Uh-oh! Better do some fast-talking," I thought. Unless we convinced him otherwise, this was it. We would all be escorted to the interrogation room for questioning, and Rinpoche would be caught in limbo at the Delhi Airport. We could not subject him to this fate.

"This *is* the boy's ID, sir," I tried. "He's too young to get an IC. He's a monk at our monastery, and these are the papers that Tibetans under twelve years of age use for travel. It's true!" I engaged every emotion that I could muster, but there was no reaction from the official.

"Just keep going, Marya," I told myself, "at least he's allowing you to explain."

"We just came from Nepal, and they were fine with these papers. No one gave us any trouble at the Kathmandu airport!" I held out the paper. "See, they stamped it. C'mon, we have to go!" I followed this with a drawn-out, "Pleeeease!" tapping into every ounce of feminine charm I had.

The poor chap stared long and hard at me, and I smiled pleadingly. Then he shifted his attention to Rinpoche, Miguel, and Thupten. Rinpoche looked innocent. Miguel was our rock. Thupten exemplified a lama's self-confidence. What a team!

The immigration officer bit his lips and cast his eyes downward in careful consideration.

Meanwhile, the Russians and the Indian officials battled on, their loud voices filling the void in our own negotiation. There were too many bodies to shuffle into a back room and there were no expeditious procedures to grant them asylum.

Finally, after what felt like another aeon, the inspector silently conceded. With an upturned palm, he gestured for our paperwork. Miguel rapidly handed it to him. We remained very still, barely breathing, lest he change his mind.

*Tat-tat-tat-tat-tat…*he made imprints all over Rinpoche's paperwork with each of his many stamps.

"Enjoy your stay in India!" he said, acting pleased with his decision.

I let out a gleeful cry. "Oh, thank you! Thank you very much! You deserve a promotion. We're going to write a letter of recommendation for you!"

We tried not to appear too eager as we raced off to pick up our luggage. Our bags had been meticulously placed together with other unclaimed items next to the carousel which had long since stopped running. Everyone was gone and it was eerily quiet.

As we headed towards the departure aisle leading to the exit, I was astonished to catch sight of Customs Officers flanking the aisle. Why would so many still be there when no passengers remained?

We had nothing to declare. Our bags were mostly filled with care packages that had nothing of monetary value. So, we headed straight for the Green Line designating that there were no imported items to declare. We smiled and acknowledged the first set of men.

"Japanese? You come from Japan?" they asked me.

I gave the same answers to these standard questions. "Hawai'i, Chinese! Bye, bye!" I replied with a big grin and a little wave of the hand.

Immediately, the men started chattering in Hindi. They jabbed each other and laughed amongst themselves like schoolboys. We joined their joyousness—indeed, it was nearly time to celebrate.

Rinpoche decided that he wanted to play, and for the first time since the Dram border, he acted like a little boy. He jumped up on the luggage cart, and balanced himself on the top of bags closest to the front wheels. The kid wanted a ride.

Miguel, relishing the moment, picked up his pace and started pushing the trolley as if in a race for the finish line. Another seven or eight men guarded the exit, but their tough persona was no match for the charm of this delightful scene. Everyone clapped as Rinpoche flew by—it seemed as if he were on a palanquin on the rooftop of the world!

The double doors parted, and we saw the beaming faces of our monks. Venerable Thupten Ngodup, the Nechung Medium accompanied by Venerable Tenzin Choephel, and other assistants were there. How we had waited for this moment!

Just then, two officers approached us. "Do you have anything to declare?"

"Nope, nothing! Nothing at all!" Miguel and I answered together, and handed them our customs forms. They reached for the slips of paper, and, with that characteristic head gesture, signaled us through.

Pushed forward by a fresh breeze of energy, we sailed through the exit gates—the last of eighteen checkpoints. The entire road to freedom had been extraordinary and miraculous!

Arrival at Nechung

We headed for Nechung Monastery in Dharamsala in Himachal Pradesh at the foothills of the Himalayas of northern India. It was a glorious welcome. The entire road from the main gate of Gangchen Kyishong to the monastery was festooned with banners and crowds of people bowing in respect with offering scarves in their hands. Auspicious symbols were sketched in powdered lime on the ground each step of the way. Rich incense aromas and billows of cedar, juniper, and sandalwood drifted toward us as we arrived at Nechung.

The deep resonance of Tibetan horns filled the mountain air. The Nechung monks were lined up at the monastery entrance and down the steps to the monastic gate. They were dressed in their best robes and ceremonial hats. Our senior monks were at the head of the procession with tears of happiness in their eyes. It was joyous, beautiful, and moving.

Nechung Choktrul Rinpoche was home.

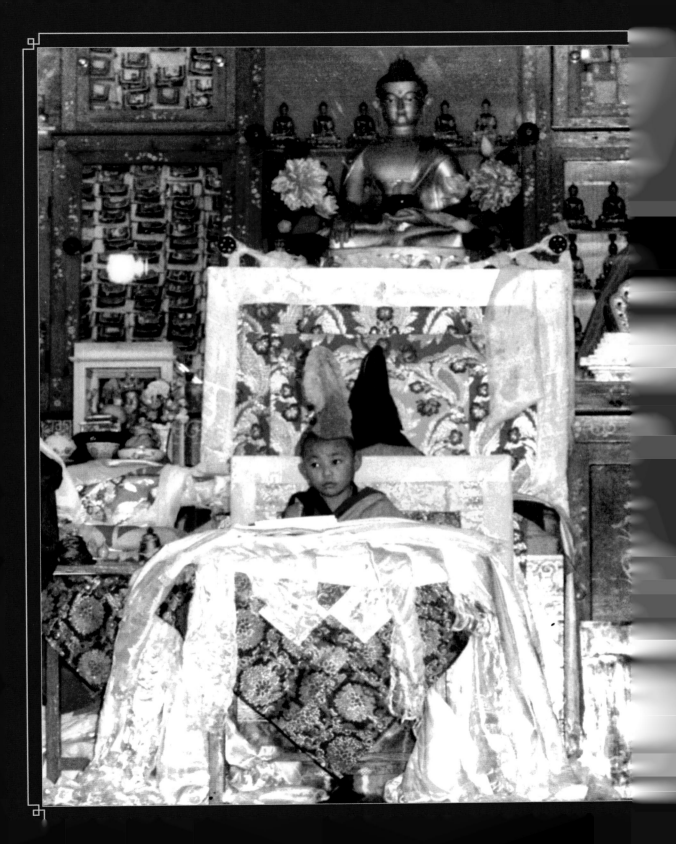

THE ENTHRONEMENT

On March 13, 1995, Nechung Choktrul Rinpoche received his novice vows from His Holiness the Dalai Lama in Dharamsala, India. This was his formal ordination ceremony, an important moment in the life of a monk. There are thirty-two precepts for a novice monk, including the root vows of celibacy and abstaining from killing, lying, stealing, and intoxicants. In the customary manner, His Holiness ordained three boys at a time, and Rinpoche received his vows with two other lamas. Several other boys from Nechung Monastery were ordained on the same day.

Nechung Choktrul Rinpoche and the monks returned to the monastery in the afternoon and were greeted by the familiar sound of ceremonial horns and trumpets from the rooftop. They filed into the main temple hall and took their respective places. Rinpoche sat on his throne, flanked by the other monks in the order of their seniority. Venerable Thupten Ngodup, the Seventeenth Nechung Kuten, the Vajracharya Thupten Damchoe, and the monastery's senior monks all presented Rinpoche with silk *kata* offering scarves. The next to go up were Rinpoche's family members—his mother, grandmother, and uncle—who came from Tibet for the occasion. Lastly, it was Tiapala, Miguel and I, representing the Nechung household, followed by monks and other guests. Ceremonial rice and tea were offered, and good fortune prayers were recited before Rinpoche was escorted back to his quarters.

The enthronement was scheduled two days later on Wednesday, March 15, 1995. The occasion was attended by several hundred invited guests, including representatives of the Tibetan Government-in-Exile, assistants of various high lamas, administrators from monasteries, and members of the Nechung community from Lhasa, Dharamsala, Nepal, the U.S. mainland, Europe, and Hawai'i. Many of Tiapala's relatives also came from Ladakh.

Hand-painted auspicious symbols of wheels and conches decorated the pathways outside the monastery. Festive banners with the appliquéd knot of eternity fluttered merrily in the mountain breezes. Rhododendrons were in full bloom on this beautiful spring day.

The morning began with Khamtrul Rinpoche bestowing an initiation from a *terma* called "Sunlight of Interdependence." He gave a brief talk on Dzogchen, saying, in the ultimate sphere of reality, there is no duality such as good and bad. However, since we live in a phenomenal world where everything is relative to causes and conditions, it is important to create the interdependent conditions for auspiciousness and good fortune.

He also gave an introduction to the *terma*—a Dharma treasure revealed by the previous Terton Sogyal Rinpoche during the time of the Thirteenth Dalai Lama. Though Sogyal Rinpoche had the *terma* in his possession, it remained sealed, needing a key element to open it; which in this case, were several strands of a woman's blond hair. With the persistence and collaboration of the Thirteenth Dalai Lama, who realized that the *terma* would be of great benefit in the future, an attempt to procure this rare item (in Tibet) was made.

One early morning, a crow—manifestation of Sogyal Rinpoche's personal protector—was set free from the temple rooftops. Around its neck were pearls, gold, and other precious gems. Ten days later, they witnessed the return of the crow, very weak, with tattered feathers, as though he had traveled an extensive distance. The strands of jewels were missing from his neck and in their place were golden strands of hair!

With this essential substance, the *terma* was opened, to reveal many teachings, including "Sunlight of Interdependence." Sogyal Rinpoche gave the oral transmission to Aben Tulku, who transmitted it to Khamtrul Rinpoche, the third holder of the lineage. This *terma* has strong associations with the West, and Khamtrul Rinpoche laughed about how he had teased the present Dalai Lama about the interdependence of this treasure and his influence in the West.

After the initiation and a short break, the actual enthronement ceremony took place. Several Nechung monks and Miguel escorted Rinpoche from his quarters to the main temple hall. After prostrating, Rinpoche ascended the throne to sit in front of the whole assembly of monks and attendees. The image of Shakyamuni Buddha was directly behind him, surrounded by all the deities and lamas of the lineage.

In the traditional manner, prayers for auspiciousness were recited; tea and sweet rice served, and gifts were offered to Rinpoche's family as symbols of gratitude and friendship. Rinpoche's mother wept tears of joy, extremely moved by the moment.

Arhat prayers for longevity were recited as numerous guests filed up to present *katas* and offerings to Nechung Choktrul Rinpoche and his family. The heap of white scarves was so high that at times it was hard to see Rinpoche behind it! What a momentous, unforgettable occasion!

EPILOGUE

Nechung Choktrul Rinpoche is now thirty-five years old. He has lived in northern India since leaving Tibet in September 1993 at the age of eight. His primary home has been Nechung Monastery in Dharamsala in Himachal Pradesh. For over a decade at Nechung, he memorized prayers from the general Buddhist texts, learned ritual practices specific to the monastery, and attended philosophy classes there.

In 2007, Rinpoche entered Mindrolling Monastery located in Clement Town, a small Tibetan settlement a day's drive from Dharamsala. There he completed a nine-year program on Buddhist Sutra and Tantra. As an ordained Buddhist monk, he received thorough training in a formal college setting with strict ethical discipline and educational standards.

Annually, Rinpoche and the Mindrolling monks took breaks from their studies. During these periods, he attended further teachings from lineage lamas and joined the Nyingma Prayer Festival in Bodhgaya, the site of the Buddha's enlightenment. He spent the late winter and early spring months at Nechung Monastery and participated in the monastery's annual ceremonies. After graduating in 2016, he served as an adjunct professor at Mindrolling for three consecutive years; this tenure ended in 2019.

Rinpoche has visited Nechung Dorje Drayang Ling in Wood Valley, Hawai'i nine times. The first was in April 1994, a few months after he left Tibet, during His Holiness the Dalai Lama's second visit to the temple. The most recent stay was in the spring of 2019. At that time, he was in residence for ten weeks and taught classes on the basics of Buddhist practice. He has also attended rituals and taught at the Nechung centers in New York, San Francisco, and Los Angeles.

Nechung Choktrul Rinpoche has not seen his father since their farewell at the Dram border in 1993. His father continues to work as a government employee in Tibet. He has not risked his livelihood and his family's security by taking a leave of absence. His mother and grandmother were able to acquire the necessary paperwork for travel from Lhasa to India via Nepal, and came to see him on three occasions, including his enthronement.

Rinpoche speaks with his family by phone on occasion, but only when they call him on a secure line. Tibetans continue to fear surveillance by Chinese authorities and repercussions if sensitive subject matter is overheard. Consequently, they do not breathe the name of the Dalai Lama, nor discuss Buddhism or politics.

Between September 2002 and January 2010, eight official delegations of personal envoys for His Holiness the Dalai Lama have met with Chinese officials. These meetings created an official platform for the Tibetan and Chinese governments to have an open dialogue on issues of concern, although overall progress and benefit is uncertain.

In 2011, His Holiness retired from an active role in politics. A democratic process was initiated to elect officials for the Central Tibetan Administration (Tibetan Government-in-Exile), and there is widespread participation amongst the Tibetans. A Sid-Gyong, or political leader, elected by the Tibetan community worldwide, has been serving as the political successor to His Holiness.

In many ways, the human rights situation in Tibet has not improved. Severe repression of self-determination, speech, and religion continues unabated. In recent years, over one hundred-fifty monks, nuns, and laypersons of all ages have martyred themselves in acts of self-immolation due to desperation and frustration with the ongoing occupation.

Moreover, the Chinese government tightly controls spiritual and cultural matters and now claims to be the only authority to choose lamas' reincarnations. This usurped authority is invalid and has never been within the scope of Chinese jurisdiction.

Although autonomy for Tibet has not been achieved to date, His Holiness the Dalai Lama remains optimistic that change will come.

Nechung Dorje Drayang Ling Monastery, Dharamsala, Himachal Pradesh, India

Nechung Choktrul Rinpoche on monastery rooftop, circa February 1997

Nechung Choktrul Rinpoche at Maui Dharma Center, Island of Maui

H.H. the Dalai Lama with Marya and Miguel upon
his arrival at the temple on April 17, 1994

Nechung Kuten, Nechung Choktrul Rinpoche and monks awaiting His Holiness the Dalai Lama's arrival at Nechung Dorje Drayang Ling on April 17, 1994.

Nechung Dorje Drayang Ling, Wood Valley, Island of Hawai'i

Nechung Choktrul Rinpoche with Marya and Miguel at Gyuto Monastery,
Dharamsala, India, July 2016

Nechung Choktrul Rinpoche at Nechung Dorje Drayang Ling,
Hawai'i, April 2019

ACKNOWLEDGEMENTS

His Holiness the Fourteenth Dalai Lama is recognized by innumerable people throughout the world as a man of peace sharing his message of kindness and selflessness. For Tibetans, he is a manifestation of infinite compassion, a tireless leader guiding his people and keeping Tibetan culture alive and flourishing. On a personal level, through his teachings and exemplary behavior, His Holiness has inspired us to cultivate altruistic intention and actions, core principles that he has instilled in us over the decades. Furthermore, I offer our utmost gratitude for his invaluable advice in the search and discovery of the reincarnation of Nechung Rinpoche which led to the events described in this book.

It is our teacher-student relationship with Nechung Rinpoche, the Venerable Thupten Konchok Palzangpo (1917–1983) that set forth the conditions for us to be closely affiliated with Nechung Dorje Drayang Ling Monastery. Henceforth, we became members of the search party for his reincarnation. Rinpoche imparted teachings that ranged from the ordinary to the profound, and we were given the opportunity to live, study, and work with a lama of high caliber day and night. This experience is something that one can only dream of and is rarely possible nowadays. I will forever treasure those precious years.

I am grateful for all the teachings and initiations of our numerous root and lineage gurus. Over fifty lamas have visited and taught at our remote temple and retreat on the Island of Hawai'i, some on multiple occasions. In particular, we are thankful for the support and blessings of the late Khenpo Jigme Phuntsok Rinpoche and Khamtrul Rinpoche, for our mission to find Nechung Rinpoche in Tibet.

I thank the Seventeenth Nechung Kuten, Venerable Thupten Ngodup. As the current Medium of Tibet's Chief State Oracle, he has the formidable role of going into trance to convey the Nechung Oracle's message when consulted on important matters of religion and state, including the identification of lamas' reincarnations.

I also wish to acknowledge the kindness of the Vajracharya Thupten Phuntsok and Kushog Wangyal (Venerable Thupten Sherab), the late senior monks of Nechung Monastery. Their trust and encouragement made our active participation in the quest for Rinpoche's reincarnation possible.

Recognition needs to be given to the late Venerable Lobzang Toldan "Tiapala" for his years of dedication at the temple from 1984 to 2016, especially serving as a caretaker during our many trips abroad.

Much credit goes to Venerable Thupten who fostered the contacts in Tibet that gave us the ability to integrate into the close-knit community of Lhasa. Thupten's communication skills and partnership were essential to the ultimate success of the search, discovery, and escape. His fearlessness and patriotism are exemplary and incomparable.

Venerable Tenzin Choephel's (Kushog Karma) assistance was indispensable for the young Rinpoche's flight from Nepal to India. He also helped with the painstaking task of fact-checking historical references, correcting Tibetan phonetics, and the glossary for this book. For all this, I offer my heartfelt appreciation.

My deepest gratitude goes to our friends in Tibet who provided courageous assistance. With their unwavering support and strength, we negotiated the most precarious of circumstances. Their knowledge and personal connections were instrumental in securing the facts and resources necessary for the accomplishment of our goal.

I offer my appreciation for the encouragement from all those who read the manuscript: Sophia Schweitzer and Julie Falicki for their reading of the first draft; John and Maile Bay for their editorial suggestions; and Catherine Robbins and Debbie Uchida for their constructive remarks.

I am grateful to Tom Peek who guided me through the manuscript revision process; Cynthia Col and Genelle Izumi for reading the finished manuscript and for their editing skills; Garret Izumi for his meticulous work on the photographs that were taken by numerous photographers over the decades; and Claire Flint Last for the cover design and layout of this book.

Lastly, a very special thanks to Glenda Izumi for her enthusiasm, diligence, and whose invaluable assistance was vital for the completion of this project. Every one of these friends inspired me to share this story with all who may be interested.

Needless to say, I could not have embarked on this amazing life journey, including all these adventures, without my beloved husband, Miguel. Our shared experiences go beyond what can be expressed in words. The interdependence of conditions generated by our relationship created the auspiciousness of everything that has manifested, including our life-long work at our temple and retreat in Hawai'i. The merit resulting from anything that I have done must be shared with him.

May our joint efforts, great, medium or small, be of limitless benefit to numerous living beings throughout the world!

—Marya Waifoon Schwabe
Wood Valley, Island of Hawai'i
November 1, 2020

The Symbolism
of the Tibetan Flag

- In the center stands a magnificent snow-clad mountain, which represents the great nation of Tibet, widely known as the Land of Snows.

- Across the dark blue sky, six red beams spread, representing the original ancestral lineages of the Tibetan people. The combination of the two-colored beams symbolizes the protection of the spiritual teachings and secular life by the dark blue *(Palden Lhamo)* and red *(Nechung Dorje Drakden)* guardian protectors with which Tibet has a special connection.

- At the tip of the snow mountain, the sun with its rays brilliantly shining in all directions represents the equal enjoyment of freedom, spiritual and material happiness, and prosperity by all beings in the land of Tibet.

- On the slopes of the mountain proudly stand a pair of snow lions blazing with the manes of fearlessness, which represents the country's victorious accomplishment of a unified spiritual and secular life.

- The three-sided yellow border represents the flourishing of the Buddha's teachings. The side without a border represents Tibet's openness to non-Buddhist thought.

- The beautiful, radiant three-colored jewel held aloft represents the ever-present reverence held by the Tibetan people towards the Three Supreme Jewels (the Buddhist objects of refuge: Buddha, Dharma and Sangha).

- The two-colored swirling jewel held between the two lions represents the people guarding and cherishing the self discipline of correct ethical behavior, principally represented by the practices of the ten exalted virtues and the sixteen humane modes of conduct.

Courtesy of International Campaign for Tibet

Statement of
His Holiness the Dalai Lama

On the Fiftieth Anniversary of the Tibetan National Uprising Day Central Tibetan Administration (CTA)

Today is the fiftieth anniversary of the Tibetan people's peaceful uprising against communist China's repression in Tibet. Since last March, widespread peaceful protests have erupted across the whole of Tibet. Most of the participants were youths born and brought up after 1959, who have not seen or experienced a free Tibet. However, the fact that they were driven by a firm conviction to serve the cause of Tibet that has continued from generation to generation is indeed a matter of pride. It will serve as a source of inspiration for those in the international community who take keen interest in the issue of Tibet. We pay tribute and offer our prayers for all those who died, were tortured and suffered tremendous hardships including during the crisis last year, for the cause of Tibet since our struggle began.

Around 1949, communist forces began to enter northeastern and eastern Tibet (Kham and Amdo) and by 1950, more than 5000 Tibetan soldiers had been killed. Taking the prevailing situation into account, the Chinese government chose a policy of peaceful "liberation, "which in 1951 led to the signing of the 17-Point Agreement and its annexation. Since then, Tibet has come under the control of the People's Republic of China. However, the Agreement clearly mentions that Tibet's distinct religion, culture and traditional values would be protected.

Between 1954 and 1955, I met with most of the senior Chinese leaders in the Communist Party, government and military, led by Chairman Mao Zedong, in Beijing. When we discussed ways of achieving the social and economic development of Tibet, as well as maintaining Tibet's religious and cultural heritage, Mao Zedong and all the other leaders agreed to establish a preparatory committee to pave the way for the implementation of the autonomous region, as stipulated in the Agreement, rather than establishing a military administrative commission. From about 1956 onwards, however, the situation took a turn for the worse with the imposition of ultra-leftist policies in Tibet. Consequently, the assurances given by higher authorities were not implemented on the ground. The forceful implementation of the so-called "democratic reform" in the Kham and Amdo regions of Tibet, which did not accord with prevailing conditions, resulted in immense chaos and destruction. In Central Tibet, Chinese officials forcibly and deliberately violated the terms of the 17-Point Agreement, and their heavy-handed tactics increased day by day. These desperate developments left the Tibetan people with no alternative but to launch a peaceful uprising on 10 March 1959. The Chinese authorities responded with unprecedented force that led to the killing, arrests and imprisonment of tens of thousands of Tibetans in the following months. Consequently, accompanied by a small party of Tibetan government officials including some Kalons (Cabinet Ministers), I escaped into exile in India. Thereafter, nearly a hundred thousand Tibetans fled into exile in India, Nepal and Bhutan. During the escape and the months that followed they faced unimaginable hardship, which is still fresh in Tibetan memory.

Having occupied Tibet, the Chinese communist government carried out a series of repressive and violent campaigns that have included "democratic reform," class struggle, communes, the Cultural Revolution, the imposition of martial law, and more recently the patriotic reeducation and the strike-hard campaigns. These thrust Tibetans into such depths of suffering and hardship that they literally experienced hell on earth. The immediate result of these campaigns was the deaths of hundreds of thousands of Tibetans. The lineage of the Buddha Dharma was severed. Thousands of religious and cultural centers such as monasteries, nunneries and temples were razed to the ground. Historical buildings and monuments were demolished. Natural resources have been indiscriminately exploited. Today, Tibet's fragile environment has been polluted, massive deforestation has been carried out and wildlife, such as wild yaks and Tibetan antelopes, are being driven to extinction.

These 50 years have brought untold suffering and destruction to the land and people of Tibet. Even today, Tibetans in Tibet live in constant fear and the Chinese authorities remain constantly suspicious of them. Today, the religion, culture, language and identity, which successive generations of Tibetans have considered more precious than their lives, are nearing extinction; in short, the Tibetan people are regarded like criminals deserving to be put to death. The Tibetan people's tragedy was set out in the late Panchen Rinpoche's 70,000-character petition to the Chinese government in 1962. He raised it again in his speech in Shigatse in 1989 shortly before he died, when he said that what we have lost under Chinese communist rule far outweighs what we have gained. Many concerned and unbiased Tibetans have also spoken out about the hardships of the Tibetan people.

Even Hu Yaobang, the Communist Party Secretary, when he arrived in Lhasa in 1980, clearly acknowledged these mistakes and asked the Tibetans for their forgiveness. Many infrastructural developments such as roads, airports, railways, and so forth, which seem to have brought progress to Tibetan areas, were really done with the political objective of sinicising Tibet at the huge cost of devastating the Tibetan environment and way of life.

As for the Tibetan refugees, although we initially faced many problems such as great differences of climate and language and difficulties earning our livelihood, we have been successful in reestablishing ourselves in exile. Due to the great generosity of our host countries, especially India, Tibetans have been able to live in freedom without fear. We have been able to earn a livelihood and uphold our religion and culture. We have been able to provide our children with both traditional and modern education, as well as engaging in efforts to resolve the Tibet issue. There have been other positive results too. Greater understanding of Tibetan Buddhism with its emphasis on compassion has made a positive contribution in many parts of the world.

Immediately after our arrival in exile I began to work on the promotion of democracy in the Tibetan community with the establishment of the Tibetan Parliament-in-Exile in 1960. Since then, we have taken gradual steps on the path to democracy and today our exile administration has evolved into a fully functioning democracy with a written charter of its own and a legislative body. This is indeed something we can all be proud of.

Since 2001, we have instituted a system by which the political leadership of Tibetan exiles is directly elected through procedures similar to those in other democratic systems. Currently, the directly elected Kalon Tripa's (Cabinet Chairperson) second term is underway. Consequently, my daily administrative responsibilities have reduced and today I am in a state of semi-retirement. However, to work for the just cause of Tibet is the responsibility of every Tibetan, and as long as I live, I will uphold this responsibility.

As a human being, my main commitment is in the promotion of human values; this is what I consider the key factor for a happy life at the individual, family and community level. As a religious practitioner, my second commitment is the promotion of inter-religious harmony. My third commitment is of course the issue of Tibet. This is firstly due to my being a Tibetan with the name of "Dalai Lama"; more importantly, it is due to the trust that Tibetans both inside and outside Tibet have placed in me. These are the three important commitments, which I always keep in mind.

In addition to looking after the well-being of the exiled Tibetan community, which they have done quite well, the principal task of the Central Tibetan Administration has been to work towards the resolution of the issue of Tibet. Having laid out the mutually beneficial Middle-Way policy in 1974, we were ready to respond to Deng Xiaoping when he proposed talks in 1979. Many talks were conducted and fact-finding delegations dispatched. These however, did not bear any concrete results and formal contacts eventually broke off in 1993.

Subsequently, in 1996-97, we conducted an opinion poll of the Tibetans in exile, and collected suggestions from Tibet wherever possible, on a proposed referendum, by which the Tibetan people were to determine the future course of our freedom struggle to their full satisfaction. Based on the outcome of the poll and the suggestions from Tibet, we decided to continue the policy of the Middle-Way.

Since the re-establishment of contacts in 2002, we have followed a policy of one official channel and one agenda and have held eight rounds of talks with the Chinese authorities. As a consequence, we presented a Memorandum on Genuine Autonomy for the Tibetan People, explaining how the conditions for national regional autonomy as set forth in the Chinese constitution would be met by the full implementation of its laws on autonomy. The Chinese insistence that we accept Tibet as having been a part of China since ancient times is not only inaccurate, but also unreasonable. We cannot change the past no matter whether it was good or bad. Distorting history for political purposes is incorrect.

We need to look to the future and work for our mutual benefit. We Tibetans are looking for a legitimate and meaningful autonomy, an arrangement that would enable Tibetans to live within the framework of the People's Republic of China. Fulfilling the aspirations of the Tibetan people will enable China to achieve stability and unity. From our side, we are not making any demands based on history. Looking back at history, there is no country in the world today, including China, whose territorial status has remained forever unchanged, nor can it remain unchanged.

Our aspiration that all Tibetans be brought under a single autonomous administration is in keeping with the very objective of the principle of national regional autonomy. It also fulfills the fundamental requirements of the Tibetan and Chinese peoples. The Chinese constitution and other related laws and regulations do not pose any obstacle to this and many leaders of the Chinese Central Government have accepted this genuine aspiration. When signing the 17-Point Agreement, Premier Zhou Enlai acknowledged it as a reasonable demand. In 1956, when establishing the Preparatory Committee for the "Tibet Autonomous Region," Vice-Premier Chen Yi pointing at a map said, if

Lhasa could be made the capital of the Tibet Autonomous Region, which included the Tibetan areas within the other provinces, it would contribute to the development of Tibet and friendship between the Tibetan and Chinese nationalities, a view shared by the Panchen Rinpoche and many Tibetan cadres and scholars. If Chinese leaders had any objections to our proposals, they could have provided reasons for them and suggested alternatives for our consideration, but they did not. I am disappointed that the Chinese authorities have not responded appropriately to our sincere efforts to implement the principle of meaningful national regional autonomy for all Tibetans, as set forth in the constitution of the People's Republic of China.

Quite apart from the current process of Sino-Tibetan dialogue having achieved no concrete results, there has been a brutal crackdown on the Tibetan protests that have shaken the whole of Tibet since March last year. Therefore, in order to solicit public opinion as to what future course of action we should take, the Special Meeting of Tibetan exiles was convened in November 2008. Efforts were made to collect suggestions, as far as possible, from the Tibetans in Tibet as well. The outcome of this whole process was that a majority of Tibetans strongly supported the continuation of the Middle-Way policy. Therefore, we are now pursuing this policy with greater confidence and will continue our efforts towards achieving a meaningful national regional autonomy for all Tibetans.

From time immemorial, the Tibetan and Chinese peoples have been neighbors. In future too, we will have to live together. Therefore, it is most important for us to coexist in friendship with each other.

Since the occupation of Tibet, the Communist China has been publishing distorted propaganda about Tibet and its people. Consequently, there are, among the Chinese populace, very few people who have a true understanding about Tibet. It is, in fact, very difficult for them to find the truth. There are also ultra-leftist Chinese leaders who have, since last March, been undertaking a huge propaganda effort with the intention of setting the Tibetan and Chinese peoples apart and creating animosity between them. Sadly, as a result, a negative impression of Tibetans has arisen in the minds of some of our Chinese brothers and sisters. Therefore, as I have repeatedly appealed before, I would like once again to urge our Chinese brothers and sisters not to be swayed by such propaganda, but, instead, to try to discover the facts about Tibet impartially, so as to prevent divisions among us. Tibetans should also continue to work for friendship with the Chinese people.

Looking back on 50 years in exile, we have witnessed many ups and downs. However, the fact that the Tibet issue is alive and the international community is taking growing interest in it is indeed an achievement. Seen from this perspective, I have no doubt that the justice of Tibet's cause will prevail, if we continue to tread the path of truth and non-violence.

As we commemorate 50 years in exile, it is most important that we express our deep gratitude to the governments and peoples of the various host countries in which we live. Not only do we abide by the laws of these host countries, but we also conduct ourselves in a way that we become an asset to these countries. Similarly, in our efforts to realize the cause of Tibet and uphold its religion and culture, we should craft our future vision and strategy by learning from our past experience.

I always say that we should hope for the best, and prepare for the worst. Whether we look at it from the global perspective or in the context of events in China, there are reasons for us to hope for a quick resolution of the issue of Tibet. However, we must also prepare ourselves well in case the Tibetan struggle goes on for a long time. For this, we must focus primarily on the education of our children and the nurturing of professionals in various fields. We should also raise awareness about the environment and health, and improve understanding and practice of non-violent methods among the general Tibetan population.

I would like to take this opportunity to express my heartfelt gratitude to the leaders and people of India, as well as its Central and State Governments, who despite whatever problems and obstacles they face, have provided invaluable support and assistance over the past 50 years to Tibetans in exile. Their kindness and generosity are immeasurable. I would also like to express my gratitude to the leaders, governments and people of the international community, as well as the various Tibet Support Groups, for their unstinting support.

May all sentient beings live in peace and happiness.

—The Dalai Lama
10 March 2009

Courtesy of www.dalailama.com

AN EXPLANATION OF REINCARNATION

by H.H. the Dalai Lama

Introduction

My fellow Tibetans, both in and outside Tibet, all those who follow the Tibetan Buddhist tradition, and everyone who has a connection to Tibet and Tibetans: due to the foresight of our ancient kings, ministers and scholar-adepts, the complete teaching of the Buddha, comprising the scriptural and experiential teachings of the Three Vehicles and the Four Sets of Tantra and their related subjects and disciplines flourished widely in the Land of Snow. Tibet has served as a source of Buddhist and related cultural traditions for the world. In particular, it has contributed significantly to the happiness of countless beings in Asia, including those in China, Tibet and Mongolia.

In the course of upholding the Buddhist tradition in Tibet, we evolved a unique Tibetan tradition of recognizing the reincarnations of scholar-adepts that has been of immense help to both the Dharma and sentient beings, particularly to the monastic community.

Since the omniscient Gedun Gyatso was recognized and confirmed as the reincarnation of Gedun Drub in the fifteenth century and the Gaden Phodrang Labrang (the Dalai Lama's institution) was established, successive reincarnations have been recognized. The third in the line, Sonam Gyatso, was given the title of the Dalai Lama. The Fifth Dalai Lama, Ngawang Lobsang Gyatso, established the Gaden Phodrang Government in 1642, becoming the spiritual and political head of Tibet. For more than 600 years since Gedun Drub, a series of unmistaken reincarnations has been recognized in the lineage of the Dalai Lama.

The Dalai Lamas have functioned as both the political and spiritual leaders of Tibet for 369 years since 1642. I have now voluntarily brought this to an end, proud and satisfied that we can pursue the kind of democratic system of government flourishing elsewhere in the world. In fact, as far back as 1969, I made clear that concerned people should decide whether the Dalai Lama's reincarnations should continue in the future. However, in the absence of clear guidelines, should the concerned public express a strong wish for the Dalai Lamas to continue, there is an obvious risk of vested political interests misusing the reincarnation system to fulfill their own political agenda. Therefore, while I remain physically and mentally fit, it seems important to me that we draw up clear guidelines to recognize the next Dalai Lama, so that there is no room for doubt or deception. For these guidelines to be fully comprehensible, it is essential to understand the system of Tulku recognition and the basic concepts behind it. Therefore, I shall briefly explain them below.

Past and future lives

In order to accept reincarnation or the reality of Tulkus, we need to accept the existence of past and future lives. Sentient beings come to this present life from their previous lives and take rebirth again after death. This kind of continuous rebirth is accepted by all the ancient Indian spiritual traditions and schools of philosophy, except the Charvakas, who were a materialist movement. Some modern thinkers deny past and future lives on the premise that we cannot see them. Others do not draw such clear-cut conclusions on this basis.

Although many religious traditions accept rebirth, they differ in their views of what it is that is reborn, how it is reborn, and how it passes through the transitional period between two lives. Some religious traditions accept the prospect of future life, but reject the idea of past lives.

Generally, Buddhists believe that there is no beginning to birth and that once we achieve liberation from the cycle of existence by overcoming our karma and destructive emotions, we will not be reborn under the sway of these conditions. Therefore, Buddhists believe that there is an end to being reborn as a result of karma and destructive emotions, but most Buddhist philosophical schools do not accept that the mind-stream comes to an end. To reject past and future rebirth would contradict the Buddhist concept of the ground, path and result, which must be explained on the basis of the disciplined or undisciplined mind. If we accept this argument, logically, we would also have to accept that the world and its inhabitants come about without causes and conditions. Therefore, as long as you are a Buddhist, it is necessary to accept past and future rebirth.

For those who remember their past lives, rebirth is a clear experience. However, most ordinary beings forget their past lives as they go through the process of death, intermediate state and rebirth. As past and future rebirths are slightly obscure to them, we need to use evidence-based logic to prove past and future rebirths to them.

There are many different logical arguments given in the words of the Buddha and subsequent commentaries to prove the existence of past and future lives. In brief, they come down to four points: the logic that things are preceded by things of a similar type, the logic that things are preceded by a substantial cause, the logic that the mind has gained familiarity with things in the past, and the logic of having gained experience of things in the past.

Ultimately all these arguments are based on the idea that the nature of the mind, its clarity and awareness, must have clarity and awareness as its substantial cause. It cannot have any other entity such as an inanimate object as its substantial cause. This is self-evident. Through logical analysis we infer that a new stream of clarity and awareness cannot come about without causes or from unrelated causes. While we observe that mind cannot be produced in a laboratory, we also infer that nothing can eliminate the continuity of subtle clarity and awareness.

As far as I know, no modern psychologist, physicist, or neuroscientist has been able to observe or predict the production of mind either from matter or without cause. There are people who can remember their immediate past life or even many past lives, as well as being able to recognize places and relatives from those lives. This is not just something that happened in the past. Even today there are many people in the East and West, who can recall incidents and experiences from their past lives. Denying this is not an honest and impartial way of doing research, because it runs counter to this evidence. The Tibetan system of recognizing reincarnations is an authentic mode of investigation based on people's recollection of their past lives.

How rebirth takes place

There are two ways in which someone can take rebirth after death: rebirth under the sway of karma and destructive emotions and rebirth through the power of compassion and prayer. Regarding the first, due to ignorance negative and positive karma are created and their imprints remain on the consciousness. These are reactivated through craving and grasping, propelling us into the next life. We then take rebirth involuntarily in higher or lower realms. This is the way ordinary beings circle incessantly through existence like the turning of a wheel. Even under such circumstances ordinary beings can engage diligently with a positive aspiration in virtuous practices in their day-to-day lives. They familiarize themselves with virtue that at the time of death can be reactivated providing the means for them to take rebirth in a higher realm of existence. On the other hand, superior Bodhisattvas, who have attained the path of seeing, are not reborn through the force of their karma and destructive emotions, but due to the power of their compassion for sentient beings and based on their prayers to benefit others. They are able to choose their place and time of birth as well as their future parents. Such a rebirth, which is solely for the benefit of others, is rebirth through the force of compassion and prayer.

The meaning of Tulku

It seems the Tibetan custom of applying the epithet 'Tulku' (Buddha's Emanation Body) to recognized reincarnations began when devotees used it as an honorary title, but it has since become a common expression. In general, the term Tulku refers to a particular aspect of the Buddha, one of the three or four described in the Sutra Vehicle. According to this explanation of these aspects of the Buddha, a person who is totally bound by destructive emotions and karma has the potential to achieve the Truth Body (Dharmakaya), comprising the Wisdom Truth Body and Nature Truth Body. The former refers to the enlightened mind of a Buddha, which sees everything directly and precisely, as it is, in an instant. It has been cleared of all destructive emotions, as well as their imprints, through the accumulation of merit and wisdom over a long period of time. The latter, the Nature Truth Body, refers to the empty nature of that all-knowing enlightened mind. These two together are aspects of the Buddhas for themselves. However, as they are not directly accessible to others, but only amongst the Buddhas themselves, it is imperative that the Buddhas manifest in physical forms that are accessible to sentient beings in order to help them. Hence, the ultimate physical aspect of a Buddha is the Body of Complete Enjoyment (Sambhogakaya), which is accessible to superior Bodhisattvas, and has five definite qualifications such as residing in the Akanishta Heaven. And from the Body of Complete Enjoyment are manifested the myriad Emanation Bodies or Tulkus (Nirmanakaya), of the Buddhas, which appear as gods or humans and are accessible even to ordinary beings. These two physical aspects of the Buddha are termed Form Bodies, which are meant for others.

The Emanation Body is three-fold: a) the Supreme Emanation Body like Shakyamuni Buddha, the historical Buddha, who manifested the twelve deeds of a Buddha such as being born in the place he chose and so forth; b) the Artistic Emanation Body which serves others by appearing as craftsmen, artists and so on; and c) the Incarnate Emanation Body, according to which Buddhas appear in various forms such as human beings, deities, rivers, bridges, medicinal plants, and trees to help sentient beings. Of these three types of Emanation Body, the reincarnations of spiritual masters recognized and known as 'Tulkus' in Tibet come under the third category. Among these Tulkus there may be many who are truly qualified Incarnate Emanation Bodies of the Buddhas, but this does not necessarily apply to all of them. Amongst the Tulkus of Tibet there may be those who are reincarnations of superior Bodhisattvas, Bodhisattvas on the paths of accumulation and preparation, as well as masters who are evidently yet to enter these Bodhisattva paths. Therefore, the title of Tulku is given to reincarnate Lamas either on the grounds of their resembling enlightened beings or through their connection to certain qualities of enlightened beings.

As Jamyang Khyentse Wangpo said: "Reincarnation is what happens when someone takes rebirth after the predecessor's passing away; emanation is when manifestations take place without the source's passing away."

Recognition of Reincarnations

The practice of recognizing who is who by identifying someone's previous life occurred even when Shakyamuni Buddha himself was alive. Many accounts are found in the four Agama Sections of the Vinaya Pitaka, the Jataka Stories, the Sutra of the Wise and Foolish, the Sutra of One Hundred Karmas and so on, in which the Tathagata revealed the workings of karma, recounting innumerable stories about how the effects of certain karmas created in a past life are experienced by a person in his or her present life. Also, in the life stories of Indian masters, who lived after the Buddha, many reveal their previous places of birth. There are many such stories, but the system of recognizing and numbering their reincarnations did not occur in India.

The system of recognizing reincarnations in Tibet

Past and future lives were asserted in the indigenous Tibetan Bon tradition before the arrival of Buddhism. And since the spread of Buddhism in Tibet, virtually all Tibetans have believed in past and future lives. Investigating the reincarnations of many spiritual masters who upheld the Dharma, as well as the custom of praying devotedly to them, flourished everywhere in Tibet. Many authentic scriptures, indigenous Tibetan books such as the Mani Kabum and the Fivefold Kathang Teachings and others like the Books of Kadam Disciples and the Jewel Garland: Responses to Queries, which were recounted by the glorious, incomparable Indian master Dipankara Atisha in the eleventh century in Tibet, tell stories of the reincarnations of Arya Avalokiteshvara, the Bodhisattva of Compassion. However, the present tradition of formally recognizing the reincarnations of masters first began in the early thirteenth century with the recognition of Karmapa Pagshi as the reincarnation of Karmapa Dusum Khyenpa by his disciples in accordance with his prediction. Since then, there have been seventeen Karmapa incarnations over more than nine hundred years.

Similarly, since the recognition of Kunga Sangmo as the reincarnation of Khandro Choekyi Dronme in the fifteenth century there have been more than ten incarnations of Samding Dorje Phagmo. So, among the Tulkus recognized in Tibet there are monastics and lay tantric practitioners, male and female. This system of recognizing the reincarnations gradually spread to other Tibetan Buddhist traditions, and Bon, in Tibet. Today, there are recognized Tulkus in all the Tibetan Buddhist traditions, the Sakya, Geluk, Kagyu and Nyingma, as well as Jonang and Bodong, who serve the Dharma. It is also evident that amongst these Tulkus some are a disgrace.

The omniscient Gedun Drub, who was a direct disciple of Je Tsongkhapa, founded Tashi Lhunpo Monastery in Tsang and took care of his students. He passed away in 1474 at the age of 84. Although initially no efforts were made to identify his reincarnation, people were obliged to recognize a child named Sangye Chophel, who had been born in Tanak, Tsang (1476), because of what he had to say about his amazing and flawless recollections of his past life. Since then, a tradition began of searching for and recognizing the successive reincarnations of the Dalai Lamas by the Gaden Phodrang Labrang and later the Gaden Phodrang Government.

The ways of recognizing reincarnations

After the system of recognizing Tulkus came into being, various procedures for going about it began to develop and grow. Among these some of the most important involve the predecessor's predictive letter and other instructions and indications that might occur; the reincarnation's reliably recounting his previous life and speaking about it; identifying possessions belonging to the predecessor and recognizing people who had been close to him. Apart from these, additional methods include asking reliable spiritual masters for their divination as well as seeking the predictions of mundane oracles, who appear through mediums in trance, and observing the visions that manifest in sacred lakes of protectors like Lhamo'i Latso, a sacred lake south of Lhasa.

When there happens to be more than one prospective candidate for recognition as a Tulku, and it becomes difficult to decide, there is a practice of making the final decision by divination employing the dough-ball method (zen tak) before a sacred image while calling upon the power of truth.

Emanation before the passing away of the predecessor

Usually a reincarnation has to be someone's taking rebirth as a human being after previously passing away. Ordinary sentient beings generally cannot manifest an emanation before death (ma-dhey tulku), but superior Bodhisattvas, who can manifest themselves in hundreds or thousands of bodies simultaneously, can manifest an emanation before death. Within the Tibetan system of recognizing Tulkus there are emanations who belong to the same mind-stream as the predecessor, emanations who are connected to others through the power of karma and prayers, and emanations who come as a result of blessings and appointment.

The main purpose of the appearance of a reincarnation is to continue the predecessor's unfinished work to serve Dharma and beings. In the case of a Lama who is an ordinary being, instead of having a reincarnation belonging to the same mind-stream, someone else with connections to that Lama through pure karma and prayers may be recognized as his or her emanation. Alternatively it is possible for the Lama to appoint a successor who is either his disciple or someone young who is to be recognized as his emanation. Since these options are possible in the case of an ordinary being, an emanation before death that is not of the same mind-stream is feasible. In some cases, one high Lama may have several reincarnations simultaneously, such as incarnations of body, speech and mind and so on. In recent times, there have been well-known emanations before death, such as Dudjom Jigdral Yeshe Dorje and Chogye Trichen Ngawang Khyenrab.

Using the Golden Urn

As the degenerate age gets worse, and as more reincarnations of high Lamas are being recognized, some of them for political motives, increasing numbers have been recognized through inappropriate and questionable means, as a result of which huge damage has been done to the Dharma.

During the conflict between Tibet and the Gurkhas (1791–93) the Tibetan Government had to call on Manchu military support. Consequently, the Gurkha military was expelled from Tibet, but afterwards Manchu officials made a 29-point proposal on the pretext of making the Tibetan Government's administration more efficient. This proposal included the suggestion of picking lots from a Golden Urn to decide on the recognition of the reincarnations of the Dalai Lamas, Panchen Lamas and Hutuktus, a Mongolian title given to high Lamas. Therefore, this procedure was followed in the case of recognizing some reincarnations of the Dalai Lama, Panchen Lama and other high Lamas. The ritual to be followed was written by the Eighth Dalai Lama Jampel Gyatso. Even after such a system had been introduced, this procedure was dispensed with for the Ninth, Thirteenth and myself, the Fourteenth Dalai Lama.

Even in the case of the Tenth Dalai Lama, the authentic reincarnation had already been found and in reality this procedure was not followed, but in order to humor the Manchus it was merely announced that this procedure had been observed.

The Golden Urn system was actually used only in the cases of the Eleventh and Twelfth Dalai Lamas. However, the Twelfth Dalai Lama had already been recognized before the procedure was employed. Therefore, there has only been one occasion when a Dalai Lama was recognized by using this method. Likewise, among the reincarnations of the Panchen Lama, apart from the Eighth and the Ninth, there have been no instances of this method being employed. This system was imposed by the Manchus, but Tibetans had no faith in it because it lacked any spiritual quality. However, if it were to be used honestly, it seems that we could consider it as similar to the manner of divination employing the dough-ball method (zen tak).

In 1880, during the recognition of the Thirteenth Dalai Lama as the reincarnation of the Twelfth, traces of the Priest-Patron relationship between Tibet and the Manchus still existed. He was recognized as the unmistaken reincarnation by the Eighth Panchen Lama, the predictions of the Nechung and Samye oracles, and by observing visions that appeared in Lhamo'i Latso; therefore the Golden Urn procedure was not followed. This can be clearly understood from the Thirteenth Dalai Lama's final testament of the Water-Monkey Year (1933) in which he states:

"As you all know, I was selected not in the customary way of picking lots from the golden urn, but my selection was foretold and divined. In accordance with these divinations and prophecies I was recognized as the reincarnation of the Dalai Lama and enthroned."

When I was recognized as the Fourteenth incarnation of the Dalai Lama in 1939, the Priest-Patron relationship between Tibet and China had already come to an end. Therefore, there was no question of any need to confirm the reincarnation by employing the Golden Urn. It is well-known that the then Regent of Tibet and the Tibetan National Assembly had followed the procedure for recognizing the Dalai Lama's reincarnation taking account of the predictions of high Lamas, oracles and the visions seen in Lhamoi Latso; the Chinese had no involvement in it whatever. Nevertheless, some concerned officials of the Kuomintang later cunningly spread lies in the newspapers claiming that they had agreed to forego the use of the Golden Urn and that Wu Chung-tsin presided over my enthronement, and so on. This lie was exposed by Ngabo Ngawang Jigme, the Vice-Chairman of the Standing Committee of the National People's Congress, who the People's Republic of China considered to be a most progressive person, at the Second Session of the Fifth People's Congress of the Tibet Autonomous Region (31st July 1989). This is clear, when, at the end of his speech, in which he gave a detailed explanation of events and presented documentary evidence, he demanded:

"What need is there for the Communist Party to follow suit and continue the lies of the Kuomintang?"

Deceptive strategy and false hopes

In the recent past, there have been cases of irresponsible managers of wealthy Lama-estates who indulged in improper methods to recognize reincarnations, which have undermined the Dharma, the monastic community and our society. Moreover, since the Manchu era Chinese political authorities repeatedly engaged in various deceitful means using Buddhism, Buddhist masters and Tulkus as tools to fulfill their political ends as they involved themselves in Tibetan and Mongolian affairs. Today, the authoritarian rulers of the People's Republic of China, who as communists reject religion, but still involve themselves in religious affairs, have imposed a so-called re-education campaign and declared the so-called Order No. Five, concerning the control and recognition of reincarnations, which came into force on 1st September 2007. This is outrageous and disgraceful. The enforcement of various inappropriate methods for recognizing reincarnations to eradicate our unique Tibetan cultural traditions is doing damage that will be difficult to repair.

Moreover, they say they are waiting for my death and will recognize a Fifteenth Dalai Lama of their choice. It is clear from their recent rules and regulations and subsequent declarations that they have a detailed strategy to deceive Tibetans, followers of the Tibetan Buddhist tradition and the world community. Therefore, as I have a responsibility to protect the Dharma and sentient beings and counter such detrimental schemes, I make the following declaration.

The next incarnation of the Dalai Lama

As I mentioned earlier, reincarnation is a phenomenon which should take place either through the voluntary choice of the concerned person or at least on the strength of his or her karma, merit and prayers. Therefore, the person who reincarnates has sole legitimate authority over where and how he or she takes rebirth and how that reincarnation is to be recognized. It is a reality that no one else can force the person concerned, or manipulate him or her. It is particularly inappropriate for Chinese communists, who explicitly reject even the idea of past and future lives, let alone the concept of reincarnate Tulkus, to meddle in the system of reincarnation and especially the reincarnations of the Dalai Lamas and Panchen Lamas. Such brazen meddling contradicts their own political ideology and reveals their double standards. Should this situation continue in the future, it will be impossible for Tibetans and those who follow the Tibetan Buddhist tradition to acknowledge or accept it.

When I am about ninety I will consult the high Lamas of the Tibetan Buddhist traditions, the Tibetan public, and other concerned people who follow Tibetan Buddhism, and re-evaluate whether the institution of the Dalai Lama should continue or not. On that basis we will take a decision. If it is decided that the reincarnation of the Dalai Lama should continue and there is a need for the Fifteenth Dalai Lama to be recognized, responsibility for doing so will primarily rest on the concerned officers of the Dalai Lama's Gaden Phodrang Trust. They should consult the various heads of the Tibetan Buddhist traditions and the reliable oath-bound Dharma Protectors who are linked inseparably to the lineage of the Dalai Lamas. They should seek advice and direction from these concerned beings and carry out the procedures of search and recognition in accordance with past tradition. I shall leave clear written instructions about this. Bear in mind that, apart from the reincarnation recognized through such legitimate methods, no recognition or acceptance should be given to a candidate chosen for political ends by anyone, including those in the People's Republic of China.

—The Dalai Lama
Dharamsala
September 24, 2011

Courtesy of www.dalailama.com

GLOSSARY

Abbreviations

CID	Central Intelligence Department
CTS	China Travel Service
FIT	Foreign Independent Traveler
IC	Identity Certificate
LTWA	Library of Tibetan Works and Archives
NORI	No Objection to Return to India
PLA	People's Liberation Army
PRC	People's Republic of China

Buddhist Terms

Avalokiteshvara
Bodhisattva of Compassion (Tibetan: Chenrezig).

Bardo
An intermediate state, often in relation to the period between death and rebirth.

Bodhisattva
Someone motivated to achieve enlightenment for the sake of benefiting living beings.

Bum Tsok
Bum (one hundred thousand) Tsok (offerings), indicating that the offering verses are recited one hundred thousand times by the assembled participants during a prayer ritual.

Buddha Dharma
Doctrine of the Buddha.

Chod
A meditative practice for eliminating karmic debt and realizing the wisdom of selflessness.

Circumambulation
The practice of walking in a clockwise direction around temples, sacred sites, and stupas as a devotional activity.

Dharma
Teachings of the Buddha and the spiritual path that transforms and endows the mind and behavior with positive qualities.

Dorje
(Sanskrit: vajra) symbolizes immutability, steadfastness, and indestructibility.

Empowerment
see Initiation.

Five Wisdom Buddhas
Vairocana, Aksobhya, Ratnasambhava, Amitabha, and Amoghasiddhi are the Five Wisdom Buddhas, symbolic of wisdom of reality, mirror-like wisdom, wisdom of equality, wisdom of discernment, and all-accomplishing wisdom respectively.

Initiation
Sometimes referred to as empowerment, this is conferred by a qualified lama who has received and accomplished the lineage of the practice.

1. A permission (Tibetan: je-nang) initiation bestows the body, speech, and mind blessings of the deity and grants the practitioner permission to visualize a particular deity, recite the mantra, and meditate on the nature of mind.

2. An empowerment (Tibetan: wong) is more elaborate, and most often associated with higher tantras. It generally has four main parts: vase, secret, wisdom, and word empowerments.

Kalachakra
This is an Anuttarayoga (highest yoga) tantra, symbolic of a balance of elements in the outer world and inner body. Kalachakra (Tibetan: Due-Khor) means "wheel of time." As of 2017, His Holiness the Fourteenth Dalai Lama has bestowed thirty-four Kalachakra empowerments dedicated to world peace. The first was given at the Norbu Lingka in Lhasa, Tibet in May 1954, and the most recent was in January 2017 in Bodhgaya, India.

Karma
Results produced by causal actions.

Kushog
Venerable One, an honorific term for some monastics.

Kuten
A human medium who serves as a channel for a protector entity and may verbally communicate messages or predictions during a trance.

Lama
La (high)—exalted in realization, exceptional in teaching, outstanding in moral character; Ma (mother)—someone who cares for all living beings with love and kindness like a mother for her only child. Sometimes a person may be called a lama if he/she engages in a lengthy retreat or if they don monastic robes, but a lama in the true sense should have the qualities as described.

Lineage
There are four main lineages in Tibetan Buddhism—one "old" and three "new." The oldest lineage, Nyingma, was established in the eighth century; subsequently, various teachers founded the newer lineages—Sakya, Kagyu and Gelug. Each has respective sub-traditions; there are also other schools such Jonang and Bodong.

Maitreya
The future Buddha.

Mandala

1. A symbolic offering of everything precious in the universe, there can be reference to a thirty-seven aspect mandala presentation or an abbreviated seven-part mandala.

2. The celestial abode of a deity, with the main Buddha or deity in the center, surrounded by a retinue, offering gods and goddesses, protectors, symbols, etc.

Manjushri

Bodhisattva of Wisdom—in general, Manjushri has five aspects: Golden Manjushri, Youthful Manjushri, White Manjushri, Blue Manjushri, and Manjushri Seated upon a Lion. There is also a black Manjushri as appeared to Je Tsongkhapa in a vision.

Mantra

The word mantra means protection of mind from ordinary perception and view of reality. Mantras are also Sanskrit syllables associated with various Buddhas and deity yoga to be recited during various phases of meditation and ritual.

Mudra

A symbolic hand gesture used while making offerings and invocations, etc.

Nechung Choekyong

The Nechung Protector Dorje Drakden—Nechung Choekyong and Palden Lhamo are the two principal protectors of Tibet and the Dalai Lamas. Nechung Choekyong in trance is also called the Nechung Oracle. Facilitating these trances is one of the primary functions of Nechung Monastery, in addition to performing daily recitations and rituals associated with the Nechung Choekyong.

Nechung Kuten

The Medium of the Nechung Choekyong (*see* Kuten).

Nechung Oracle

see Nechung Choekyong.

Ngondro

Preliminary contemplative and meditative practices for purification and accumulation of merit.

Palden Lhamo
A female protectress, Palden Lhamo is one of the two principal state protectors.

Pehar
The supernatural entity that Padmasambhava "bound to oath" to be the powerful guardian protector.

Phowa
Transference of consciousness at the time of death, ideally to a pure realm.

Prostration
The Tibetan tradition utilizes body (physical prostration), speech (recitation of refuge prayers), and mind (visualization of objects in refuge in their true nature).

Refuge
The threshold into Buddhism is taking refuge in the Three Jewels—the Buddha (symbol of awakened enlightenment), the Dharma (teachings), and the Sangha (monastics and spiritual community).

Rinpoche
Precious One—Rinpoche is a title given to a person with outstanding qualities. Often synonymous with lama, Rinpoche is accompanied by another name to identify a specific lama.

Sangha
Spiritual community (Tibetan: Ge-dun)—Those who aspire for virtue, often monastics or a dharma support group. Sangha also refers to the Bodhisattva sangha, such as Avalokiteshvara, Manjusri, Vajrapani, etc., or the Arhat sangha (the highest order of ordained disciples of the Buddha).

Shakyamuni
The Buddha of the current time, whose teachings are still taught, studied, and practiced by Buddhists around the world.

Sky burial
The practice of offering human remains to vultures after a person has passed.

Stupa
A monument symbolic of the enlightened mind.

Tantra
An esoteric class of teachings and practices—generally divided into: Kriya (action), Carya (performance), Yoga, and Annuttarayoga (highest yoga) Tantras. There are also Father, Mother, and Non-dual Tantras.

Terma
A sacred object or practice that is hidden or "buried" by Padmasambhava, to be revealed by a Terton in a future time to bring benefit to the world and living beings.

Terton
Someone who has the strong karmic connection and ability to "reveal" terma treasures or sacred objects.

Three Yanas
1. Theravadin is a practice where the practitioner seeks self-liberation and includes the precepts of ordination.

2. Mahayana is the great path that focuses on altruism and benefiting others, both in thought and action.

3. Vajrayana is the tantric path, where one trains to pierce the illusory veil of existence and view the world and sentient beings as deities in their natural pristine state.

Tsok
1. Accumulation of merit and wisdom.

2. Congregation—a gathering of people and/or offerings.

3. A ceremony during which foods and offerings are presented, and people gather for recitations, prayers, and ritual.

Tulku
Emanation body or the reincarnation of a lama.

Vajra

see Dorje.

Vajrakilaya Tantra

A tantra and practice to overcome outer, inner, and secret obstructions that give rise to full realization.

Vajrayana

The tantric or secret mantra path with numerous methods and levels of training and practice.

Yoga

Commonly known as physical yogas for fitness and spirituality; it can also represent the various aspects of Buddhist Tantra.

Yogi/Yogini

An accomplished practitioner of various yogas.

Cultural Terms

Butter Tea

A traditional Tibetan beverage—black tea churned with milk, butter, and a pinch of salt.

Chuba

A dress for women, often worn over a wrap-style blouse; men's chubas have long sleeves and are worn over shirts.

Dzi

Natural dzi stones are believed to bestow good fortune and health, as well as possess mystical attributes such as protection from physical and psychic harms. The original source of these beads is a mystery. While the traditional, antique beads are greatly preferred, new modern-made dzi are gaining in popularity.

Kata

A long scarf that is presented as an offering to teachers, shrines, and holy places. Katas are usually silk or rayon in white, but can be in primary colors, and are used for special occasions.

Losar

Tibetan New Year falls on the first day of the first lunar month; this date varies yearly in the western calendar.

Mo

A divination performed using various methods such as dice, beads, mirror, etc.

Momo

Meat, cheese or vegetable dumplings.

Namaste

A respectful Indian greeting.

Sha-dreh

Meat stew served with rice.

Tashi Delek

A Tibetan greeting—Tashi (good fortune), De (happiness), Lek (goodness).

Thangka

Sacred art, traditionally a scrolled painting or a silk, embroidered appliqué featurings images of Buddhas, spiritual teachers, and deities.

Tsampa

Flour from parched roasted barley, a staple food of Tibetans.

Yar-Tsa Gun-Bu

A chameleon-like medicinal herb found at high altitudes in the mountains of Tibet; Cordyceps Sinensis is its scientific name.

Eminent Personages

Dordrak Rigzin Chenmo
The head of Jangter, a sub-tradition of the Nyingma lineage, and head lama of Dorje Drak Monastery.

Drikung Rinpoche
The two head lamas, Drikung Chetsang Rinpoche and Drikung Chungtsang Rinpoche, of Drikung Monastery renowned for Phowa practice.

Gampopa
"The Physician from Gampo" Sonam Rinchen (1079–1153) was the main student of Milarepa and a highly regarded Tibetan Buddhist teacher who codified his own master's teachings which form the foundation of the Kagyu educational tradition.

Ganden Tripa
The head of the Gelug lineage, one of the four main traditions of Tibetan Buddhism.

Gedhun Choekyi Nyima
In 1995, His Holiness the Dalai Lama identified Gedhun Choekyi Nyima, a boy in Tibet, to be the reincarnation of the last Panchen Lama who passed away in 1989. However, the boy quickly disappeared into Chinese custody, and to this day his welfare and whereabouts are unknown.

Gyalsay Rinpoche
A peer of the previous Nechung Rinpoche who presided at the Bum Tsok prayer ceremony in Lhasa during our visit in the summer of 1987.

Karmapa
The head of the Karma Kagyu lineage, the current Karmapa is the seventeenth reincarnation.

Khamtrul Rinpoche

A master of the Nyingma lineage, he served as the secretary of the Department of Religious and Cultural Affairs of the Central Tibetan Administration (Tibetan Government-in-Exile) and later established Chime Gatsal Ling, a monastery in lower Dharamsala.

Khenpo Jigme Phuntsok

A highly respected contemporary master and great abbot (1933–2004) who established the seat of learning, Larung Gar Monastery in eastern Tibet. At one time, it had 10,000 monastics and lay practitioners from Tibet and China. His previous reincarnation was Terton Sogyal Lerab Lingpa.

Lobsang Jigme

Served as the Sixteenth Nechung Kuten from 1945 to 1984.

Machig Labdron

The "Singular Mother Torch from Lab" (1055–1149) is a reincarnation of Yeshe Tsogyal, and the renowned eleventh century Tibetan tantric Buddhist master and yogini that originated several Tibetan lineages of the Vajrayana practice of Chod. The Chod tradition developed by Machig Labdron is "a radical synthesis of the Prajnaparamitra tradition and tantra guru yoga that 'cuts' through the ego."

Nagarjuna

Tibetan: mGon-po kLu-grub (c. 150–c. 250 CE) is widely considered one of the most important Buddhist philosophers. Along with his disciple Aryadeva, he is known to be the founder of the Madhyamaka school of Mahayana Buddhism. Nagarjuna is also credited with developing the philosophy of the Prajnaparamita sutras. He served as the head of the Nalanda University in many capacities.

Ogyen Thinley Choephel

The first Nechung Rinpoche, he was the abbot of Mindrolling Monastery who left Mindrolling in the 1800s and took residence at Nechung Monastery in Lhasa, Tibet.

Padmasambhava

A master from India known for his supernatural powers, Padmasambhava, often called Guru Rinpoche, was invited to Tibet (with Abbot Shantarakshita) by Tibet's Emperor Trisong Deutsen in the eighth century to help establish and disseminate the tenets of Buddhism. Under their leadership, Samye—the first monastic institution—was constructed and the first monks ordained.

Panchen Lama

Considered to be the human manifestation of Buddha Amitabha, the Panchen Lama is the head of Tashilhungpo Monastery in Shigatse and one of the highest reincarnations of Tibetan Buddhism. Traditionally, his reincarnation is recognized by the Dalai Lama.

Patrul Rinpoche

Dza Patrul Orgyen Jigme Chokyi Wangpo (1808–1887), an enlightened master, who, though he lived the life of a vagabond, was one of the most illustrious spiritual teachers of the nineteenth century. His principal teacher, Jigme Gyalwe Nyugu, was one of the foremost students of Jigme Lingpa. He received the teachings on the preliminary practices of the Longchen Nyingtik, as well as many other important transmissions from Jigme Gyalwe Nyugu. Among his many beautiful writings, *The Words of My Perfect Teacher* is a classic text, studied to the present day.

Shantarakshita

Tibetan: Shyiwa Tsho (725–788), also called Khenpo Bodhisattva or Bodhisattva Abbot, this Indian master was abbot of the Buddhist University of Nalanda. He was invited to Tibet by King Trisong Deutsen where he founded the Monastic Institute of Samye and ordained the first seven monks, thus establishing the Tibetan sangha.

Shantideva

Shantideva (c. 685CE–c. 763 CE) was an Indian Buddhist monk and scholar at Nalanda. He was one of the greatest philosophers and poets of all time, reflecting on the overall structure of Buddhist moral commitments. Shantideva was a prince from Saurashtra, a western coastal region that now forms part of the Indian state of Gujarat. He was an adherent of the Madhyamaka philosophy of Nagarjuna.

Shugsep Jetsun Rinpoche
A highly regarded female master in Tibet, a Chod practitioner, and the teacher to many lamas and monastics, including the previous Nechung Rinpoche and Nechung monks in Tibet

Terton Ratna Lingpa
A highly revered mystic and master of Buddhism in Tibet (1403–1479), Nechung Rinpoche is considered to be the reincarnation of Ratna Lingpa.

Terton Sogyal Orgyen Lerab Lingpa
see Khenpo Jigme Phuntsok

Thupten Konchok
The previous Nechung Rinpoche, Thupten Konchok (1917–1983) was recognized by the Thirteenth Dalai Lama to be the reincarnation of Ogyen Thinley Choephel, the abbot from Mindrolling Monastery.

Thupten Ngodup
The Medium of the Chief State Oracle, Thupten Ngodup was confirmed to be the Seventeenth Nechung Kuten in 1987.

Trisong Deutsen
One of the greatest leaders in Tibetan history (c. eighth century), King Trisong Deutsen, along with Padmasambhava and Shantarakshita, was responsible for the early dissemination of Buddhism in Tibet.

Tsongkhapa
Je Tsongkhapa—Lobsang Drakpa was the founder of the Gelug lineage of Tibetan Buddhism and established Ganden Monastery in 1409.

Zungjuk Rinpoche
The lama who escaped from Tibet with the previous Nechung Rinpoche in 1962.

People

Amdo Lungdok
A political activist who lived in Lhasa, Tibet. He helped to organize the Bum Tsok ceremony at the Jokhang in 1987.

Chambray and Junior
The young men who helped navigate the young Rinpoche through security at the Tibetan border.

Chiang Kai-shek
China's civil war was fought between the Communists led by Mao Zedong and the Nationalists led by Chiang Kai-shek, who later was exiled to Taiwan.

Dekyi and Samten
The daughter and son-in-law of our contacts and confidants in Lhasa, Tibet.

Drikung
A sub-tradition of the Kagyu lineage of Tibetan Buddhism. Also the nickname given to a monk from Drikung Monastery, India who traveled with us to Lhamo Latso, the visionary lake and other pilgrimage sites.

Jampa Soepa-la
An elderly monk of Nechung Monastery in Tibet.

Jamspal
Tiapala's childhood friend from Ladakh, India.

Kalden and Khandro
Nechung Choktrul Rinpoche's parents.

Khenrab and Yudron
Our main contacts and confidants in Lhasa who were instrumental in the discovery of Nechung Rinpoche's reincarnation.

Kunsang Lama
An entrepreneur from Kathmandu, Nepal who did business in Tibet.

Lobsang Dawa
Assistant to the previous Nechung Rinpoche in Tibet.

Nyima and Migmar
Tibetans living in Switzerland with whom we traveled from the Tibetan border to Kathmandu, Nepal.

Rabgye-la and Tsewang-la
Monks of Nechung Monastery in Tibet.

Tenzin Choephel
A senior monk and director at Nechung Monastery in Dharamsala, India; widely known as Kushog Karma, he generated the necessary paperwork for the young Rinpoche's flight from Kathmandu, Nepal to Delhi, India.

Tenzin Geyche
His Holiness the Dalai Lama's personal secretary in-exile for many decades.

Tenzin Lodoe
A monk from Nechung Monastery, Dharamsala, India, whose parents and siblings were key figures in the search for Nechung Rinpoche's reincarnation.

Thupten
The monk from Nechung Monastery in Dharamsala, India with whom we conducted the search and discovery of Nechung Rinpoche's reincarnation and ultimately accompanied the young lama out of Tibet together.

Thupten Phuntsok
One of the senior-most monks who escaped Tibet and was responsible for the reestablishment of Nechung Monastery in India.

Thupten Sherab
Known as Kushog Wangyal, he was one of the monks who escaped Tibet and was instrumental for the reestablishment of Nechung Monastery in India.

Tiapala

Nickname of Lobzang Toldan, the monk attendant of the previous Nechung Rinpoche; Tiapala lived at the temple in Wood Valley, Hawai'i from 1984 to 2016.

Tsering and Drolma

The couple who joined us on the excursion to Lhamo Latso and pilgrimage sites.

Places

Chamseng Latso

A remote lake located beyond Lhamo Latso.

Chandigarh

Serves as a union territory and city, and is the capital for the states of Punjab and Haryana, India.

Chengdu

An industrialized city in the province of Sichuan in Western China, with an airport that has flights to Lhasa, Tibet.

Chimphu

A mountain near Samye where retreatants meditated and practiced in caves prior to 1959.

Chokhor Gyal

A monastery located close to Lhamo Latso, the visionary lake.

Cholung

The place where Je Tsongkhapa engaged in retreat.

Dharamsala

A town in the Kangra District of Himachal Pradesh in northern India, Dharamsala is the home of His Holiness the Dalai Lama and the seat of the Central Tibetan Administration (Tibetan Government-in-Exile).

Drepung Monastery

Drepung was the largest monastic institution in Tibet with seven colleges prior to 1959. The first monks of Nechung Monastery in Lhasa came from the Deyang College of Drepung.

Dram

The crossing at Zhangmu on the Tibetan border between Tibet and Nepal.

Gangchen Kyishong

The seat of the Central Tibetan Administration (Tibetan Government-in-Exile), Gangchen Kyishong is located in the central part of Dharamsala. Nechung Monastery is located here, below the Library of Tibetan Works and Archives.

Hebori

A hill close to Samye Monastery where Pehar was "bound to oath" by Guru Padmasambhava.

Jokhang

Considered to be the most sacred temple in Tibet, Jokhang is located in the Barkhor area of Lhasa in Central Tibet.

Lhamo Latso

A visionary lake which is located in the mountains southeast of Lhasa. Search parties for the reincarnations of important lamas may journey to Lhamo Latso in hopes of having a vision that would lead to the discovery of the unmistaken reincarnation.

Riwo Tse Nga

The Five-Peak Mountain (Chinese: Wu Tai Shan) in China, considered to be the earthly abode of Manjushri, the Bodhisattva of Wisdom.

Sakya

A district in the Tsang province, also one of the four main lineages of Tibetan Buddhism.

Samye Monastery
The first monastic institution built in Tibet in the eighth century, Samye is located in the Chimphu Valley. Instrumental in its establishment was King Trisong Deutsen, Abbot Shantarakshita, and Guru Padmasambhava. Hebori Hill and the Chimphu caves are nearby.

Shing Lung Gonpa
Wood Valley Temple—the first name Nechung Rinpoche gave to his temple in the Ka'u District on the Island of Hawai'i.

Spituk (Pethup)
A important monastery in Ladakh, India.

Tashi Lhunpo Monastery
A monastery in Tsang, founded by the First Dalai Lama, it served as the seat of the Panchen Lamas.

Thekchen Choling
The main temple in Dharamsala, located close to the residence of H.H. the Dalai Lama.

Tsethang
The capital of the Yarlung region.

Tshurpu Monastery
The seat of the Karmapas, head of the Karma Kagyu lineage.

Zhangmu
The border town at Dram on the Tibetan border, entryway to and from Nepal.

TIBET
CULTURAL MAP

EAST TURKESTAN

Ulugh Muztagh
(6973)

Kunlun Gyalmo
(7167)

Ruthok

Gertse

Purong Gangri
(6929)

Gar

Nganglong Kangri
(6720)

Tsonyi

U-TSANG

Tsada

Senge Kha bab

Gegye

Siling
Tso

Gang Rinpoche
(Mt. Kailash 6638)

Tsochen

Trari
Namtso

Kering
Tso

Palgo

Langchen Khabab

Shentsa

Nyenchen Thanglha
(7162)

Macha Tsangpo

Drongpa

Lunpo Gangri
(7095)

Tshurphu

Tashi
Lhunpo

Menri

Saga

Tachok Khabab

She Thongmon

Ngamring

Nyem

Kyirong

Lhatse

Shigatse

Yarlung Tsangpo

NEPAL

Bumchu

Sakya

Gyantse

Panam

Yamdrok
Yutso

Lhod

Dingri

Tingkye

Gampa

Nyalam

Chomolungma
(Mt. Everest 8848)

Dromo

Ga
Punsu

BHUTA

LEGEND

- ⦿ Capital
- ⊙ Town
- 🛕 Monastery
- ▲ Major Peak
- — International Boundaries

INDIA

CHINA

AMDO

Tsaidam

Themchen

Dola

Semnyi

Terlenkha

Kangtsa

Serkhok

Pari

Gonlung

Wulan

Dashi

Siling

Gonlung

Tso
Ngonpo

Tongkor

Kumbum

Kamalog

Gormo

Gome

Tulan

Chentsa

Labrang Tashi Kyil

Mangra

Sangchu

Batse

Tsegor Thang

Tsekhog

Yadzi

Chone

Matoe

Gepa Sumdo

Luchu

Tso
Kyareng

Amnye Machen
(6282)

Machen

Yulgan

Thewo

Drugchu

Chumarleb

Gade

Machu

Dzöge

Namphel

Tridu

Chigdril

Taktsang
Lhamo Kirti

Zatoe

Darlag

Pema

Ngaba

Sungchu

Yulshul/Kyegudo

Sershul

Kirti

Trochu

chen

Derge

Dzamthang

Nangchen

Nyagchu

Serthar

Barkham

Tengchen

Jomda

Dzogchen

Chuchen

Tashiling

Driru

Gyalmo Ngulchu

Palpung

KHAM

Drakgo

Rongdrag

Lhari

Palbar

Chamdo

Palyül

Tawu

Karze

Muchu

Riwoche

Gonjo

Nyagrong

po

Gyalha Peri
(72194)

Lhorong

Drakyab

Markham

Lithang

Chaksam

Nyagchu

Minyak Gangkar (7556)

epung

Minling

Pashöd

Pome

Bathang

Lithang Ganden
Thubten Choekorling

Nyagchu

Gyesur

Nang

Namchag Barwa
(7282)

Dzogang

Dabpa

Kawa Karpo (6718)

Lhuntse

Riwonyi (6882)

Zayul

Derong

Mili

rdo

Dechen

Gyalthang
Sumtsenling

Balung

MYANMAR

THE TIBET MUSEUM

© THE TIBET MUSEUM, 2020

About Marya and Miguel

Marya Schwabe began studying Buddhism in 1974, together with her husband Miguel, at a temple in Wood Valley on the Island of Hawai'i. The temple was founded for Nechung Rinpoche, the reincarnate lama of Nechung Monastery, the institution that houses the Chief State Oracle of Tibet. From 1975 to 1983, Marya and Miguel lived and worked closely with Rinpoche. Under his tutelage, they immersed themselves in Buddhism and learned spoken and classical Tibetan at the remote sanctuary.

Nechung Rinpoche encouraged them to learn Tibetan so they could comprehend the profundity of the Buddhist philosophy from the source. He foresaw that they would study with many lamas who were not fluent in English. True to Rinpoche's prescience, Marya organized visits and teaching programs for over fifty lamas, including His Holiness the Dalai Lama in 1980 and 1994, from all the major lineages of Tibetan Buddhism, to the temple and other centers. She has had the rare opportunity to study with and translate for many of these extraordinary teachers. The subjects range from foundational practices, the highest yoga tantras, and Dzogchen.

Since the 1970s, Marya has also served as the temple administrative director, managing the business, outreach, and public relations; while Miguel has utilized his skills to develop and maintain the infrastructure, buildings, and grounds. They have traveled extensively in Asia and currently reside and work at Nechung Dorje Drayang Ling in Hawai'i.

His Holiness the Dalai Lama with Marya and Miguel,
Nechung Dorje Drayang Ling in Hawai'i, April 18, 1994

Made in the USA
Middletown, DE
02 September 2024

60314845R00177